Toward a
General Theory of
the First Amendment

Toward a General Theory of the First Amendment

Thomas I. Emerson

VINTAGE BOOKS
A Division of Random House

New York

Contents

Introduction

‖ NO ONE CONCERNED WITH
freedom of expression in the United States today can fail to be
alarmed by the unsatisfactory state of First Amendment doctrine.
Despite the mounting number of decisions and an even greater
volume of comment, no really adequate or comprehensive theory
of the First Amendment has been enunciated, much less agreed
upon. Proponents of the "absolute" or "literal" interpretation of
the First Amendment have failed to define the bounds of their
position or to account for such apparent exceptions to the absolute test as the law of libel, the application of child labor laws to
the distribution of literature, and the regulation of election campaigns. Their views have therefore been dismissed as impractical
or illogical, or both. At the other end of the spectrum, the
"balancing" test has tended to reduce the First Amendment,
especially when a legislative judgment is weighed in the balance,
to a limp and lifeless formality. Among intermediate positions,
the "clear and present danger" test is the best known; yet not
only has this formula often been ignored, but it was discarded in
the Smith Act cases and at any rate is hardly applicable to many
of the issues which now arise, such as the extent of the protection afforded by the First Amendment from the legislative
investigating power. Other efforts to formulate an overall theory
have not met outstanding success. Nor has doctrine been evolved
to deal with some of the newer problems, where the issue is not
pure restraint on government interference but rather the use of
governmental power to encourage freedom of expression or the
actual participation by government itself in the realm of
expression.

This failure to develop a satisfactory theory of the First
Amendment is hardly surprising. The issues are controversial and
the problems complex. The Supreme Court did not seriously

commence the task of interpretation until a few decades ago, beginning with the *Schenck* case in 1919. And rapidly changing conditions in the country have presented the issues in new and more difficult forms. Irrespective of the causes, however, there is grave danger in the present situation. Not only are courts and the legal profession in sharp conflict but the public is seriously confused and the first amendment is threatened with disintegration. Under the circumstances, one further attempt to state an acceptable theory may perhaps be pardoned.

The first task is to bring together all the basic considerations which must enter into any formulation of First Amendment doctrine that goes beyond the merely verbal level. The fundamental purpose of the First Amendment was to guarantee the maintenance of an effective system of free expression. This calls for an examination of the various elements which are necessary to support such a system in a modern democratic society. Some of these elements found early articulation in the classic theory of free expression, as it developed over the course of centuries; others are the outgrowth of contemporary conditions. More specifically, it is necessary to analyze (I) what it is that the First Amendment attempts to maintain: the function of freedom of expression in a democratic society; (II) what the practical difficulties are in maintaining such a system: the dynamic forces at work in any governmental attempt to restrict or regulate expression; and (III) the role of law and legal institutions in developing and supporting freedom of expression. These three elements are the basic components of any comprehensive theory of the First Amendment viewed as a guarantee of a system of free expression.

The second task is to formulate legal doctrine which takes into account these basic factors, which gives legal effect to the fundamental decisions made in adopting the First Amendment, and which provides the courts with guidelines sufficiently specific and legal in character as to enable them to perform their judicial function in supporting the system. We must therefore undertake (IV) a statement of the general principles upon which such legal doctrine must be based, and (V) an attempt at a formulation of some detailed rules of law that should govern the various types of First Amendment problems which arise in our society today.

In this preliminary effort I have not attempted to do more

than sketch broadly the various propositions put forward, stating them in abbreviated, at times conclusory and indeed tentative form.

This essay was originally published in the *Yale Law Journal* in 1963. In making it more generally available in book form at the present time, I have not undertaken to revise it. There have been important decisions of the Supreme Court in the interval, but they have not appreciably changed the issues or substantially altered my approach to the problems. Excerpts from the more significant of these decisions are set out in the Appendix. On the whole they tend in the direction of the views advanced in this book. But, as the fourteen opinions in the 1966 obscenity cases make clear, they have scarcely ended the search for a comprehensive and effective theory of the First Amendment.

The major literature in the field is cited at several points in the text. The debt of the writer to much of this material, while only infrequently acknowledged by specific footnoting, is obvious.

No attempt is made in this essay to treat the provisions of the First Amendment which relate to freedom of religion.

*Toward a
General Theory of
the First Amendment*

The First Amendment

‖ CONGRESS SHALL MAKE NO law respecting an establishment of religion, or prohibiting the free exercise thereof; or abridging the freedom of speech, or of the press, or the right of the people peaceably to assemble, and to petition the Government for a redress of grievances.

1 ‖ The Function of Freedom of Expression in a Democratic Society

‖ THE RIGHT OF THE INDIVIDUAL to freedom of expression has deep roots in our history. But the concept as we know it now is essentially a product of the development of the liberal constitutional state. It is an integral part of the great intellectual and social movement beginning with the Renaissance which transformed the Western world from a feudal and authoritarian society to one whose faith rested upon the dignity, the reason and the freedom of the individual. The theory in its modern form has thus evolved over a period of more than three centuries, being applied under different circumstances and seeking to deal with different problems. It is sufficient for our purposes to restate it in its final, composite form, as it comes to us today.

The values sought by society in protecting the right to freedom of expression may be grouped into four broad categories. Maintenance of a system of free expression is necessary (1) as a method of assuring individual self-fulfillment, (2) as a means of attaining the truth, (3) as a method of securing participation by the members of the society in social, including political, decision-making, and (4) as a means of maintaining the balance between stability and change in the society. We consider these in their affirmative aspects, without regard at this time to the problems of limitation or reconciliation with other values.[1]

[1] Major sources in the development of the theory include: John Milton, *Areopagitica* (1644); John Locke, *Two Treatises of Government* (1690); *Essay Concerning Human Understanding* (1690); and *Letters on Toleration* (1690); the writings of Thomas Jefferson and James Madison; John

Individual Self-Fulfillment

THE RIGHT TO FREEDOM of expression is justified first of all as the right of an individual purely in his capacity as an individual. It derives from the widely accepted premise of Western thought that the proper end of man is the realization of his character and potentialities as a human being. Man is distinguished from other animals principally by the qualities of his mind. He has powers to reason and to feel in ways that are unique in degree if not in kind. He has the capacity to think in abstract terms, to use language, to communicate his thoughts and emotions, to build a culture. He has powers of imagination, insight and feeling. It is through development of these powers that man finds his meaning and his place in the world.

The achievement of self-realization commences with develop-

Stuart Mill, *On Liberty* (1859); Walter Bagehot, *The Metaphysical Basis of Toleration* (1874); the decisions of Holmes, Brandeis and many other Supreme Court justices; Zechariah Chafee, Jr., *Free Speech in the United States* (Cambridge, Mass., Harvard University Press, 1941) and *The Blessings of Liberty* (Philadelphia, J. B. Lippincott, 1956); Harold Joseph Laski, *Authority in the Modern State* (New Haven, Conn., Yale University Press, 1919) and *Liberty in the Modern State* (New York, The Viking Press, 1948); Alexander Meiklejohn, *Political Freedom* (New York, Harper and Row, 1960). The best reference to the English and American material of the seventeenth and eighteenth centuries is Leonard W. Levy, *Legacy of Suppression* (Cambridge, Mass., Harvard University Press, 1960). For bibliography through the middle of 1958, see Thomas I. Emerson and David Haber, *Political and Civil Rights in the United States*, Vol. 1, Ch. 3 (Buffalo, N.Y., Dennis and Co., 1958). Later material includes Mortimer Adler, *The Idea of Freedom* (New York, Doubleday, 1958, 1961); Walter Gellhorn, *American Rights* (New York, Macmillan, 1960); Herbert Muller, *Issues of Freedom* (New York, Harper and Row, 1960); O. Kirchheimer, *Political Justice* (Princeton, N.J., Princeton University Press, 1961); Oscar and Mary F. Handlin, *The Dimensions of Liberty* (Cambridge, Mass., Harvard University Press, 1961). Material from the social sciences which tends to support some of the basic assumptions of the theory includes Erich Fromm, *Escape from Freedom* (New York, Holt, Rinehart and Winston, 1941), *Man for Himself* (New York, Holt, Rinehart and Winston, 1947) and *The Sane Society* (New York, Holt, Rinehart and Winston, 1955); Karl Mannheim, *Man and Society in an Age of Reconstruction* (New York, Harcourt, Brace and World, 1951); Lewis A. Coser, *The Functions of Social Conflict* (New York, Free Press of Glencoe, 1956); William Kornhauser, *The Politics of Mass Society* (New York, Free Press of Glencoe, 1959); Christian Bay, *The Structure of Freedom* (Stanford, Stanford University Press, 1958).

ment of the mind. But the process of conscious thought by its very nature can have no limits. An individual can neither tell where it may lead nor anticipate its end. Moreover, it is an *individual* process. Every man is influenced by his fellows, dead and living, but his mind is his own and its functioning is necessarily an individual affair.

From this it follows that every man—in the development of his own personality—has the right to form his own beliefs and opinions. And it also follows that he has the right to express these beliefs and opinions. Otherwise they are of little account. For expression is an integral part of the development of ideas, of mental exploration and of the affirmation of self. The power to realize his potentiality as a human being begins at this point and must extend at least this far if the whole nature of man is not to be thwarted.

Hence suppression of belief, opinion and expression is an affront to the dignity of man, a negation of man's essential nature. What Milton said of licensing of the press is equally true of any form of restraint over expression: it is "the greatest displeasure and indignity to a free and knowing spirit that can be put upon him."[2]

The right to freedom of expression derives secondly from basic Western notions of the role of the individual in his capacity as a member of society. Man is a social animal, necessarily and probably willingly so. He lives in company with his fellow men; he joins with them in creating a common culture; he is subject to the necessary controls of society and particularly of the state. His right to express his beliefs and opinions in this role as a member of his community follows from two fundamental principles. One is that the purpose of society and of its more formal aspect, the state, is to promote the welfare of the individual. Society and the state are not ends in themselves; they exist to serve the individual. The second is the principle of equality, formulated as the proposition that every individual is entitled to equal opportunity to share in common decisions which affect him.

From these concepts there follows the right of the individual to access to knowledge; to shape his own views; to communicate his needs, preferences and judgments; in short, to participate in formulating the aims and achievements of his society and his

[2] John Milton, *Areopagitica*, Vol. 21 (New York, E. P. Dutton, 1927).

state. To cut off his search for truth, or his expression of it, is thus to elevate society and the state to a despotic command and to reduce the individual to the arbitrary control of others. The individual, in short, owes an obligation to cooperate with his fellow men, but that responsibility carries with it the right to freedom in expressing himself.

Two basic implications of the theory need to be emphasized. The first is that it is not a general measure of the individual's right to freedom of expression that any particular exercise of the right may be thought to promote or retard other goals of the society. The theory asserts that freedom of expression, while not the sole or sufficient end of society, is a good in itself, or at least an essential element in a good society. The society may seek to achieve other or more inclusive ends—such as virtue, justice, equality, or the maximum realization of the potentialities of its members. These problems are not necessarily solved by accepting the rules for freedom of expression. But, as a general proposition, the society may not seek to solve them by suppressing the beliefs or opinions of individual members. To achieve these other goals it must rely upon other methods: the use of counter-expression and the regulation or control of conduct which is not expression. Hence the right to control individual expression, on the ground that it is judged to promote good or evil, justice or injustice, equality or inequality, is not, speaking generally, within the competence of the good society.

The second implication, in a sense a corollary of the first, is that the theory rests upon a fundamental distinction between belief, opinion and communication of ideas on the one hand, and different forms of conduct on the other. For shorthand purposes we refer to this distinction hereafter as one between "expression" and "action." As just observed, in order to achieve its desired goals, a society or the state is entitled to exercise control over action—whether by prohibiting or compelling it—on an entirely different and vastly more extensive basis. But expression occupies a specially protected position. In this sector of human conduct, the social right of suppression or compulsion is at its lowest point, in most respects nonexistent.

This marking off of the special area of expression is a crucial ingredient of the basic theory for several reasons. In the first place, thought and communication are the fountainhead of all expression of the individual personality. To cut off the flow at the source is to dry up the whole stream. Freedom at this point is essential to all other freedoms. Hence society must withhold its right of suppression until the stage of action is reached. Secondly, expression is normally conceived as doing less injury to other social goals than action. It generally has less immediate consequences, is less irremediable in its impact. Thirdly, the power of society and the state over the individual is so pervasive, and construction of doctrines, institutions and administrative practices to limit this power so difficult, that only by drawing such a protective line between expression and action is it possible to strike a safe balance between authority and freedom.

Attainment of Truth

IN THE TRADITIONAL THEORY, freedom of expression is not only an individual but also a social good. It is, to begin with, the best process for advancing knowledge and discovering truth.

Considered in this aspect, the theory starts with the premise that the soundest and most rational judgment is arrived at by considering all facts and arguments which can be put forth in behalf of or against any proposition. Human judgment is a frail thing. It may err in being subject to emotion, prejudice or personal interest. It suffers from lack of information and insight, or inadequate thinking. It can seldom rest at the point any single person carries it, but must always remain incomplete and subject to further extension, refinement, rejection or modification. Hence an individual who seeks knowledge and truth must hear all sides of the question, especially as presented by those who feel strongly and argue militantly for a different view. He must consider all alternatives, test his judgment by exposing it to opposition, make full use of different minds to sift the true from the false. Conversely, suppression of information, discussion, or the clash of opinion prevents one from reaching the most rational judgment, blocks the generation of new ideas, and tends to perpetuate error. This is the method of the Socratic dialogue employed on a universal scale.

The process is a continuous one. As further knowledge becomes available, as conditions change, as new insights are revealed, the judgment is open to reappraisal, improvement or abandonment.

The theory demands that discussion must be kept open no matter how certainly true an accepted opinion may seem to be. Many of the most widely acknowledged truths have turned out to be erroneous. Many of the most significant advances in human knowledge—from Copernicus to Einstein—have resulted from challenging hitherto unquestioned assumptions. No opinion can be immune from challenge.

The process also applies regardless of how false or pernicious the new opinion appears to be. For the unaccepted opinion may be true or partially true. And there is no way of suppressing the false without suppressing the true. Furthermore, even if the new opinion is wholly false, its presentation and open discussion serves a vital social purpose. It compels a rethinking and retesting of the accepted opinion. It results in a deeper understanding of the reasons for holding the opinion and a fuller appreciation of its meaning.

The only justification for suppressing an opinion is that those who seek to suppress it are infallible in their judgment of the truth. But no individual or group can be infallible, particularly in a constantly changing world.

It is essential to note that the theory contemplates more than a process for arriving at an individual judgment. It asserts that the process is also the best method for reaching a general or social judgment. This is true in part because a social judgment is made up of individual judgments. It will therefore be vitally conditioned by the quality of the individual judgments which compose it. More importantly, the same reasons which make open discussion essential for an intelligent individual judgment make it imperative for rational social judgments. Through the acquisition of new knowledge, the toleration of new ideas, the testing of opinion in open competition, the discipline of rethinking its assumptions, a society will be better able to reach common decisions that will meet the needs and aspirations of its members.

Participation in Decision-Making

THE THIRD MAIN FUNCTION of a system of freedom of expression is to provide for participation in decision-making through a process of open discussion which is available to all members of the community. Conceivably the technique of reaching the best common judgment could be limited to an elite, or could be extended to most members of the society, excluding only those who were felt to be clearly unworthy. In its earlier forms the theory was often so restricted. But as the nineteenth century progressed, it came to be accepted that all men were entitled to participate in the process of formulating the common decisions.

This development was partly due to acceptance of the concept that freedom of expression was a right of the individual, as discussed previously. But it was also inherent in the logic of free expression as a social good. In order for the process to operate at its best, every relevant fact must be brought out, every opinion and every insight must be available for consideration. Since facts are discovered and opinions formed only by the individual, the system demands that all persons participate. As John Stuart Mill expressed it, "If all mankind minus one, were of one opinion, and only one person were of the contrary opinion, mankind would be no more justified in silencing that one person, than he, if he had the power, would be justified in silencing mankind."[3]

But in addition to these reasons, the right of all members of society to form their own beliefs and communicate them freely to others must be regarded as an essential principle of a democratically organized society. The growing pressures for democracy and equality reinforced the logical implications of the theory and demanded opportunity for all persons to share in making social decisions. This is, of course, especially true of political decisions. But the basic theory carried beyond the political realm. It embraced the right to participate in the building of the whole culture, and included freedom of expression in religion, literature, art, science and all areas of human learning and knowledge.

In the field of political action, as just mentioned, the theory of freedom of expression has particular significance. It is through the political process that most of the immediate decisions on the survival, welfare and progress of a society are made. It is here that the state has a special incentive to repress opposition and often wields a more effective power of suppression. Freedom of

---

[3] John Stuart Mill, *On Liberty and Other Essays,* Vol. 20 (New York, The Book League of America, 1929).

expression in the political realm is usually a necessary condition for securing freedom elsewhere. It is in the political sector, therefore, that the crucial battles over free expression are most often fought.

As the general theory makes clear, freedom of discussion in public affairs serves an important function regardless of whether the political structure of a nation is democratic or not. Every government must have some process for feeding back to it information concerning the attitudes, needs and wishes of its citizens. It must, therefore, afford some degree of freedom at least to some of its citizens, to make known their wants and desires. Indeed, in a more formal aspect—as a petition for redress of grievances—this right of communicating to the government in power was one of the earliest forms of political expression. The Magna Carta and the Bill of Rights of 1689, for instance, were promulgated in response to such petitions. In general, the greater the degree of political discussion allowed, the more responsive is the government, the closer is it brought to the will of its people, and the harder must it strive to be worthy of their support.

The crucial point, however, is not that freedom of expression is politically useful, but that it is indispensable to the operation of a democratic form of government. Once one accepts the premise of the Declaration of Independence—that governments derive "their just powers from the consent of the governed"— it follows that the governed must, in order to exercise their right of consent, have full freedom of expression both in forming individual judgments and in forming the common judgment. Together with the argument for freedom of religious belief, this proposition was the one most frequently and most insistently urged in support of freedom of expression.[4]

The proponents of freedom of political expression often addressed themselves to the question whether the people were competent to perform the functions entrusted to them, whether they could acquire sufficient information or possessed sufficient capacity for judgment. The men of the eighteenth century, with their implicit faith in the power of reason and the perfectibility of man, entertained few doubts on this score. Political theorists

---

[4] The implications of this argument have been developed most fully in our times by Dr. Alexander Meiklejohn. See his *Political Freedom*.

of the nineteenth and twentieth centuries have been more cautious. And there was some disagreement as to whether the right of political expression could safely be extended to societies which had not reached a certain point in the development of education and culture. But these problems were actually questions concerning the viability of democracy itself. And once a society was committed to democratic procedures, or rather in the process of committing itself, it necessarily embraced the principle of open political discussion.

Balance Between Stability and Change

THE TRADITIONAL DOCTRINE of freedom of expression, finally, embodies a theory of social control. The principle of open discussion is a method of achieving a more adaptable and at the same time more stable community, of maintaining the precarious balance between healthy cleavage and necessary consensus. This may not always have been true, and may not be true of many existing societies. But where men have learned how to function within the law, an open society will be the stronger and more cohesive one.

The reasons supporting this proposition can only be stated here in summary form. In the first place, suppression of discussion makes a rational judgment impossible. In effect it substitutes force for logic. Moreover, coercion of expression is likely to be ineffective. While it may prevent social change, at least for a time, it cannot eradicate thought or belief; nor can it promote loyalty or unity. As Bagehot observed, "Persecution in intellectual countries produces a superficial conformity, but also underneath an intense, incessant, implacable doubt."[5]

Furthermore, suppression promotes inflexibility and stultification, preventing the society from adjusting to changing circumstances or developing new ideas. Any society, and any institution in society, naturally tends toward rigidity. Attitudes and ideas become stereotyped; institutions lose their vitality. The result is mechanical or arbitrary application of outworn principles, mounting grievances unacknowledged, inability to conceive new approaches, and general stagnation. Opposition

---

[5] Walter Bagehot, "The Metaphysical Basis of Toleration," in *Works of Walter Bagehot,* Vol. 2 (Hutton ed. 1889), pp. 339, 357.

serves a vital social function in offsetting or ameliorating this normal process of bureaucratic decay.

Again, suppression of expression conceals the real problems confronting a society and diverts public attention from the critical issues. It is likely to result in neglect of the grievances which are the actual basis of the unrest, and thus prevent their correction. For it both hides the extent of opposition and hardens the position of all sides, thus making a rational compromise difficult or impossible. Further, suppression drives opposition underground, leaving those suppressed either apathetic or desperate. It thus saps the vitality of the society or makes resort to force more likely. And finally it weakens and debilitates the majority whose support for the common decision is necessary. For it hinders an intelligent understanding of the reasons for adopting the decision and, as Mill observed, "beliefs not grounded on conviction are likely to give way before the slightest semblance of an argument."[6] In short, suppression of opposition may well mean that when change is finally forced on the community it will come in more violent and radical form.

The argument that the process of open discussion, far from causing society to fly apart, stimulates forces that lead to greater cohesion also rests upon the concept of political legitimation. Stated in narrower and perhaps cruder terms, the position is that allowing dissidents to expound their views enables them "to let off steam." The classic example is the Hyde Park meeting, where any person is permitted to say anything he wishes to whatever audience he can assemble. This results in a release of energy, a lessening of frustration and a channeling of resistance into courses consistent with law and order. It operates, in short, as a catharsis throughout the body politic.

The principle of political legitimation, however, is more broadly fundamental. It asserts that persons who have had full freedom to state their position and to persuade others to adopt it will, when the decision goes against them, be more ready to accept the common judgment. They will recognize that they have been treated fairly, in accordance with rational rules for social living. They will feel that they have done all within their power, and will understand that the only remaining alternative is to abandon the ground rules altogether through resort to force,

[6] Mill, p. 42, *op. cit. supra* note 3, Ch. I.

a course of action upon which most individuals in a healthy society are unwilling to embark. In many circumstances they will retain the opportunity to try again and will hope in the end to persuade a majority to their position. Just as in a judicial proceeding where due process has been observed, they will feel that the resulting decision, even though not to their liking, is the legitimate one.[7]

In dealing with the problem of social control, supporters of free expression likewise emphasize that the issue must be considered in the total context of forces operating to promote or diminish cohesion in a society. By and large, they theorize, a society is more likely to be subject to general inertia than to volatile change. Hence resistance to the political order is unlikely to reach the stage of disorder unless a substantial section of the population is living under seriously adverse or discriminatory conditions. Only a government which consistently fails to relieve valid grievances need fear the outbreak of violent opposition. Thus, given the inertia which so often characterizes a society, freedom of expression, far from causing upheaval, is more properly viewed as a leavening process, facilitating necessary social and political change and keeping a society from stultification and decay.

Moreover, the state retains adequate powers to promote political unity and suppress resort to force. For one thing, it shares the right to freedom of expression with its citizens. While there may be some limits on this power, the state is normally in a much better position to obtain information and in a much more authoritative position from which to communicate its official views than the ordinary citizen or group of citizens. More importantly, the state possesses the authority to restrict or compel action. The right with which we are concerned, as already noted, extends only to expression; when the stage of action is reached, the great power of the state becomes available for regulation or prohibition. And finally, the state has not only the power but also the obligation to control the conditions under which freedom of expression can function for the general welfare. This includes not only responsibility for eliminating griev-

---

[7] For a discussion of the notion of legitimization, as operating in the judicial process, see Charles Lund Black, *The People and the Court* (New York, Macmillan, 1960), pp. 56-86.

ances which may give rise to disorder but also a responsibility for maintaining economic and social conditions under which the ground rules of democracy can operate.

Proponents of the theory acknowledge that the process of full discussion, open to all, involves some risks to the society that practices it. At times there may be substantial delay in the working out of critical problems. There can be no ironclad guarantee that in the end a decision beneficial to society will be reached. The process, by encouraging diversity and dissent, does at times tend to loosen the common bonds that hold society together and may threaten to bring about its dissolution. The answer given is that the stakes are high and that the risks must be run. No society can expect to achieve absolute security. Change is inevitable; the only question is the rate and the method. The theory of freedom of expression offers greater possibilities for rational, orderly adjustment than a system of suppression. Moreover, they urge, as the lesson of experience, that the dangers are usually imaginary; that suppression is invoked more often to the prejudice of the general welfare than for its advancement. To this they add that the risks are the lesser evil, that the alternatives are worse, that the only security worth having is that based on freedom.

Thus the theory of freedom of expression involves more than a technique for arriving at better social judgments through democratic procedures. It comprehends a vision of society, a faith and a whole way of life. The theory grew out of an age that was awakened and invigorated by the idea of a new society in which man's mind was free, his fate determined by his own powers of reason, and his prospects of creating a rational and enlightened civilization virtually unlimited. It is put forward as a prescription for attaining a creative, progressive, exciting and intellectually robust community. It contemplates a mode of life that, through encouraging toleration, skepticism, reason and initiative, will allow man to realize his full potentialities. It spurns the alternative of a society that is tyrannical, conformist, irrational and stagnant. It is this concept of society that was embodied in the first amendment.

It is not within the scope of this book to demonstrate the soundness of the traditional theory underlying freedom of expression, or its viability under modern conditions. The writer believes that such a demonstration can be made. But the significant point here is that we as a nation are presently committed to the theory, that alternative principles have no substantial support, and that our system of freedom of expression must be based upon and designed for the realization of the fundamental propositions embodied in the traditional theory.

2 ‖ *The Dynamics of Limitation*

‖ IN CONSTRUCTING AND MAIN-
taining a system of freedom of expression, the principal problems and major controversies have arisen when the attempt is made to fit the affirmative theory—that is, the affirmative functions served by the system—into a more comprehensive scheme of social values and social goals. The crucial issues have revolved around the question of what limitations, if any, ought to be imposed upon freedom of expression in order to reconcile that interest with other individual and social interests sought by the good society. Most of our efforts in the past to formulate rules for limiting freedom of expression have been seriously defective through failure to take into consideration the realistic context in which such limitations are administered. The crux of the problem is that the limitations, whatever they may be, must be applied by one group of human beings to other human beings. In order to take adequate account of this factor it is necessary to have some understanding of the forces in conflict, the practical difficulties in formulating limitations, the state apparatus necessary to enforce them, the possibility of distorting them to attain ulterior purposes, and the impact of the whole process upon achieving an effective system of free expression.

The starting point is a recognition of the powerful forces that impel men toward the elimination of unorthodox expression. Most men have a strong inclination to suppress opposition even where differences in viewpoint are comparatively slight. But a system of free expression must be framed to withstand far greater stress. The test of any such system is not whether it tolerates minor deviations but whether it permits criticism of the fundamental beliefs and practices of the society. And in this area the drives to repress, both irrational and rational, tend to become overwhelming.

The human propensity to curb unwanted criticism has long been noted by the theorists of freedom of expression. Thus John Stuart Mill, early in his essay *On Liberty,* remarked:

> The disposition of mankind, whether as rulers or as fellow-citizens, to impose their own opinions and inclinations as a rule of conduct on others, is so energetically supported by some of the best and by some of the worst feelings incident to human nature, that it is hardly ever kept under restraint by anything but want of power.[1]

The strong innate drive to suppress deviant opinion has also been stressed in modern studies of the authoritarian personality. An attack upon cherished premises tends to create anxiety, especially in those who have a strong inner need for certainty. The deviant opinion is felt as a threat to personal security. And the response tends to be fear, hatred or a similar emotion, from which springs a compulsion to eliminate the source of the danger. In such circumstances it is natural to turn to the state for protection against the supposed evil. Such factors play a prominent part in the formulation of restrictions upon expression and, equally important, in their administration.[2]

It is necessary to take into account not only the psychology of the orthodox but also the psychology of the dissented. Persons who stand up against society and challenge the traditional view often have strong feelings for the issues they raise. Others may be influenced by inner tensions which make it difficult for them to "adjust" to the prevailing order. In any event, the dissent is often not pitched in conventional terms; nor does it follow customary standards of polite expression. This tends to increase the anxiety and hostility of the orthodox and thus compounds the problem.[3]

Apart from these inner compulsions at work in a system which undertakes to limit freedom of expression, difficulties arise at the more rational level. To many people their immediate and personal affairs are the most vivid and most compelling. Those who currently dominate a society naturally cling to their eco-

---

[1] Mill, p. 18, *op. cit. supra* note 3, Ch. I.

[2] See, *e.g.,* T. W. Adorno, Else Frenkel-Brunswik, Levinson & Sanford, *The Authoritarian Personality* (New York, Harper and Row, 1950), pp. 654-726.

[3] See, *e.g.,* Mill, pp. 63-65, *op. cit. supra* note 3, Ch. I.

nomic, political and social position of advantage. Vested interests in the status quo or in the continuing ignorance of other people tend to take precedence over the broader interests of society as a whole. Forces of this nature vigorously resist the expression of new ideas or the pressures of the underprivileged who would change existing conditions in the society.

Nor is the longer-run logic of the traditional theory immediately apparent to untutored participants in political conflict. As Justice Holmes put it:

> Persecution for the expression of opinions seems to me perfectly logical. If you have no doubt of your premises or your power and want a certain result with all your heart you naturally express your wishes in law and sweep away all opposition. To allow opposition by speech seems to indicate that you think the speech impotent, as when a man says that he has squared the circle, or that you do not care wholeheartedly for the result, or that you doubt either your power or your premises.[4]

Suppression of opinion thus may seem an entirely plausible course of action. Toleration may appear inconsistent with maintaining order or achieving other ends desired by the majority or the group in power. The dialectics of freedom and order are not always perceived; the apparent paradox is not always readily resolved.

That full understanding and readiness to accept the theory of freedom of expression tends to be an acquired attitude is apparent from the entire history of free expression. It has been common for individuals and groups who demanded freedom of expression for themselves to insist that it be denied to others. Until the nineteenth century most of the theoretical supporters of freedom of expression took this position. And even those who urged a broader view have sought to impose restrictions upon their opponents when they achieved power. Thomas Jefferson himself, after being elected President, wrote to Governor McKean of Pennsylvania objecting to the "licentiousness" and "lying" of the Federalist press and saying, "I have therefore long thought that a few prosecutions of the most prominent offenders would have a wholesome effect in restoring the integrity of the

[4] *Abrams v. United States,* 250 U.S. 616, 630 (1919) (dissenting opinion.

presses."[5] It is not surprising then that few nations in the past have succeeded in maintaining any substantial degree of freedom of expression, and that even those have suffered serious relapses in times of pressure.

Similar attitudes prevail in our own times. Studies of public support for freedom of expression reveal an alarmingly high proportion of the population who are unwilling to apply the basic principles of the theory in practice. One such study by the Gallup Poll in 1953, for instance, showed that 67 per cent of those queried thought that a person "known to favor communism" should not be allowed to make a speech in their city or town. Only 29 per cent thought that such a person should be permitted to speak, and 4 per cent had no opinion. Another study by Samuel Stouffer in 1955 concluded that the willingness to grant freedom of speech to Communists was a function less of political views or economic status than of the degree of education.[6]

Taking all these factors into account, it is clear that the problem of maintaining a system of freedom of expression in a society is one of the most complex any society has to face. Self-restraint, self-discipline and maturity are required. The theory is essentially a highly sophisticated one. The members of the society must be willing to sacrifice individual and short-term advantage for social and long-range goals. And the process must operate in a context that is charged with emotion and subject to powerful conflicting forces of self-interest.

These considerations must be weighed in attempting to construct a theory of limitations. A system of free expression can be successful only when it rests upon the strongest possible commitment to the positive right and the narrowest possible basis for exceptions. And any such exceptions must be clear-cut, precise and readily controlled. Otherwise the forces that press toward restriction will break through the openings, and freedom of expression will become the exception and suppression the rule.

A second major element in the problem is the inherent diffi-

[5] Letter to Governor McKean, Feb. 19, 1803, in *The Writings of Thomas Jefferson,* Vol. 8 (Ford ed. 1897), pp. 216, 218.
[6] Gallup Poll, printed in Washington *Post,* Dec. 5, 1953, p. 16, col. 6; S. A. Stouffer, *Communism, Conformity, and Civil Liberties* (Gloucester, Mass., Peter Smith, 1955), pp. 89-90. See also Seymour M. Lipset, *Political Man* (New York, Doubleday, 1960), pp. 109-111.

culty of framing limitations on expression. Expression in itself is not normally harmful, and the objective of the limitation is not normally to suppress the communication as such. Those who seek to impose limitation on expression do so ordinarily in order to forestall some anticipated effect of expression in causing or influencing other conduct. It is difficult enough to trace the effect of the expression after the event. But it is even more difficult to calculate in advance what its effect will be. The inevitable result is that the limitation is framed and administered to restrict a much broader area of expression than is necessary to protect against the harmful conduct feared. In other words, limitations of expression are by nature an attempt to prevent the possibility of certain events occurring rather than a punishment of the undesired conduct after it has taken place. To accomplish this end, especially because the effect of the expression is so uncertain, the prohibition is bound to cut deeply into the right of expression.

Moreover, the infinite varieties and subtleties of language and other forms of communication make it impossible to construct a limitation upon expression in definite or precise terms. It is not easy to frame a prohibition against certain forms of conduct; but to formulate a prohibition which will embrace the multiplicity of words and meanings which might influence conduct can only be done through language exceedingly broad in scope. Men for generations have found ingenious ways to evade mechanical formulae of censorship. The allegory and the historical allusion are only two of the devices that have been used for such purposes. In order to accomplish what the framers of the limitation seek, the limitation must be couched in a sweeping generalization. This means, of course, that a wide area of expression is brought within the reach of the limitation and enormous discretionary power placed in the hands of those who administer it.

This brings us to a third factor in the dynamics of limitation —the apparatus required for administration and enforcement. Those who are assigned this task already have or soon develop a tendency to pursue it with zeal. At the very least they have a job to do, the continued existence of which depends upon their activeness in performing it. Often their efficiency and possibility of advancement are measured in terms of their success, which means success in restricting expression. Prosecution of unpopular opinion is frequently an important avenue of political advancement and hence has a special appeal for the politically ambitious. While there has been little study of the psychology of the censor, security officer and investigator, experience demonstrates that many of those attracted to these positions are likely to be more than ordinarily influenced by the fears, prejudices or emotions which furnish the driving force for suppression. Much of the day-to-day work of administration is controlled by persons in the lower echelons of a bureaucracy, where narrow adherence to rigid rules, fear of superiors, and sensitivity to pressures carry the application of restrictions to their extreme limits. And the accompanying techniques of enforcement in the area of expression—the investigations, surveillance, searches and seizures, secret informers, voluminous files on the suspect —all tend to exercise a repressive influence on freedom of expression.

Other features of the administration of a limitation on expression press in the same direction. Thus the very bringing of a prosecution or other governmental proceeding, even where it is not successful, or the simple fact of investigating, can have the most serious impact. The essential point is that the forces inherent in any system of administration tend to drive to excess, and the mere existence of an enforcement apparatus is in itself restrictive.

A fourth element in the practical administration of limitations on freedom of expression is that the objectives of the limitation are readily subject to distortion and to use for ulterior purposes. Many persons do not easily separate the conduct or threatened conduct of those who express unwanted ideas from their expression of hated and feared opinions. Thus opposition to the conduct or to the potential conduct readily merges into suppression of opinion. The irresistible drive is not only to oppose the action sought by the minority group but to suppress their advocacy of it. Frequently prosecution of unpopular opinion is used as a screen for opposing necessary social change. And often the limitation becomes a weapon in a political struggle, employed primarily for partisan advantage.

Finally, in analyzing limitations on freedom of expression, there must be taken into account the whole impact of restriction on the healthy functioning of a free society. Limitations are seldom applied except in an atmosphere of public fear and hysteria. This may be deliberately aroused or may simply be the inevitable accompaniment of repression. Under such circumstances the doctrines and institutions for enforcing the limitations are subjected to intense pressures. Moreover, while some of the more hardy may be willing to defy the opposition and suffer the consequences, the more numerous are likely to be unwilling to run the risks. Similarly, persons whose cooperation is needed to permit the full flow of open discussion—those who own the means of publication or the facilities for communication —are likely to be frightened into withholding their patronage and assistance.

The dangers of attempting to eliminate what many consider the abuses of freedom of expression were constantly stressed in the struggles to establish an effective system of free expression. James Alexander, the original lawyer for Peter Zenger, who was barred from representing him at the trial, put the point in words that are frequently echoed:

> These abuses of Freedom of Speech are the excrescences of Liberty. They ought to be suppressed; but to whom dare we commit the care of doing it? An evil Magistrate, entrusted with a power to punish Words, is armed with a Weapon the most destructive and terrible. Under the pretense of pruning off the exuberant branches, he frequently destroys the tree.[7]

We lack adequate studies of the dynamics of limiting freedom of expression at various times and places throughout our history. Nevertheless, upon the basis of available material concerning the two outstanding eras of suppression in our past—the period of the Alien and Sedition laws and the First World War—the following conclusions seem warranted:[8]

[7] Philadelphia *Gazette,* Nov. 17, 1737, quoted in Leonard W. Levy, *Legacy of Suppression,* p. 135. For the similar and better known statement of Madison, see James Madison, "Report on the Virginia Resolutions," *Elliot's Debates,* Vol. 4 (1888), p. 571.

[8] The best historical account of the Alien and Sedition laws is J. M. Smith, *Freedom's Fetters* (Ithaca, N.Y., Cornell University Press, 1956). See also J. Miller, *Crisis in Freedom* (Boston, The Atlantic Monthly Press, 1951). Both books contain bibliographies. On the World War II period, Zechariah Chafee, Jr., *Free Speech in the United States* contains the fullest and most realistic discussion of the process of repression in actual operation. For additional material see the bibliography in Thomas I. Emerson and David Haber, *Political and Civil Rights in the United States,* Vol. 1, pp. 290-292.

(1) There was a consistent tendency to overestimate the need for restriction upon freedom of expression. No one now questions that the Alien and Sedition Acts were not required to preserve internal order or to protect the country against any external danger. The restrictions of World War I are also now widely acknowledged to have been unnecessary for achieving similar objectives during that period.[9] The immediate inclination of those in power to restrict expression is likely to take precedence over a more sophisticated judgment to allow longer-range national factors to come into play.

(2) The forces generated in the administration of limitations on freedom of expression tended to push application of the measures to extremes. This lack of moderation—of sober and reasoned administration—was characteristic of both the Alien and Sedition laws and the World War I restrictions.

(3) The difficulties in framing definite and precise limitations were not solved in either period. The language of restriction—whether couched as a limitation on subject matter or on the type of utterance—remained vague and unruly. Nor did the safeguards designed to mitigate the effect of the limitation operate effectively. Neither the defense of truth, the requirement of intent, nor the assurance of jury trial afforded the speaker any substantial protection.

(4) In both periods, administration of the limitations resulted in the creation of an enforcement apparatus which embodied practices most obnoxious to a free society. These included the use of informers, professional witnesses, excessive searches and seizures, government surveillance of broad areas of political expression, and unfair treatment of offenders and suspects.

(5) In practice the restrictions were employed to achieve objectives quite different from the theoretical purposes of the laws. Under the guise of assuring internal order or protection against external danger, the limitations were in fact utilized as a weapon to achieve political and economic ends sought by the group in control of administration. The Alien and Sedition laws became a major weapon in the Federalist effort to wipe out all political opposition and suppress the egalitarian ideas of the

---

[9] Even a past member of the Maryland Committee on Subversive Activities, Frank Ober, one of the leading restrictionists in the World War II period, believes that the "dangers from subversive organizations at the time of World War I were much exaggerated." *American Bar Association Journal,* Vol. 34 (1948), pp. 645, 742.

French Revolution. The World War I restrictions operated not only to curtail criticism of the war and the methods by which it was conducted, but also to crush the growth of all forms of socialist ideology.

(6) The social gains attributable to the restrictions proved to be minimal. In neither period was the security or welfare of the country appreciably enhanced. Nor did the limitations succeed in achieving national unity or social cohesion.

(7) On the other hand, the social losses were heavy. The impact of the restrictions was felt not only by those convicted, but by many who were merely prosecuted, and by countless others who could not accurately judge the boundaries imposed on freedom or who were fearful to take the risk. Enforcement of the restrictions tended to conceal the real issues facing the nation and to divert public attention and resources from their solution. Perhaps most serious of all, the administration of the restrictions resulted in corruption of the entire political atmosphere. The example of illegal and uncivilized methods employed by the government, the bitterness and hostility evoked by enforcement of limitations on expression alone, the encouragement given to public fear and prejudice, all operated to destroy the possibility of rational political discourse.

Similar conclusions can be drawn from other periods in our past, including the suppression of discussion of the slavery issue in the decades prior to the Civil War and the repression of unorthodox views in many localities during the eighteenth and nineteenth centuries.[10] The more recent wave of restrictions that followed World War II, on which we do not yet have the full perspective of history, will undoubtedly be judged in the same light by future generations. The lesson of experience, in short, is that the limitations imposed on discussion, as they operate in practice, tend readily and quickly to destroy the whole structure of free expression. They are very difficult to keep in

---

[10] On the slavery issue see R. B. Nye, *Fettered Freedom* (East Lansing, Michigan State University Press, 1949); on infringements of civil liberties in local areas see Leon Whipple, *The Story of Civil Liberty in the United States* (New York, Vanguard Press, 1927). Generally, see the materials collected in Emerson and Haber, Vol. 1, pp. 279-285, *op cit. supra* note 8, Ch. II; and J. P. Roche, "American Liberty: An Examination of the 'Tradition' of Freedom," in *Aspects of Liberty,* Milton R. Konvitz and Clinton Rossiter, Editors (Ithaca, N.Y., Cornell University Press, 1958), p. 129.

hand; the exceptions are likely to swallow up the theory. Maintenance of a system of free expression, therefore, is not an easy task. This is especially true as we confront the conditions of today. We have tended over the years to refine and delineate more carefully the restrictions we seek to impose. But the new problems arising out of modern industrial society make the issue more delicate and troublesome than at any time in our history.

3 ‖ The Role of Law and
Legal Institutions in
Maintaining a System of Free Expression

‖ THE AMERICAN PEOPLE HAVE frequently been warned that they must not count too heavily upon the legal system for the preservation of democratic liberties. Judge Learned Hand, one of the most eloquent exponents of this view, has made the point in the strongest language:

> I often wonder whether we do not rest our hopes too much upon constitutions, upon laws and upon courts. These are false hopes; believe me, these are false hopes. Liberty lies in the hearts of men and women; when it dies there, no constitution, no law, no court can save it; no constitution, no law, no court can even do much to help it. While it lies there it needs no constitution, no law, no court to save it.[1]

Certainly this admonition must be taken to heart. Obviously, a perfect set of legal rules and an ideal array of judicial institutions could not by themselves assure an effective system of free expression. Many other factors are critical. There must be a substantial consensus on the values and goals of the society—some minimum area of agreement or acquiescence. The economic structure must provide a certain standard of material welfare, shared broadly by all elements of the population. Political institutions must have some basis in the traditions of the people, must receive some degree of acceptance, must prove reasonably effective in meeting the problems of the society, and must remain capable of adjustment and change. Other institu-

[1] Irving Dilliard, Editor, *The Spirit of Liberty, Papers and Addresses of Learned Hand* (New York, Alfred A. Knopf, 1959), p. 144.

tions, such as private corporations and labor organizations, must permit communication on a diverse scale in important areas of decision-making. There must be some feeling of security in relation to other nations or societies. The educational system, the media of communication, and similar institutions molding public opinion must have some capacity to produce mature and independent members of the local and national community. The general philosophy, attitudes and mental health of the citizenry must be favorable. In short, basic conditions for a viable democratic society must be present.

Yet surely Judge Hand has overstated the case. The legal system is not so peripheral to the maintenance of free expression as his words imply. The experience of mankind demonstrates the contrary. Wherever the principles of free expression have prevailed in a society, they have been closely supported by law and legal institutions. This is particularly true, of course, in the United States. The main elements of that role, especially as it has changed in recent years, must be kept in mind in formulating a satisfactory theory of the First Amendment.

The General Role of Law

THE LEGAL SYSTEM IS, of course, one of the most effective instruments available to a society for controlling the behavior of its members so as to realize the values and goals sought by that society. Because of certain characteristics of a system of free expression, the role of law is of peculiar significance in any social effort to maintain such a system.

First, a system of free expression is designed to encourage a necessary degree of conflict within a society. To be sure, it attempts to avoid resort to force or violence by channeling this conflict into the area of expression and persuasion. And it contemplates that a longer-range consensus will ultimately be achieved. Yet, because it recognizes the right of the citizen to disagree with, arouse, antagonize and shock his fellow citizens and the government, such an arrangement of human affairs is hardly likely to be self-operating. In its short-term effects it may indeed be highly volatile. Hence the system needs the legitimizing and harmonizing influence of the legal process to keep it in successful balance.

Other features of a system of free expression likewise demonstrate the need for buttressing it through law and legal institutions. The full benefits of the system can be realized only when the individual knows the extent of his rights and has some assurance of protection in exercising them. Thus the governing principles of such a system need to be articulated with some precision and clarity. Doubt or uncertainty negates the process. Furthermore, the theory rests upon subordination of immediate interests in favor of long-term benefits. This can be achieved only through the application of principle, not by ad hoc resolution of individual cases. And it requires procedures adequate to relieve immediate pressures and facilitate objective consideration. All these elements a legal system is equipped to supply.

Further, as already observed, the theory of freedom of expression is a sophisticated and even complex one. It does not come naturally to the ordinary citizen, but needs to be learned. It must be restated and reiterated not only for each generation but for each new situation. It leans heavily upon understanding and education, both for the individual and the community as a whole. The legal process is one of the most effective methods for providing the kind of social comprehension essential for the attainment of society's higher and more remote ideals.

Finally, the principles of the system must be constantly reshaped and expanded to meet new conditions and new threats to its existence. This requires the deliberate attention of an institution entrusted with that specific obligation and possessing the expertise to perform such a function.

The function of the legal process is not only to provide a means whereby a society shapes and controls the behavior of its individual members in the interests of the whole. It also supplies one of the principal methods by which a society controls itself, limiting its own powers in the interests of the individual. The role of law here is to mark and guard the line between the sphere of social power, organized in the form of the state, and the area of private right. The legal problems involved in maintaining a system of free expression fall largely into this realm. In essence, legal support for such a system involves the protection of individual rights against interference or unwarranted control by the government. More specifically, the legal structure must provide:

(1) Protection of the individual's right to freedom of expression against interference by the government in its efforts to achieve other social objectives or to advance its own interests. This has been in the past the main area of legal concern, and it remains so, although other phases of the problem are assuming increasing importance.

(2) The use and simultaneous restriction of government in regulating conflicts between individuals or groups within the system of free expression itself; in protecting individuals or groups from nongovernmental interference in the exercise of their rights; and in eliminating obstacles to the effective functioning of the system.

(3) Restriction of the government insofar as the government itself participated in the system of expression.

All these requirements involve control over the state. The use of law to achieve this kind of control has been one of the central concerns of freedom-seeking societies over the ages. Legal recognition of individual rights, enforced through the legal process, has become the core of free society.[2]

One must recognize, of course, that the legal system can be used to undermine or destroy freedom of expression. Often in the past, and still in the present, the judicial process has served the function of legitimizing action that is wholly contrary to the elemental principles of free expression. Indeed, even in the police state, infringements of political freedom are normally accomplished in the name of the law. Yet this fact does not lessen, but rather emphasizes, the power of law and legal institutions as an instrument of social persuasion and control. It underlines the warning that the legal system is not by itself sufficient to guarantee free expression. But it also furnishes evidence that without the support of the legal structure the values of such a system are not likely to prevail in the community.[3]

[2] Generally, on the development of constitutionalism, see Charles Howard McIlwain, *Constitutionalism: Ancient and Modern* (Ithaca, N.Y., Cornell University Press, 1958).

[3] For an excellent account of the uses of legal process to thwart a system of free expression, see O. Kirchheimer, *Political Justice*.

It should be noted that Judge Hand's view of law is not the only one which accords a lesser role to law and legal institutions in the protection of individual rights than the position taken in this article. The entire range of approaches, from sociological jurisprudence to the extremes of legal realism, implies some denial of the separate effect of law in shaping or

The Role of Judicial Institutions

THE CAPACITY of the legal order to protect freedom of expression hinges in great part upon the institutions entrusted with the function of translating into legal form and enforcing the basic principles of the system. These institutions have deep roots in the Anglo-American legal process. But much of their form and even more of their quality has taken shape only in recent times. This development has proceeded further in the United States than in any other country. It represents, indeed, one of the major contributions of our political system to the democratic way of life.

The main legal institutions upon which we rely for implementing the principles of free expression are (1) a written constitution, embodying an express (if general) statement of the rights guaranteed to the individual; (2) an independent judiciary possessing the power of judicial review over legislative and executive action; and (3) an independent bar. This is not the place for a detailed treatment of the historical background or special function of each of these institutions. But the role played by the judiciary—the most important of the three—merits brief examination.

At the outset, it is essential to narrow the issue and establish a fundamental distinction. We are not dealing here with any general function of our judicial institutions to foster the whole range of freedoms in a democratic society. Nor are we dealing

---

achieving social goals. In this view, law tends to be conceived as reflecting either historical forces or culture, or some special interest, and not as exercising in itself a substantial impact upon them. Likewise, the policy-oriented approach to law tends to be opposed to the notion of a systematic theory built around one value, or a consistent theory embodying all values from which rules can be drawn that are clearly applicable to a multiplicity of events. From this point of view, a general aim involving many conflicting values is held by the decision-maker, who resolves the conflicts as best he can in the light of the general aim, giving one or another of the values greater weight at one time than another. Hence, while there are rules under this approach, they are mostly symbolic and permit decision either way, at best prescribing only extreme outer limits. Both of these approaches, in part at least, grew out of justifications for upholding substantive economic measures of the New Deal type. *Cf.* Grant Gilmore, "Legal Realism: Its Cause and Cure," *Yale Law Journal,* Vol. 70 (1961), p. 1037. The thesis of this article is that in the field of freedom of expression, law and legal institutions can and should play a more affirmative role.

with any broad power to supervise or review all major actions of the legislative and executive branches. We are concerned with the specific function of the judiciary in supporting a system of freedom of expression. This involves the application of general principles of law to assure that the basic mechanisms of the democratic process will be respected. It does not involve supervision over the decisions reached or measures adopted as a consequence of employing democratic procedures. Responsibility for this is primarily that of the legislature. In other words, the judicial institutions are here dealing essentially with the methods of conducting the democratic process, not with the substantive results of that process. In this differentiation of function lies a generic distinction between the role of the judiciary and the role of the legislature.

Within this narrower context, the part that must be played by the courts in attaining the goal of freedom of expression can be more precisely assessed. The nature of that function is, of course, conditioned by the chief characteristics of our judicial institutions. These may be described as the independence of the judiciary from the other branches of government, its relative immunization from immediate political and popular pressures, the training and quality of its personnel, its utilization of legal procedures, and its powers of judicial review.

In the first place, the judiciary may be said to possess a special competence for dealing with the kind of issues that arise in protecting the mechanisms of the democratic process. The task to be performed is not that of initiating action, but of assuring that action is channeled through acceptable modes of procedure. Hence the judgment relies more upon the knowledge and wisdom derived from historical experience, from broad political and social theory, and from weighing basic values, than upon the kind of information and skill necessary for planning and executing specific projects of economic, political or social regulation. The courts are, in short, specialists in the field of constitutional limitation.

Moreover, if we compare the legislative and executive branches of government with the judicial, it is apparent that the judiciary is the chief institution of the state capable of affording the necessary degree of legal support for a system of free expression. The legislature is subject to the most direct, immediate and constant pressure from the majority or powerful minorities. These pressures largely concern concrete and material objectives, those closest to the daily struggle for livelihood. And the emphasis is strongly upon obtaining results rather than upon methods. Under such circumstances the forces of self-restraint are often less effective in a legislative body.

Furthermore, legislators are not normally trained or experienced in longer-range historical traditions. Although many are lawyers, they are engaged in day-to-day political struggles which occupy most of their time and attention. The politically ambitious are subject to strong partisan pulls, temptations not easily resisted. The fears, prejudices and other emotions stirred by unorthodoxy are more likely to be reflected in their deliberations. Conversely, the road to political power may run in the direction of an appeal to those very irrational motives, couched in the form of simplistic or demagogic slogans. In short, the members of legislative bodies are not likely to be convinced or skilled exponents of the fundamental rules which ultimately must guide political struggles in a democratic system.

Nor does the balance of pressure groups within the legislative institution serve adequately to assure full protection of a system of free expression. This is partly because interest groups of sufficient strength to find representation in the legislature are driven by their own immediate concerns and by the pressures on their own bureaucracy to achieve results. Partly, the reason is that in the legislative struggles of the great pressure groups there is none which represents as such the more general and unorganized interest in preserving fundamental but less immediate values, including freedom of individual expression. Civil liberties organizations and similar associations serve an important function, but their direct influence on the legislative process is not equal to that of the groups organized for economic or political objectives. It is of the essence of the theory of free expression that each single person, even though he be the only one of that view, must be protected in his right of expression. The political structure of the legislature does not fit this theory. Its internal balance is designed principally to safeguard the interests of the majority or powerful minorities. But the right of expression by such groups is least likely to need protection.

Not only has the legislative institution failed to develop within itself the conditions of self-restraint necessary for preserving freedom of individual expression, but the general balance of political forces in the nation, leaving the judicial institution to one side, is not calculated to achieve that objective. The original balance contemplated by the framers of the Constitution was between the popularly elected House of Representatives on the one hand and the Senate and President, chosen indirectly through the state legislatures, on the other. But this balance was seriously impaired by the popular election of both the Senate and the President. In a broad sense both houses of the legislature and the chief executive now represent the dominant majority or at least a coalition of impressive minorities. Nor does the other major balancing mechanism incorporated in the Constitution— the states versus the federal government—solve the problem. That balance operates through a division of areas in which each government may exercise affirmative power, but it does not prevent infringement of individual or minority rights within the allotted area of power. Consequently, only the judicial institutions remain as a counterforce not directly dependent upon the majority temporarily possessing authority.

In short, protection of interest through a balance of forces in the legislative process presupposes political strength, not only in voting power but also in the opportunity to persuade other voters and influence public opinion. Yet the assurance of this political power is one of the very problems that must be solved. Unless such power can be secured in other ways—and it does not automatically follow from a representative system—the technique of balancing forces cannot operate effectively.

This is not to say that legislatures are totally lacking in self-restraint, though much of legislative self-restraint is undoubtedly maintained by the existence of the potential judicial check. Nor is it asserted that legislatures will not normally adhere of their own volition to constitutional limitations. Nevertheless, if the legislature, even rarely, does overstep the bounds of the democratic process, it can fundamentally and irrevocably alter the contours of our society.

When we turn to the executive branch the need is even more compelling for an independent institution which, by applying rules of law that embody the fundamental principles of democratic organization, can hold governmental action in bounds. The executive may well be less vulnerable to the direct influence of a current electoral majority whose concern for concrete material objectives makes it impatient with procedural limitations based on a sophisticated abstract theory. Yet the function of the executive is to carry out social policies formulated by the legislature. Its interest is in practical problems of administration. The test of its success is in achieving results, the methods tending to become of secondary importance. Patterns of advancement and recognition press in the same direction. It is frequently subjected to legislative pressures through appropriations, investigations and similar forms of influence. The very size of the executive branch accentuates the problem. The large number of individuals exercising power; the great percentage of officials who may be poorly paid, incompetent or badly trained; the difficulty of communicating policy and maintaining standards in a large organization; and the inflexibility and disregard of human values endemic in a bureaucracy—all tend to minimize the possibility of self-restraint in the executive branch.

Furthermore, no balance of forces operates to protect minority or individual rights. Executive agencies are not usually constituted to represent various elements in a community, even if such a balance were effective. More likely they reflect a single group, or take on the quasi-independent character of a permanent civil service, more or less impervious to the subtleties of minority protection.

All experience with the operations of the executive in applying limitations to freedom of expression—from the English licensing laws to the loyalty programs of the present day—demonstrates that the executive is strongly influenced to carry such restrictions to extremes. There is far more agreement on the necessity of some judicial check upon executive than upon legislative action. On this issue, indeed, there is virtually no disagreement.

The judicial branch of government thus remains as the major institution upon which we must rely for defining and enforcing the ground rules of a system of freedom of political expression. It is our chief hope for an institutional structure which can operate somewhat removed from the political forces that temporarily wield state power, which can speak for the longer-range interests of the community at large, and which is thereby in a position to afford significant protection to individual rights of expression.[4]

The Role of Law and Judicial Institutions in a Modern Democratic Society

THE ROLE OF LAW and judicial institutions in maintaining a system of freedom of expression has up to this point been described in general and somewhat abstract terms. We have been inclined to think of these matters as they appeared to the framers of the Constitution or as they emerged with the evolution of the Supreme Court during the nineteenth century. In order to understand their full significance, however, it is necessary to examine more specifically how law and judicial institutions operate amid the concrete realities of the present day. It is apparent that the conditions of freedom in the United States, including freedom of expression, are quite different under twentieth century mass democracy than they were under nineteenth century economic liberalism. And the role of law and judicial institutions has been changing decisively also. As we shall see, the new conditions of American democracy make novel and increased demands upon the legal structure; at the same time they make possible more effective legal support for the realization of individual rights. The failure to recognize these developments has been responsible for much of the uncertainty and hesitation in formulating a comprehensive theory of the part which law and the judiciary must play in supporting a system of free expression. It is possible here to sketch this evolution only in briefest outline.

Throughout the nineteenth century the role of the legal system in directly protecting freedom of expression was a relatively narrow one. The main business of the courts was with property relations, especially with the problem of maintaining a free and unobstructed market which would allow full rein to the creative energies of the people. In constitutional terms this meant concern about state or local interference with a nation-wide market. In common law terms it involved concentration on enforcement of

[4] For a recent analysis of the function of our judicial institutions in terms of the political power structure, see Martin Shapiro, "Judicial Modesty, Political Reality, and Preferred Position," *Cornell Law Quarterly*, Vol. 47 (1962), p. 175.

voluntary economic arrangements and the development of legal techniques which facilitated the operation of the marketplace. The chief function of the courts in the area of individual rights lay in the protection afforded in the process of applying the criminal law. Freedom of expression was more the by-product of the economic and political system than the result of deliberate articulation and enforcement of legal doctrine by the courts. Freedom of association was a natural outgrowth of existing conditions. The mechanisms of communication were left to the operation of the general system of laissez-faire. The federal government had no occasion to restrict individual expression except in a military emergency, and here its powers were seldom contested in the courts. Federal authority did not extend to control over most state, local or nongovernmental interference. The state legal systems were entrusted with protection of speech against violent interference by private persons, a task not always adequately performed, but otherwise were seldom called upon to deal with issues of individual expression. All this accounts for the fact that legal implementation of individual rights in free expression lagged well behind the general theory.

Even after 1870, when it became manifest that economic and political laissez-faire in the United States was breaking down, the courts played only a minor role in supporting the right to freedom of expression, or indeed most other individual rights. Well into the twentieth century, judicial attention centered upon issues of property relations. The major constitutional development was the expansion of the due process clause of the Fourteenth Amendment to protect liberty of contract and to restrict governmental efforts to deal with the problems of economic concentration and the abuses of rising industrialism. Legal problems outside the field of constitutional law concerned primarily such matters as corporate structure and financing. Although the Fourteenth Amendment gave the federal courts control over state and local action, the Supreme Court, after the collapse of Reconstruction, exercised its authority beyond the field of property relations only in a minor fashion until the second quarter of the twentieth century. It is typical of the lack of judicial protection of individual rights that the conviction of the Haymarket anarchists, under an extreme application of the doctrine of guilt by association, was remedied (in part) not by the courts but by Governor Altgeld's exercise of executive power. Not until the concern over national security in World War I and its aftermath forced the issue did the courts start to become aware of the new role that was being thrust upon them.[5]

The changes which have taken place and which are still in progress are all essentially the product of technological advances. These changes, in their economic, social and political aspects, are industrialization, urbanization and the proliferation of organization. Their impact upon freedom of expression and the function of law may be summarized roughly as follows:

(1) Industrialization has fundamentally altered the former relationships between property holding and the achievement of individual rights. Concentration of economic power has destroyed the whole structure of numerous independent economic units and eliminated the economic base from which individuals were able to assert their rights against the government and against private power groups. Geographical escape has been cut off. Moreover, the system of free expression can no longer rely for its main support upon the incentive provided by a rising property-holding interest. The driving force must be sought elsewhere. Those groups which now have most to gain from maintaining a fully open society—labor, small farmers, white collar, professional and consumer groups—cannot achieve this objective by insisting on the inviolability of property rights. On the contrary, their interest in change and mobility must be pursued through the force of mass public opinion and political action. Thus, realization of their rights now depends upon the existence of law, not its absence; upon affirmative protection of the legal system, not negative resistance to state authority.

(2) The expansion of organization in our society has left the unorganized sectors peculiarly vulnerable to infringement of their rights. Freedom of expression within the organized group (including the government) by the nonbelonging individual, by the small group, and in connection with the organization of new groups, faces overwhelming hazards. In our highly conformist

[5] See J. Willard Hurst, *Law and the Conditions of Freedom in the Nineteenth-Century United States* (Madison, University of Wisconsin Press, 1956); Roche, p. 145, *supra* note 10, Ch. II. See also Calvin Woodard, "Reality and Social Reform: The Transition from Laissez-Faire to the Welfare State," *Yale Law Journal*, Vol. 72 (1962), p. 286.

society it is from these sources that much of the social value in freedom of expression springs. Yet these deviant individuals and groups, lacking any other base, must find vindication of their rights primarily in resort to the judicial process.

(3) Large-scale and pervasive government, operating on a new order of magnitude and function, poses greater and more subtle threats to individual rights. The government has become an overpowering antagonist in any clash between state and individual. The exercise of authority in many areas, imposing social controls which are acceptable in themselves, tends in actual operation also to circumscribe freedom of expression. Perhaps most important, the danger of distorting legitimate powers for illegitimate purposes has become acute.

(4) Just as the government is now a more formidable foe, so is it a more necessary ally. The breakdown of laissez-faire extends not only to the economic but to other spheres, and our system of free expression is no longer self-operating. The complexities of modern society have introduced into the free marketplace of ideas blockages and distortions that can only be removed by affirmative social controls. The situation is indeed paradoxical. Freedom of expression is by its very nature laissez-faire; it implies absence of government control. Yet the conditions under which freedom of expression can successfully operate in modern society require more and more governmental regulation.

(5) The far-reaching developments of the twentieth century have brought with them new challenges to our feelings of security and competence, and new difficulties in achieving a necessary consensus amid rapid change. Internally, our society is being compelled to face drastic adjustments to novel conditions, major modifications of our whole economic, political and social structure. Externally, we face a fundamental alteration in our relations with the rest of the world. The pace is urgent. Yet as our society has grown older and more institutionalized its rigidities have increased; there has been a crystallization of vested interests and ideas. Pressing against these inflexibilities of the status quo, the insistent forces of change tend to arouse in the body politic anxiety, fear, hostility, frustration and bewilderment. Ofttimes these irrational responses are deliberately stimu-

lated. Probably never before has our society confronted greater possibility of cleavage and disruption.

(6) One of the most significant features of the movement from nineteenth century laissez-faire liberalism to twentieth century mass democracy has been the change in the nature of the political process, particularly the impact of mass public opinion. Because of increased literacy and education, the growth of widespread, rapid communication and the influence of the mass media, public opinion has become broader, more uniform, less independent. Because political issues are more complex, more dependent on specific information not available to the general public, and more remote, public opinion has become more apathetic, less well informed, less focused on precise issues, and less confident. Hence, in mass democracy, public opinion has become more susceptible to manipulation. Frequently this manipulation tends to be demagogic in character, employing broad and often irrational appeals, utilizing slogans and myths, or evoking a scapegoat as an alternative to facing reality. Thus there is much greater need in a mass democracy for countervailing judicial power to protect nonconforming individuals and small minority groups, both in their relations with the legislature and the executive and in their participation in large voluntary associations. There is need also to make as effective as possible the efforts of those leadership groups that are committed to a system of individual rights, whose main weapons are found in an appeal to rational principle and the force of law.

(7) Finally, the evolution of modern society has meant greater participation by the government itself in political expression. Widespread resort to direct coercion by the state is compatible neither with a democratic society nor, in the long run, with a technological society. Modern government strives to achieve unity and control more by the manipulation of public attitudes and opinion than by direct application of official sanctions. Hence, as the area of its control has expanded, the state's interest in affirmative measures of education, persuasion and manipulation has correspondingly increased. Such activities by the state raise obvious problems for a system of free expression, especially where the government possesses a monopoly or quasi-monopoly, as in the field of education. These issues, of course,

cannot be solved exclusively by the application of constitutional doctrines or by the workings of judicial institutions. But in any effort to regulate or control direct participation by the government in political expression the courts, from their relatively independent position as mediators between government and the individual, will necessarily play a growing part.

All these developments have placed upon law and judicial institutions a greater responsibility for the maintenance of a system of freedom of expression. It is important to add, however, that many of the same factors operate to improve the possibility that this burden can be successfully assumed.

In the first place, industrialization, urbanization and particularly the resulting advance in organizational skill have greatly increased the willingness and capacity of our society to make deliberate use of social power and institutions to achieve social results. Our institutions for applying objective criteria to the solution of controversial issues have grown in scope and prestige. This is reflected particularly in the growing use of law and legal institutions as a method of resolving conflicts in different areas and among differing elements. There is abundant evidence of this development. The progress of administrative law—in which legislators, government attorneys, private practitioners, the bench and the law schools have all cooperated—has brought most government activity within the framework of legal standards and procedures, subject to judicial supervision. As a result, many powers formerly exercised outside the legal system have now been brought within it. Large sectors of labor-management relations, once the arena of sharpest conflict, have been reduced to legal order, a spectacular evolution from the turmoil over "government by injunction" of a few decades ago. The decision of the Supreme Court in the recent apportionment case, bringing the judiciary into the settlement of hotly fought controversies over basic units of representation, is another indication of the remarkable change. Only sixteen years before, the decision had gone the other way and such issues were left to be fought without judicial guidance or control. Thus the consistent trend of our society has been that relations between the state, private centers of power and the individual have become more and more defined and enforced through the elaboration of legal procedures.

Life in our cities has tended to make relations between individuals far more impersonal. Yet this has also had the effect of relieving direct local pressures against dissenting opinion, a problem for which the eighteenth and nineteenth centuries never found a successful solution. At the same time it permits association on a wider scale with persons holding like views or pursuing the same limited objectives. Centralization of government, by removing protection of individual rights from the tensions and hazards of "direct democracy," has had a comparable effect. Under urbanization and centralization not only have legal rules and institutions become more necessary, but they are better adapted to safeguarding the rights of individual dissenters. Where private or governmental controls are applied to individuals at close range, in a situation where relations are face-to-face and highly personal, they are less subject to legal restraint. But where there is opportunity for the law to resolve conflicts growing out of more remote and impersonal relations, legal institutions operate to better advantage. The formulation and application of abstract general rules—the essence of the legal process—are much more effective in such a context.

Centralization of government has also resulted in far more extensive national control over state and local infringement of individual rights. Since in recent times our experience has been that such infringement is the more likely to occur the lower the level of government, expansion of federal jurisdiction represents a substantial gain. And quite apart from the propensity of the various levels to violate personal liberty, the very existence of another layer of judicial supervision may well afford important additional protection.

Moreover, the advent of mass democracy does not mean that the problem of safeguarding dissenting expression is beyond solution. The increasing literacy, education, skills and material welfare which accompany industrialization are also potential sources of support for democratic institutions. These, indeed, provide the incentive and the power for preserving an open and advancing society. Further, in a modern technological community, as previously noted, social control by sheer force and repression is ultimately impossible under any system which can be called democratic. Certainly such measures cannot be used against a substantial minority, and consequently in one sense the dimensions of the problem are reduced. The task remaining for laws and judicial institutions—that of protecting the rights of individuals and small minorities—is at least one of more manageable proportions.

Finally, the changed relationship of this country to the rest of the world has also brought certain benefits to our own system of individual rights. Our power and influence in world affairs rest in great part upon the appeal of our tradition and practice of personal freedom. The desire—indeed the need—to preserve this "image" of America has frequently spurred us to greater efforts and has noticeably strengthened the position of the judiciary as guardian of the heritage.

To summarize the discussion up to this point, the central issue posed by the twentieth century for our system of free expression is the development of methods for maintaining that system, not as a self-adjusting by-product of laissez-faire, but as a positive and deliberate function of the social process. The underlying theory of freedom of expression remains unaltered. But the legal foundations by which the theory is to be realized have fundamentally changed. What is needed is a consciously formulated structure of protection, embracing legal doctrines that are operationally workable and utilizing legal institutions that are equipped to handle the problem. The conditions for successfully accomplishing this task exist. Its achievement presents a basic challenge for our time.

The Role of the Supreme Court

INASMUCH AS THE Supreme Court stands at the apex of our judicial institutions and is by far the most influential of them all, it is perhaps desirable to add a few words specifically concerning the role of that body.[6]

[6] The place of the Supreme Court in our political structure has, of course, been the subject of unending comment and controversy. Most of this discussion has not focused on the precise issue before us—the function of the Supreme Court in supporting a system of freedom of expression—and hence is largely irrelevant to our present purposes. Only a fraction of the literature dealing with the manner in which the Supreme Court should exercise its powers of judicial review can be cited here. The so-called "passivist" approach derives primarily from James B. Thayer, "The Origin and Scope of the American Doctrine of Constitutional Law," *Harvard Law Review*, Vol. 7 (1893), p. 129, and is represented by Learned Hand, *The Bill of Rights* (Cambridge, Mass., Harvard Univer-

What has been said about judicial institutions in general applies with particular force to the Supreme Court. The character of the individual rights and social values at stake, the kind of forces loosed in prescribing limitations, the necessity for support by law, especially under conditions of mass democracy, all demand that the Court play a positive, indeed almost an aggressive role in this area. By the very nature of the problem—the protection of individual rights against a majority acting through the legislature or the executive—an attitude of "passivism" on the part of the one institution expressly assigned the protecting role cannot meet the requirements of the situation.

The objections urged against an "activist" role for the Supreme Court have, as Judge Hand himself recognized, the least application where the purpose of review is to safeguard a system of freedom of expression.[7] The argument that the courts lack the competence to assume an active role, that they are by nature unsuited for such a task, seems clearly without foundation in this area; on the contrary, for reasons already noted, judicial institutions are peculiarly equipped to deal with these issues. The contention that reliance upon judicial review fosters irresponsibility in other institutions of government and in the public carries little weight here in light of the political realities of today and our irreversible commitment to the practice. The position

sity Press, 1958); R. Jackson, *The Supreme Court in the American System of Government* (New York, Harper and Row, 1955); Paul A. Freund, *The Supreme Court of the United States* (Gloucester, Mass., Peter Smith, 1961); Herbert Wechsler, "Toward Neutral Principles of Constitutional Law," *Harvard Law Review*, Vol. 73 (1959), p. 1, reprinted in *Principles, Politics and Fundamental Law* (Cambridge, Mass., Harvard University Press, 1961); R. G. McCloskey, *The American Supreme Court* (Chicago, University of Chicago Press, 1960); Wallace Mendleson, *Justices Black and Frankfurter* (Chicago, University of Chicago Press, 1961); A. M. Bickel, *The Least Dangerous Branch* (Indianapolis, Bobbs-Merrill, 1962). The so-called "activist" position is represented by William Douglas, *The Right of the People* (New York, Doubleday, 1958); W. W. Rostow, "The Democratic Character of Judicial Review," *Harvard Law Review*, Vol. 66 (1952), p. 193; Edmond N. Cahn, "The Firstness of the First Amendment," *Yale Law Journal*, Vol. 65 (1956), p. 464; Fred Rodell, "Judicial Activists, Judicial Self-Deniers, Judicial Review and the First Amendment," *Georgia Law Journal*, Vol. 47 (1959), p. 483; R. S. McKay, "The Preference for Freedom," *New York University Law Review*, Vol. 34 (1959), p. 1182; Charles Lund Black, *The People and the Court* (New York, Macmillan, 1960); Shapiro, *supra* note 4, Ch. III.

[7] Hand, p. 69, *op. cit. supra* note 6, Ch. III.

that utilization of judicial review in this area is undemocratic is based upon the assumption that democracy is pure majoritarianism and ignores the widespread acceptance of judicial review in the United States as a crucial element in maintaining those mechanisms of the democratic process which safeguard the rights of individuals and minorities against the majority.

The objection that our judicial institutions lack the political power and prestige to perform an active role in protecting freedom of expression against the will of the majority raises more difficult questions. Certainly judicial institutions must reflect the traditions, ideals and assumptions, and in the end must respond to the needs, claims and expectations, of the social order in which they operate. They must not and ultimately cannot move too far ahead or lag too far behind. The problem for the Supreme Court is one of finding the proper degree of responsiveness and leadership, or perhaps better, of short-term and long-term responsiveness. Yet in seeking out this position the Court should not underestimate the authority and prestige it has achieved over the years. Representing the "conscience of the community," it has come to possess a very real power to keep alive and vital the higher values and goals toward which our society imperfectly strives. Our experience as a nation confirms the strength of the Court's role in this respect; with the possible exception of the eleventh amendment, the people have never changed our fundamental law to withdraw individual rights to which the Court has given sanction. In any event, the issue at stake is nothing less than the maintenance of the democratic process. Given its prestige, it would appear that the power of the Court to protect freedom of expression is unlikely to be substantially curtailed unless the whole structure of our democratic institutions is threatened. Even then, we cannot assume that the American people, if the issue were made clear to them, would choose to pursue this course of action. And surely the Court should not, in anticipation of such a turn of events or through a negative or timid attitude, abandon the leadership which history has thrust upon it.

Two corollary propositions may be added, pertaining to the attitude of the Supreme Court toward the two other major institutions of government with which it may come into opposition. In its relations with the legislature the Court should be guided by the crucial distinction between the Court's function

in reviewing issues involving the basic mechanisms of the democratic process and issues concerned with the results of that
process. In the latter sector the Supreme Court's role is necessarily limited; in the former it is vital and pervasive. The Court's
obligation to bow to the will of the legislature and the executive
is at a minimum where a serious claim to infringement of freedom of expression on the part of those institutions is presented.
In this sense, from the judicial point of view, freedom of expression should be regarded as a "preferred freedom."

In the second place, the Supreme Court should apply the same
rules to alleged interference with freedom of expression by state
(or local) governments as by the federal government. This is, of
course, the accepted doctrine of the Court, although occasionally
suggestions have been made for a relaxation of the rules in their
application to the states.[8] As heretofore observed, infringement
of freedom of expression is the more likely to occur the lower the
level of official involved, and local institutions are less capable of
maintaining individual rights than the more remote and often
better-staffed institutions at the higher levels. The objection that
national uniformity in this area constitutes an unwarranted interference with state or local rights is not sufficiently persuasive to
outweigh the advantages and the need of federal supervision.
The problem of maintaining an effective system of freedom of
expression is today a national, not to say international, problem,
and the federal courts have not been able to remain aloof.
Actually, the interference with state and local governments in
this area is minimal, for the federal government is simply
enunciating general rules of democratic procedure, not depriving
the state of any substantive authority to solve its problems
through the extensive powers available to it, or taking over the
burdens (and political power) of administration. Hence the
impact on the relative powers of the federal and state governments is small. The Supreme Court should not hesitate or pro-

---

[8] See *Beauharnais v. Illinois,* 343 U.S. 250, 287 (1952) (Jackson, J.,
dissenting); *Roth v. United States,* 354 U.S. 476, 496 (1957) (Harlan,
J., dissenting); O. John Rogge, *The First and the Fifth* (New York,
Thomas Nelson and Sons, 1960), pp. 35-53. The position is implied in
Mr. Justice Frankfurter's view of the relationship of the First Amendment
to the Fourteenth Amendment. See his opinions in *Adamson v. California,*
332 U.S. 46, 59 (1947), *Beauharnais and Sweezy v. New Hampshire,* 354
U.S. 234, 255 (1957).

ceed cautiously in enforcing the fundamental ground rules of the democratic process throughout the nation.

This brief attempt to appraise the role of the Supreme Court has necessarily proceeded at a highly abstract level. The propositions urged are not sufficient to decide any particular case. But they do represent an approach, an attitude, a philosophy. As such they constitute a critical point of departure.

4 ‖ *The Formulation of Legal Doctrine: In General*

‖ THE ATTAINMENT OF FREE-
dom of expression is not the sole aim of the good society. As the
private right of the individual, freedom of expression is an end
in itself, but it is not the only end of man as an individual. In its
social and political aspects, freedom of expression is primarily a
process or a method for reaching other goals. It is a basic element in the democratic way of life, and as a vital process it
shapes and determines the ends of democratic society. But it is
not through this process alone that a democratic society will
attain its ultimate ends. Any theory of freedom of expression
must therefore take into account other values, such as public
order, justice, equality and moral progress, and the need for
substantive measures designed to promote those ideals. Hence
there is a real problem of reconciling freedom of expression with
the other values and objectives sought by the good society.

All institutions of society are necessarily involved in this
process of reconciliation. We are concerned here, however, with
the role of law and judicial institutions. And this requires that, to
the extent the courts participate in the process, the principles of
reconciliation must be expressed in the form of legal doctrine.

The major source of legal doctrine is, of course, the First
Amendment. Other constitutional provisions—such as the requirement of due process, the privilege against self-incrimination,
and the prohibition against unreasonable searches and seizures—
are relevant and important; a workable system of free expression
must rely upon the whole complex of legal rules designed for the
protection of individual rights.[1] But here we limit discussion to

[1] See Cahn, pp. 476-478, *supra* note 6, Ch. III.

doctrines flowing from the First Amendment. Within that framework, however, proposals for acceptable doctrine will not be confined to those previously asserted as embodying the meaning of the First Amendment or those deduced from prior decisions of the Supreme Court.

This analysis assumes as its fundamental premise the proposition that the framers of the First Amendment intended that provision to serve as the legal basis for guaranteeing an effective system of freedom of expression, and that such fundamental constitutional provisions ought to be interpreted vitally to meet the requirements of the present day. In framing legal doctrine to carry out this basic purpose, the analysis necessarily incorporates by reference our previous discussion of the function of freedom of expression in a democratic society, the dynamics of limitation, and the role of law and legal institutions in supporting a system of freedom of expression. Each of these elements must be taken into account in formulating the basic principles of First Amendment doctrine and in constructing the specific rules to govern the various kinds of situations in which First Amendment problems are posed.

Before attempting these tasks, however, it is necessary to make a partial digression in order to examine the various theories which have from time to time been proposed for reconciling the right to freedom of expression with other social values and objectives.

A Critique of Existing Theories

AT THE OUTSET certain general theories of reconciliation which have never received any substantial support as a proper interpretation of the First Amendment are rejected. The earliest, and one of the most common in previous periods, was simply to exclude certain groups altogether from the right to freedom of expression. Thus Milton would not have extended the freedom to Catholics, atheists, or non-Christians. Locke apparently would have denied political liberty to Catholics and would have punished those who "will not own and teach the duty of tolerating all men in matters of mere religion." Some of the earlier supporters of free expression seem to have contemplated that the right should be exercised only by a relatively small elitist group.[2] Today this theory takes the form that freedom of expression should not be allowed to "anti-democratic" groups.[3] The prevailing current view, however, is that freedom of expression should be extended to all groups, even those which seek to destroy it.[4] This position is the only one consistent with the basic affirmative theory and compatible with successful administration of an effective system.

Likewise, some who support the affirmative theory have argued nevertheless that reconciliation should be framed generally in terms of the nature of the expression. Thus the old law

[2] Milton, pp. 37-38, *op. cit. supra* note 3, Ch. I; "A Treatise of Civil Power in Ecclesiastical Causes," in *The Works of John Milton*, Vol. 6 (1932), pp. 13-14; "Of True Religion, Heresie, Schism, and Toleration," *ibid.*, pp. 172-173; John Locke, "A Letter Concerning Toleration," in *The Works of John Locke*, Vol. 6 (1801), p. 45. For a discussion of the theory from Milton to the end of the eighteenth century, with emphasis on the limitations urged, see Leonard W. Levy, *Legacy of Suppression*.

[3] For expressions of this view, see Carl A. Auerbach, "The Communist Control Act of 1954: A Proposed Legal-Political Theory of Free Speech," *University of Chicago Law Review*, Vol. 23 (1956), p. 173; Evan F. M. Durbin, *The Politics of Democratic Socialism* (London, G. Routledge, 1940), pp. 275-279; Karl R. Popper, *The Open Society and Its Enemies*, Ch. 7 (New York, Harper and Row, 1952); Edward H. Carr, *The Soviet Impact on the Western World* (New York, Macmillan, 1947), pp. 13-17; Walter Lippmann, *The Public Philosophy* (New York, New American Library, 1956), pp. 96-103. See also the material cited in D. Riesman, "Civil Liberties in a Period of Transition," in *Public Policy*, Vol. 3, Carl J. Freidrich and Edward S. Mason, Editors (Cambridge, Mass., Harvard University Press, 1942), pp. 33, 52-68; G. E. G. Catlin, "On Freedom," in *Aspects of Liberty*, Milton R. Konvitz and Clinton Rossiter, Editors (Ithaca, N.Y., Cornell University Press, 1958), p. 49; W. F. Berns, *Freedom, Virtue and the First Amendment* (Chicago, Henry Regnery Co., 1957).

[4] Chafee, pp. 30-35, *op. cit. supra* note 8, Ch. II; Riesman, p. 43; *supra* note 3, Ch. IV; Meiklejohn, pp. 42-43, 57, 76-77, *op. cit. supra* note 1, Ch. I; Douglas, pp. 91-94, *op. cit. supra* note 6, Ch. III; *American Communications Ass'n v. Douds*, 339 U.S. 382, 439 (1950) (Jackson, J.); *Dennis v. United States*, 341 U.S. 494 (1951). For less clear-cut statements, see Thomas Jefferson, "First Inaugural Address, March 4, 1801," in *Life and Selected Writings of Thomas Jefferson* (New York, Random House, 1944), p. 321; John Stuart Mill, *On Liberty and Other Essays* (New York, E. P. Dutton, 1927), pp. 37, 101-110; Walter Bagehot, "The Metaphysical Basis of Toleration," in *Works of Walter Bagehot*, Vol. 2 (Hutton ed., 1889), pp. 326, 343; but *cf. ibid.* at p. 358; C. L. Becker, *Freedom and Responsibility in the American Way of Life* (New York, Random House, 1945), pp. 40-41.

of seditious libel, the suggestion that protection be extended to speech that is true but not to that which is false or misleading, limitations based on evil intent or motive, prohibition of abusive or vituperative communication, and the test of social utility, have all been urged as appropriate standards. These criteria are understandable as the product of an age when the theory was novel and could only be expected to make cautious headway against the long tradition of suppression. But they obviously cannot serve as useful standards for the present day. Some of them may be relevant, though not necessarily controlling, in particular types of situations. But as general standards they are clearly contrary to the affirmative theory, unworkable, and destructive of freedom of expression.

We come then to the major doctrines which have in recent times been enunciated by a majority or minority of the Supreme Court. It is possible to deal with them only in the briefest fashion.

Bad Tendency Test

In the earlier stages of the interpretation of the first amendment, a majority of the Supreme Court accepted the so-called "bad tendency" test. According to this doctrine, expression which had a tendency, or which the legislature could reasonably believe had a tendency, to lead to substantial evil could be prohibited. The Court in the *Gitlow* case stated the doctrine broadly, "That a State in the exercise of its police power may punish those who abuse this freedom [of speech] by utterances inimical to the public welfare, tending to corrupt public morals, incite to crime, or disturb the public peace, is not open to question." With reference to the particular issue before it—speech thought to endanger the public peace and safety—the Court held that the legislature was entitled to "extinguish the spark without waiting until it has enkindled the flame or blazed into conflagration." [5]

The bad tendency test offers virtually no protection to freedom of expression. In theory, achievement of all other social values or objectives is preferred to allowing expression where any apparent conflict between the two exists. In practice, the doctrine cuts off expression at a very early point on the road to action; significant

---

[5] *Gitlow v. New York,* 268 U.S. 652, 667, 669 (1925). See also *Whitney v. California,* 274 U.S. 357 (1927).

opposition to the government or its policies, for instance, receives no legal protection. The test has now been abandoned.[6]

Clear and Present Danger Test

In the development of Supreme Court doctrine, the bad tendency test came to be superseded by the "clear and present danger" test. As originally enunciated by Justice Holmes in the *Schenck* case the test was: "The question in every case is whether the words used are used in such circumstances and are of such a nature as to create a clear and present danger that they will bring about the substantive evils that Congress has a right to prevent." [7] The doctrine was elaborated by Justice Brandeis in his *Whitney* opinion, and was extensively employed by the Court in various types of cases until the *Douds* and *Dennis* cases in the early 1950's.[8]

The clear and present danger test represented a substantial advance over the bad tendency test and was welcomed by many supporters of freedom of expression. In theory, it protects some expression even though that expression interferes with the attainment of other social objectives, for the danger to the other interests must be immediate and clear. In practice, by drawing the line of allowable expression closer to the point of action, it opened up a wider area of protection. But there are serious objections to the test:

(1) The formula assumes that once expression immediately threatens the attainment of some valid social objective, the expression can be prohibited. But no very viable system of freedom of expression can exist under such limitations. The basic theory

[6] The *Gitlow* doctrine was urged by the government in the *Dennis* case but rejected by the Court. *Dennis v. United States,* 341 U.S. 494, 507 (1951).

[7] *Schenck v. United States,* 249 U.S. 47, 52 (1919).

[8] *Whitney v. California,* 274 U.S. 357 (1927); *American Communications Ass'n v. Douds,* 339 U.S. 382 (1950); *Dennis v. United States,* 341 U.S. 494 (1951) (reviewing the prior decisions). Several significant decisions of this period, notably those in which Chief Justice Hughes wrote the opinion, did not employ the clear and present danger test. See *De Jonge v. Oregon,* 299 U.S. 353 (1937); *Stromberg v. California,* 283 U.S. 359 (1931). A recent account of the history of the clear and present danger test, together with a collection of the previous literature discussing it, may be found in R. S. McKay, "The Preference for Freedom," *New York University Law Review,* Vol. 34 (1959), pp. 1182, 1203-1212.

contemplates that conflict with other objectives must occur, and indeed the system can be said to operate only where such conflict does take place. To permit the state to cut off expression as soon as it comes close to being effective is essentially to allow only abstract or innocuous expression. In short, a legal formula framed solely in terms of effectiveness of the expression in influencing action is incompatible with the existence of free expression.

(2) The clear and present danger test is excessively vague. As experience has shown, its application by the Court leads to no one ascertainable result. And for the main participants in the system of freedom of expression—police, prosecutors, and other officials on the one hand and the individual seeking to exercise his rights on the other—the test furnishes little clarity in advance of a judicial decision.

(3) In all but the simplest situations the factual judgment demanded of the court is difficult or impossible to make through the use of judicial procedures. If the Supreme Court had taken the factual issue seriously in the *Dennis* case, for example, and attempted to assess whether the utterances of the Communist Party actually constituted a clear and present danger, it would have been plunged into consideration of a mass of historical, political, economic, psychological and social facts concerning the position and influence of the Communist Party in the United States and abroad. This judgment would have included both evaluation and prophecy of a sort no court is competent to give. In many situations, therefore, the test cannot be intelligently applied.[9]

(4) The doctrine grew out of cases where the restriction at issue was a direct prohibition of expression by criminal or similar sanctions, and is of doubtful application to other kinds of interference with freedom of expression. In a legislative investigating case, for example, a rule allowing the committee to inquire about expression that might create a clear and present danger of some substantive evil would seem to impose no limits whatever upon

[9] Mr. Justice Douglas, alone among the justices, did make a serious attempt to apply the clear and present danger test in *Dennis,* relying for his factual material on judicial notice. See *Dennis v. United States,* 341 U.S. at 585-87. Mr. Justice Douglas has since abandoned the test, at least for most purposes. See, *e.g., Scales v. United States,* 367 U.S. 203, 262-75 (1961).

the scope of investigation into expression. And where the regulation in question is not aimed directly at punishing a particular utterance but affects freedom of expression in a more generalized or indirect way, as in a tax law or a disclosure requirement, the issues are not framed in terms of whether a specific utterance creates a specific danger. In any event, the clear and present danger test has not been applied in such cases.

(5) In the course of its development the clear and present danger test was expanded to include other factors than the immediate impact of expression in bringing about action. Thus such elements as the nature and gravity of the evil sought to be prevented, the alternatives open to the government, and the value of the expression in relation to the harm feared were taken into account. When this is done, however, the clear and present danger test becomes indistinguishable from the ad hoc balancing test, discussed next, and is subject to the same infirmities.

The clear and present danger test was abandoned by a majority of the Supreme Court in the *Dennis* case. The substitute —the gravity of the evil, discounted by its improbability— excised the main features of the original test by eliminating or minimizing the requirement that the danger be immediate and clear. The present status of the clear and present danger test is thus in some doubt. There is still some blood remaining in the doctrine, and it has continued to be used in certain types of situations.[10] But as a general test of the limits of the First Amendment, the clear and present danger test must be regarded as unacceptable.

Ad Hoc Balancing

Whereas the bad tendency test accords no weight to the values of free expression, and the clear and present danger test gives them weight only in a limited area, the ad hoc balancing test purports to give them full weight. The formula is that the court must in each case balance the individual and social interest in freedom of expression against the social interest sought by the

[10] The clear and present danger test was recently applied to invalidate a conviction for contempt of court based upon utterances alleged to interfere with a grand jury proceeding. *Wood v. Georgia,* 370 U.S. 375 (1962). The decision was by a vote of 5 to 2, but all justices participating acquiesced in the use of the test.

regulation which restricts expression. The test, first clearly enunciated in Chief Justice Vinson's opinion in the *Douds* case, has been employed by a majority of the Supreme Court in a number of subsequent decisions. It is not entirely clear whether the test is meant to be one of general application to all First Amendment issues, but it is fair to say that its supporters consider it the dominant theory.[11]

The principal difficulty with the ad hoc balancing test is that it frames the issues in such a broad and undefined way, is in effect so unstructured, that it can hardly be described as a rule of law at all. As a legal doctrine for affording judicial protection to a system of freedom of expression, it is not tenable. More specifically:

(1) The ad hoc balancing test contains no hard core of doctrine to guide a court in reaching its decision. Rather, a court is cast loose in a vast space, embracing the broadest possible range of issues, to strike a general balance in the light of its own best judgment. Not only does the test allow a court to reach either conclusion in almost every case, but the lack of structure makes it realistically impossible for a court to perform its difficult function of applying accepted and impartial rules to hold in check the unruly forces that seek to destroy a system of free expression.

[11] In addition to the opinion of Chief Justice Vinson in the *Douds* case, 339 U.S. at 394, leading opinions employing the ad hoc balancing test are those of Mr. Justice Frankfurter, concurring in the *Dennis* case, 341 U.S. at 517, and in *Communist Party v. Subversive Activities Control Bd.*, 367 U.S. 1, 4 (1961); Mr. Justice Harlan in *N.A.A.C.P. v. Alabama*, 357 U.S. 449, 451 (1958), *Barenblatt v. United States*, 360 U.S. 109, 111 (1959), and *Konigsberg v. State Bar*, 366 U.S. 36, 37 (1961); and Mr. Justice Clark, dissenting in *Talley v. California*, 362 U.S. 60, 67 (1960). The leading opinions criticizing the test are those of Mr. Justice Black in the *Barenblatt, Konigsberg,* and *Communist Party* cases, *supra,* and in *Braden v. United States,* 365 U.S. 431, 438 (1961). For comment supporting the test see Kenneth L. Karst, "Legislative Facts in Constitutional Litigation," *Supreme Court Review,* Vol. 75 (1960); Wallace Mendelson, *Justices Black and Frankfurter: Conflict in the Court* (Chicago, University of Chicago Press, 1961); Paul G. Kauper, Book Review, *Michigan Law Review,* Vol. 58 (1960), p. 619. For comment criticizing the test see H. Black, "The Bill of Rights," *New York University Law Review,* Vol. 35 (1960), p. 865; Edmond Cahn, "Mr. Justice Black and First Amendment 'Absolutes': A Public Interview," *New York University Law Review,* Vol. 37 (1962), p. 549; Alexander Meiklejohn, "The Balancing of Self-Preservation Against Political Freedom," *California Law Review,* Vol. 49 (1961), p. 4; Laurent B. Frantz, "The First Amendment in the Balance," *Yale Law Journal,* Vol. 71 (1962), p. 1424.

(2) If a court takes the test seriously, the factual determinations involved are enormously difficult and time-consuming, and quite unsuitable for the judicial process. This is even more true here than in the application of the clear and present danger test.[12]

(3) Actually, the test does not allow the judicial institution to exercise any real degree of independent judgment. As applied to date, the test gives almost conclusive weight to the legislative judgment. In the words of its chief exponent, Mr. Justice Frankfurter, the Court will not question the decision of the legislature unless that determination is "outside the pale of fair judgment." [13] It is true that the test does not necessarily compel this excessive deference to the legislature. But the operation of the test tends strongly towards that result. For a court must rest its decision on the broadest considerations of policy, which are normally the grist of legislative determination. A court is therefore in the difficult or impossible position of having either to acquiesce in the legislative judgment or to overrule the legislature on the latter's own ground. In wholesale disregard of the fundamental difference between legislative and judicial functions, the decision is necessarily framed largely in terms of policy or wisdom, rather than in terms of limitation on power.

(4) The test gives no real meaning to the First Amendment. As Mr. Justice Black has justifiably protested, it amounts to no more than a statement that the legislature may restrict expression whenever it finds it reasonable to do so, and that the courts will not restrain the legislature unless that judgment is itself unreasonable. The same degree of protection could be obtained under the due process clause, without the First Amendment. Surely the First Amendment was not intended and should not be applied to afford as little support as this for a system of free expression.

(5) The test cannot afford police, prosecutors, other government officials and the individual adequate advance notice of the

---

[12] For a summary of the factors which would have to be balanced in order to determine the issue in *Barenblatt v. United States,* 360 U.S. 109 (1959), see Laurent B. Frantz, "The First Amendment in the Balance," *Yale Law Journal,* Vol. 71 (1962), pp. 1443-1444 n. 87. The effort of the defense to introduce expert testimony on the balancing issue in a later congressional investigating committee case was rejected by the trial court. *United States v. Yellin,* 287 F.2d 292 (7th Cir.), *cert. granted,* 368 U.S. 816 (1961).

[13] *Dennis v. United States,* 341 U.S. at 540.

rights essential to be protected. Moreover, the test is unworkable from the viewpoint of judicial administration, requiring for ultimate decision an ad hoc resolution by the highest tribunal in each case. For these reasons the test is wholly incapable of coping with the dynamic forces evoked by governmental efforts at limitation of expression.

In sum, when examined in the light of our previous analysis of the elements essential to a system of freedom of expression, the ad hoc balancing test is, as a legal theory of reconciliation, illusory.

Absolute Test

The so-called "absolute" test is somewhat more unsettled in meaning than the other tests proposed, in part because its opponents have seemingly misunderstood it and in part because its supporters are not in full agreement among themselves. Two things are clear. The test is not that all words, writing and other communications are, at all times and under all circumstances, protected from all forms of government restraint. No advocate of the test, so far as this writer is aware, takes this extreme and obviously untenable position. Nor is the test necessarily one of the "literal meaning," in the sense that one need only look to the wording of the First Amendment to find immediately, on the face of the provision, the complete answer to every issue.[14]

Actually, the absolute test involves two components:

(1) The command of the First Amendment is "absolute" in the

---

[14] Some of the leading statements of the absolute position may be found in dissenting opinions and articles of Mr. Justice Black cited in note 11, Ch. IV *supra;* the concurring opinion of Mr. Justice Douglas in *Speiser v. Randall,* 357 U.S. 513, 536-537 (1958), and his dissenting opinions in *Times Film Corp. v. City of Chicago,* 365 U.S. 43, 78 (1961), and *Scales v. United States,* 367 U.S. 203, 262 (1961); Alexander Meiklejohn, *Political Freedom,* and "The First Amendment Is an Absolute," *Supreme Court Review,* Vol. 245 (1961). For a sympathetic discussion of Justice Black's position see C. Black, Jr., "Mr. Justice Black, the Supreme Court and the Bill of Rights," *Harper's Magazine,* Feb. 1961, p. 63; and Charles Alan Reich, "Mr. Justice Black and the Living Constitution," *Harvard Law Review,* Vol. 76 (1963), p. 673. For criticism of the absolute position see the opinion of Mr. Justice Harlan in the *Konigsberg* case, Mendelson, and Karst, all *supra* note 11, Ch. IV; Alexander Bickel, "Mr. Justice Black, The Unobvious Meaning of Plain Words," *The New Republic,* Mar. 14, 1960, p. 13; R. S. McKay, "The Preference for Freedom," *New York University Law Review,* Vol. 34 (1959), pp. 1182, 1193-1203.

sense that "no law" which "abridges" "the freedom of speech" is constitutionally valid. This proposition has been criticized as self-evident, though supporters of the ad hoc balancing test have at times used language which suggests disagreement with it.[15] And the proposition may not appear to carry the decision-maker very far, since it is still necessary to decide in each case the meaning of "abridge," of "the freedom of speech," and sometimes of "law." But the point being stressed is by no means inconsequential. For it insists on focusing the inquiry upon the definition of "abridge," "the freedom of speech," and if necessary "law," rather than on a general de novo balancing of interests in each case. And the text gives weight to the constitutional decision made in adopting the First Amendment by emphasizing that the entire question of reconciling social values and objectives is not reopened. This approach of "defining" rather than "balancing" narrows and structures the issue for the courts, bringing it more readily within the bounds of judicial procedures. It is true that the process of "defining" requires a weighing of various considerations, but this is not the same as open-ended "balancing." On this aspect of the absolute test all proponents of the doctrine appear to be in agreement.

(2) The absolute test includes another component. It is intended to bring a broader area of expression within the protection of the First Amendment than the other tests do. It does this by including a wider sector of government activity within the definition of "abridge," a more extensive area of expression within "the freedom of speech," and at times a broader notion of state action within the term "law." [16] It is perhaps misleading to apply the term "absolute" to this portion of the theory. As already noted, the process does not result in every communication being given unqualified immunity from restriction or regulation under the First Amendment. The characterization as "absolute" does serve the purpose, however, of emphasizing the

---

[15] See Mr. Justice Frankfurter in *Communist Party v. Subversive Activities Control Bd.*, 367 U.S. at 90-91.

[16] By way of illustration from Mr. Justice Black's opinions see, on the definition of "abridge," his dissenting opinion in *Communist Party v. Subversive Activities Control Bd.*, 367 U.S. 1, 137-38, 147-169; on the definition of "the freedom of speech" his dissenting opinion in *Dennis v. United States*, 341 U.S. 497, 579-581; and on the definition of "law" his dissenting opinion in *International Ass'n of Machinists v. Street*, 367 U.S. 740, 780, 788-791 (1961).

positive features of the constitutional guarantee and limiting the area of restraint.[17]

As to the first component of the absolute test—framing the issue as one of "defining" rather than "balancing"—the proponents of the doctrine are, in the opinion of this writer, entirely correct, though they may not have fully articulated the reasons in terms of the essential elements of a system of freedom of expression. As to the second component—the scope of the protected area of expression—the test remains in an unsatisfactory state, partly because the proponents are in disagreement over their conclusions, but primarily because they have never sufficiently defined the terms upon which its application rests. The reasons underlying a choice of definition have never been fully explored. Consequently, the test has remained not only vulnerable to attack as embodying merely "an unlimited license to talk," [18] but as essentially undeveloped and inchoate. This state of affairs is no doubt explainable, at least in part, by the fact that the absolute test has never commanded a majority of the Supreme Court and hence its supporters have never been compelled to face the responsibility of formulating its scope with precision.[19]

The upshot of this analysis of current legal doctrine attempting to reconcile competing values under the First Amendment is that the bad tendency test, the clear and present danger test, and the ad hoc balancing test do not afford adequate protection to a system of freedom of expression. Some better theory is urgently needed. The absolute test, while incorporating one basic principle of a satisfactory theory, has left a host of major issues unresolved and largely unexplored.[20]

[17] For elaboration on this point, see C. Black, Jr., "Mr. Justice Black, the Supreme Court, and the Bill of Rights," *Harper's Magazine,* Feb. 1961, p. 63.

[18] Mr. Justice Harlan in *Konigsberg v. State Bar,* 366 U.S. 36, 50 (1961).

[19] See Charles Alan Reich, "Mr. Justice Black and the Living Constitution," *Harvard Law Review,* Vol. 76 (1963), p. 673.

[20] For other efforts to frame a general theory of the First Amendment see, *e.g.,* Comment, "Legislative Inquiry into Political Activity: First Amendment Immunity from Committee Interrogation," *Yale Law Journal,* Vol. 65 (1956), p. 1159; Comment, "The Constitutional Right to Anonymity: Free Speech, Disclosure and the Devil," *Yale Law Journal,* Vol. 70 (1961), p. 1084; Charles B. Nutting, "Is the First Amendment Obsolete?," *George Washington Law Review,* Vol. 30 (1961), p. 167. For an

General Principles of First Amendment Interpretation

WE COME BACK, then, to the original problem: the formulation of a workable legal doctrine which will take into account the basic factors underlying a system of freedom of expression and which will give effect to the fundamental decision embodied in the First Amendment for reconciling freedom of expression with other social values and objectives. Upon the basis of the previous analysis, the essential principles of such a doctrine can be stated as follows:

(1) The root purpose of the First Amendment was to assure an effective system of freedom of expression in a democratic society. Its adoption and its continued acceptance imply that some fundamental decisions with respect to reconciliation have been made, that a certain major balancing of interests has already been performed. These judgments, these prior balancings, are those which necessarily flow from the decision to put into operation a system of free expression, with all the values that such a system is intended to secure, in the realistic context of the actual functioning of society and its legal institutions. It follows from our earlier analysis that the judgments made, stated in the most fundamental and general terms, were that expression must be freely allowed and encouraged; that it may not be restricted either for the direct purpose of controlling it or as a method of obtaining other social objectives; and that the attainment of such other objectives is to be achieved through regulation of action. A system of freedom of expression cannot exist on any other foundation, and a decision to maintain such a system necessarily implies a decision on these general propositions.

(2) The function of the courts is not to reopen this prior balancing but to construct the specific legal doctrines which, within the framework of the basic decision made in adopting the First Amendment, will govern the concrete issues presented in fitting an effective system of freedom of expression into the

---

effort by a political scientist, see Carr, "The Seesaw Between Freedom and Power," *University of Illinois Bulletin,* Vol. 57 (1960), p. 3. Generally, the materials dealing with First Amendment doctrine, up to 1958, are collected in Emerson and Haber, *Political and Civil Rights in the United States,* Vol. 1, Ch. III and IV.

broader structure of modern society. This problem may appropriately be formalized, as the absolutists do, in terms of defining the key elements in the First Amendment: "freedom of expression," "abridge," and "law." These definitions must be functional in character, derived from the basic considerations underlying a system of freedom of expression which have previously been set forth.

This process does, of course, involve a weighing of considerations. But the task is narrower, taking place within better defined limits, than ad hoc balancing. And it results in more specific, more tightly structured doctrine than the ad hoc balancing approach permits. While the results may not be acceptable to all absolutists, in essence it seeks to accomplish their ultimate aims.

(3) The specific legal doctrines implementing the First Amendment must be framed in the light of the dynamics of a system of freedom of expression. It is not sufficient to formulate theory in the abstract, however refined. The rules must be workable in terms of the realities of maintaining a system in the everyday world. Thus the difficulty of framing precise regulations affecting expression, and the forces that tend to distort and overextend them, must be taken into account. The need of the individual to know with some assurance what his rights are, and of government officials to know with some certainty the limits of their power, require that the legal doctrine be constructed with this object as a major consideration. And the requirement of effective judicial administration, especially as concerns the functioning of the Supreme Court, is a critical factor.

(4) Construction of a definition of "freedom of expression" centers around two major problems:

(a) The first task is to formulate in detail the distinction between "expression" and "action." As we have seen, the whole theory and practice of freedom of expression—the realization of any of the values it attempts to secure—rests upon this distinction. Hence the starting point for any legal doctrine must be to fix this line of demarcation. The line in many situations is clear. But at many points it becomes obscure. Expression often takes place in a context of action, or is closely linked with it, or is equivalent in its impact. In these mixed cases it is necessary to decide, however artificial the distinction may appear to be, whether the conduct is to be classified as one or the other. This judgment must be guided by consideration of whether the conduct partakes of the essential qualities of expression or action. In the main this is a question of whether the harm attributable to the conduct is immediate and instantaneous, and whether it is irremediable except by punishing and thereby preventing the conduct. A second factor is also significant. This is whether the regulation of the conduct is, as a practical administrative matter, compatible with a workable system of free expression, a factor discussed above. In formulating the distinction between expression and action there is thus a certain leeway in which the process of reconciling freedom of expression with other values and objectives can remain flexible. But the crucial point is that the focus of inquiry must be directed toward ascertaining what is expression, and therefore to be given the protection of expression, and what is action, and thus subject to regulation as such.[21]

(b) The second task is to delineate those sectors of social activity which fall outside the area in which, under the basic theory, freedom of expression must be maintained. For reasons which will be elaborated later, these alien sectors include certain aspects of the operations of the military, of communication with foreign countries, and of the activities of children. The problem here is not only to ascertain the areas in which freedom of expression is not intended to operate, at least in its classic form, but to construct rules governing those situations where the area of free expression and the alien area interlock.

(5) Application of the term "abridge" is not difficult in many cases. But a problem arises in certain types of situations. The main ones are where a regulation is not a direct restriction of expression but is designed to accomplish another objective, and the impact upon expression is "secondary" or "indirect"; where the regulation is concerned not with reconciling freedom of

---

[21] In formulating the distinction between "expression" and "action" some of the concepts embodied in the clear and present danger test are utilized. But the approach here differs materially from the clear and present danger approach. It is designed to protect the whole general area of expression, regardless of whether that expression creates a danger of subsequent harm. In borderline cases, however, the determination of whether the conduct is to be treated as expression or action rests upon whether the harm is immediate, whether it is irremediable, and whether regulation of the conduct is administratively consistent with maintaining a system of freedom of expression.

expression with another social objective but operates within the framework of the system itself by attempting to allocate means of communication or facilitate the working of the system; and where the government itself participates in expression. In these situations the formulation of legal doctrine involves construction of a workable definition of "abridge."

(6) The interpretation of the First Amendment in protecting the right of expression against abridgment by private (non-governmental) centers of power revolves around the definition of "law." This problem is essentially the same as that of defining the scope of "state action."

These principles are necessarily general in character. They do not, of course, automatically solve difficult concrete problems in interpretation of the First Amendment. All that is suggested is that they furnish a method of approach which places the specific issues in a functional context, yet one within the capacity of judicial institutions to manage.

5 || *The Formulation of Legal Doctrine: In Particular Areas of Freedom of Expression*

|| WE ARE NOW IN A POSITION to consider the formulation of specific legal doctrines applicable to the principal areas in which issues of freedom of expression arise in contemporary society. In the remainder of this book an attempt is made to survey all the chief problems, no matter how troublesome, and to suggest the legal doctrine by which they should be resolved. It is not possible at this time to examine at length all the considerations which compel or justify the adoption of a particular rule, or to test a proposed rule by applying it in detail to a variety of actual or potential cases. The most that can be done is to indicate how a particular doctrine may be derived from the basic principles previously stated and suggest tentative conclusions as to the form the doctrine should take. Such a hurried survey will, of course, leave many unanswered questions, doubts and disagreements. But the hope is that it will demonstrate at least how the issues ought to be framed if we are to achieve a meaningful and effective application of the First Amendment

The major areas fall into five categories: (1) freedom of belief; (2) possible conflict of the right of expression with the other individual interests; (3) possible conflict with other social interests; (4) regulation designed to facilitate the operation of the system; and (5) government participation in the process of expression.

Freedom of Belief

FREEDOM OF BELIEF concerns the right of individuals to form and hold ideas and opinions which are not communicated to others. Belief is not, strictly speaking, expression; yet it is so closely related that the safeguarding of the right to hold beliefs is essential in maintaining a system of freedom of expression. The issue involves the protection of such beliefs against government coercion, either by compelling expression of a belief or by imposing a penalty for holding one. More specifically it includes such matters as the requirement of a test oath that includes a statement of belief, legislative inquiry into matters of belief, compelling disclosure of political ideas or opinions, and the use of criminal penalties or other official sanctions to punish those who hold certain beliefs or to deprive them of benefits or privileges otherwise available.

The holding of a belief in the circumstances described is not action or directly locked with action. It must be classified as the equivalent of "expression." The prior balance struck in adopting the First Amendment—that governmental regulation must be directed specifically to action and may not generally control action through control of expression—is fully applicable. Thus any alleged conflict between the interest in free expression through protecting the right to hold beliefs, and other individual or social interests, must be deemed resolved in favor of freedom of belief. The legal doctrine, therefore, should be that the holding of a belief is afforded complete protection from state coercion.

The reasons supporting this legal rule are apparent. The attempt to coerce belief is not only one of the most destructive forms of restricting expression but it affords no substantial protection to any legitimate individual or social interest. It invades the innermost privacy of the individual and cuts off the right of expression at its source. It entails insuperable difficulties in administration. The problem of ascertaining belief, especially by the formal procedures of the law, is an impossible one and leaves the individual at the mercy of his prosecutors. The attempt calls forth all the hysteria of the witch hunt and all the apparatus of thought control. The whole process seems incompatible with the existence of free expression.

And nothing of social value is gained. The effort to suppress belief can rarely be successful. It cannot change opinions or substitute better ones. It affects chiefly those among the unorthodox who are men of principle and, by encouraging concealment and deception, destroys the whole basis of public morality. In no event can an unexpressed opinion in itself have an adverse effect upon the interests of other individuals or of society. Its indirect effect, through possible translation into subsequent action, is too remote and uncertain to warrant use of the government's immense and destructive powers of coercion.

The Supreme Court has considered the issue in two major decisions. In the *Barnette* case a majority held invalid a state statute imposing a compulsory requirement that school children recite the pledge of allegiance to the flag.[1] In the *Douds* case the Court, by an equally divided vote, upheld the validity of that part of the Taft-Hartley non-Communist affidavit which required a union officer, as a condition of his union's obtaining the benefits of the National Labor Relations Act, to state that he "does not believe in, and is not a member of or supports any organization that believes in . . . the overthrow of the United States Government by force or by any illegal or unconstitutional methods." [2] The flag salute law, certainly as to the Jehovah's Witnesses involved, required the affirmation of a belief. The Taft-Hartley provision imposed a government sanction for the mere holding of a political belief. Both constituted state coercion of belief. The appropriate principle is that stated in the famous words of Justice Jackson in the *Barnette* case:

> If there is any fixed star in our constitutional constellation, it is that no official, high or petty, can prescribe what shall be orthodox in politics, nationalism, religion or other matters of opinion or force citizens to confess by word or act their faith therein. If there are any circumstances which permit an exception, they do not now occur to us.[3]

[1] *West Va. State Bd. of Educ. v. Barnette*, 319 U.S. 624 (1943).

[2] *American Communications Ass'n v. Douds*, 339 U.S. 382 (1950). The vote was 3 to 3. The same issue arose in *Osman v. Douds*, 339 U.S. 846 (1950), where the vote was 4 to 4. See also *Killian v. United States*, 368 U.S. 231 (1961). A similar problem was raised in the Lattimore contempt case, but the decision went on other grounds. *United States v. Lattimore*, 215 F.2d 847 (D.C. Cir. 1954), *indictment dismissed*, 127 F. Supp. 405 (D.D.C. 1955), *aff'd*, 232 F.2d 334 (D.C. Cir. 1955). See also *United States v. Ballard*, 322 U.S. 78 (1944).

[3] 319 U.S. at 642. The fact that children were involved in the flag

Reconciliation With Other Individual Interests

WHERE MORE than mere belief is involved, and an idea, opinion or statement is actually communicated to others, the possibility of conflict between freedom of expression and other interests becomes more acute. Here the problem of reconciliation may be more troublesome. It becomes necessary to examine separately the various types of interests at stake and the nature of the possible conflict, and to formulate for specific types of situations the legal doctrines which will best achieve the reconciliation within the basic principles embodied in the First Amendment.

At the outset a fundamental distinction must be made between interests that are individual or private in character and interests that are social or public. Such a distinction is, of course, hard to draw with precision. Obviously, society must be concerned in some sense with all the interests of the individual; it is his welfare and achievements that make up the life of the community. Further, society must consider the relations between two or more individuals, and especially the reconciliation of conflicts between them; otherwise the solution of the controversy may disturb the public order or affect the general welfare adversely. To some degree, therefore, all conflicts will have mixed private and public implications. Nevertheless, the difference between a wrong to an individual and a wrong to the community has long been recognized in Anglo-American law. It has crucial significance in framing satisfactory principles to govern a system of freedom of expression.

Utilizing this concept, there are certain types of conflict between freedom of expression and interests that may be considered

---

salute case raises an additional issue as to the extent to which the conduct of children falls within the area of freedom of expression. The case is referred to above only in connection with the Supreme Court's attitude toward coercion of belief generally. The writer would not apply the general rules for freedom of expression to the children in the flag salute case. In his view the issue as to them is more appropriately handled as one of freedom of religion.

Whether a limited qualification of the general principle is necessary in the situation where an individual enters government service is discussed in text accompanying notes 40-41, Ch. V *infra*. And questions of the government's right to influence belief through participation in the process of expression are likewise considered in text accompanying note 53, Ch. V *infra*.

predominantly private in character. These may involve one or both of two elements. The first is where the injury to the individual is direct and peculiar to him, rather than one suffered in common with others, and where society leaves the burden of protecting the interest to the individual himself, either by way of granting him a legal cause of action or by requiring him to raise the issue and support his claim. The second is where the interest is an intimate and personal one, embracing an area of privacy from which both the government and one's neighbors ought to be excluded.

Where conflicts of this nature are involved, the problem of reconciliation takes on certain attributes not present where broader social or group interests are at stake. In the first place, the harm to the individual interest is more likely to be direct and immediate in its impact, and irremediable by resource to regulation of the subsequent conduct stimulated by the expression. For this reason communication injuring an individual interest is more readily classifiable as "action" than injury to the general social interest which is capable of protection by control of subsequent overt acts. In the second place, the government as umpire of the conflict can be more objective and impartial. Its function is to decide between two individuals, rather than under the pressures of competing social forces. Hence we need have less concern with the vagueness of the criteria for judgment, the subtlety of questions of proof, the creation of an atmosphere of partisanship or hysteria, or other possible abuses of the governmental process. Moreover, where the individual carries the burden of establishing his case, we face fewer administrative problems. It is likely there will be less resources marshaled to restrict freedom of expression; there is no risk of developing a dangerous apparatus of enforcement; the whole process of reconciliation through governmental action will be more loose, more relaxed, and more consistent with an atmosphere of freedom. Finally, when we are dealing with a question of personal privacy, we are in an area, like that of belief, where the interest involved should receive a paramount measure of protection.

In the light of these generalizations, we are in a position to examine specifically the major points at which freedom of expression may come into conflict with significant private interests.

Reputation

Of primary concern in the past has been the problem of reconciling the right of freedom of expression with the right to protection against unfair damage to reputation. A communication by one person may subject another to ridicule, hatred or contempt and thereby seriously injure him in the estimation of his fellows. The competing interest here is partly a material one; the communication may cause damage to business or professional standing or to other interests of property. But the interest is also a broader one, extending to all aspects of the personality. A member of a civilized society should have some measure of protection against unwarranted attack upon his honor, his dignity and his standing in the community.

Reconciliation of the interests at stake in this situation has been effected mainly through methods and doctrines embodied in the civil law of libel and slander. Legal action may be brought by the person injured against the offender to recover damages for statements which caused the injury; but in such a proceeding the truth of the statement made constitutes a defense. In a few jurisdictions the truth alone is not a complete defense but must be accompanied by a showing that the statements were published with good motives and for justifiable ends.[4]

Active supporters of freedom of expression have had some difficulty in fitting the law of civil libel and slander into a tightly constructed scheme of First Amendment interpretation.[5] But if one takes into account the nature of the conduct involved and the differences between reconciling freedom of expression with private rather than public interests, the problem is not insur-

[4] Fowler S. Harper and Fleming James, Jr., *Torts,* Vol. 1, § 5.20 n.6 (Boston, Little, Brown, 1956).

[5] Mr. Justice Black, for example, finds the law of libel incompatible with the First Amendment, thus eliminating it altogether in both federal and state legal systems, Edmond Cahn, "Justice Black and First Amendment 'Absolutes': A Public Interview," *New York University Law Review,* Vol. 37 (1962), pp. 549, 557-558. Dr. Meiklejohn draws a distinction between "public speech," entitled to absolute protection under the First Amendment, and "private speech," entitled only to protection against unreasonable restrictions under the due process clause. Alexander Meiklejohn, *Political Freedom,* pp. 39-42. But since libelous speech could deal with "public" as well as "private" matters, this distinction seems inadequate in respect to this problem.

mountable. First of all, as indicated above, the harm caused by this type of communication tends to be direct and instantaneous and not remediable by longer-range social processes which can prevent the injury. If we look upon loss of "reputation" as similar to loss of the use of an arm, then, even though there be a later restoration, the injury is immediate. In other words, the injury, at least in substantial part, does not flow from action resulting from the communication—action which can be intercepted by regulation addressed specifically to it—but directly from the communication itself. In this sense, therefore, true private defamation tends toward the category of "action" and hence is subject to reasonable regulation.

Other factors work toward the same resolution. The requirements of truth and good motive are, of course, exceedingly vague and difficult of application. They are not acceptable as a general measure of the limitation to freedom of expression. But in this context—in a private law suit where the opposing interest is essentially a private one—they would appear to constitute justifiable standards. The restriction on expression is imposed within narrow bounds, in a situation where the government can effectively perform the role of umpire. No serious abuses of official administration are normally encountered. The values attached to the expression, both as an individual right and as serving a social and political purpose, are likely to be of least relative significance. And the private interest protected is one of considerable moment. Under all the circumstances it is unlikely, and experience with the civil law of libel and slander confirms the theoretical point, that the limitation results in any serious impairment of the right to freedom of expression.

It is true that more difficult issues arise where the public interest becomes more directly involved, as where the person who considers his reputation impaired is a public official, a candidate for public office, or someone functioning in the public arena, such as a political commentator, an author, or one who otherwise addresses the public. If the damaging statement affects such a person purely in his private and personal capacity, the ordinary principles of libel and slander would obtain. On the other hand, if the alleged defamation relates essentially to the public performance of the person claimed to be injured, the issue is no different from the problem of criminal libel, discussed below. There remains, however, an intermediate category where the alleged defamation is mixed in character, pertaining to both private and public capacities. This occurs, for example, where the honesty of an official in connection with the discharge of his public duties is challenged. The best resolution of such a problem would appear to be through the development of a doctrine of fair comment.[6] Under such a rule, the communication would be protected if it is based upon the facts, or what a reasonable man would accept as the facts, is fair, and is not malicious. This standard of fair comment, if rigorously pressed against unpopular defendants, could cut off much public discussion. Still it may be justified if employed only in private litigation and if the judiciary accepts its obligation to act as a firm defender of the First Amendment interest. The possibility of local abuse in this situation, perhaps the chief source of concern, is substantially lessened by the supervisory powers of the federal courts, particularly the Supreme Court. All in all the problem has thus far not appeared to be a serious one, or one which the Supreme Court could not readily keep in check.

A different question is raised where freedom of expression is restricted by the law of criminal libel. This involves a criminal prosecution, brought by the government, for punishment of libelous statements. Truth has customarily not been recognized as a defense unless the accused can show in addition that the communication was made with good motives and for justifiable ends. In this respect the law of criminal libel is similar to the early law of seditious libel, prior to the statutory modification which established truth as a defense. The theory of the prosecution for criminal libel is that a public interest is involved because the publication would otherwise result in personal vengeance by the person defamed or his friends, thus leading to a breach of the peace or other public disorder. The competing interest here, therefore, is the public interest in preserving order, a matter discussed subsequently. But a brief comment may be made at this point.

According to the theory underlying criminal libel, the harm to be prevented is the action, in the nature of disorder or similar conduct, which it is feared may flow from the utterance. In this it differs from civil libel where, as we saw, there was no action

[6] Harper and James, *Torts*, Vol. 1, § 5.28 (1956).

distinct from the communication itself which could be intercepted by regulation. For this reason, the communication involved in criminal libel prosecutions can not be classified as "action." The prior balancing in favor of protecting expression, embodied in the First Amendment, here compels acceptance of the legal doctrine that criminal libel laws are invalid. And this conclusion would stand whether truth is accepted as a complete defense or the standard remains in its present form. In earlier times, when honor was more often defended by force of arms, the problem of preserving the peace may have been more difficult. But under modern conditions, when the rule of law is generally accepted as a substitute for private physical measures, it can hardly be urged that the maintenance of peace requires a criminal prosecution for private defamation. Society has other means at its disposal for achieving its goal, methods which are effective in comparable kinds of private disputes. On the other hand, in the context of a public prosecution the dangers in punishing expression under the necessarily loose standards invoked are, for reasons already stated,[7] great. Criminal libel, when resorted to, can only result in suppressing unpopular expression. It would not be greatly different in its impact than employment of the law of seditious libel.

For much the same reasons group libel statutes do not square with an effective system of free expression. In addition, this type of legislation creates an especially acute dilemma. If truth is not allowed as a defense to the prosecution, clearly the infringement upon expression would cut very deep; but if proof of truth is permitted, the prosecution provides a wider, a more dramatic, and a partially official forum for publication of the alleged defamatory statements.

The Supreme Court has not squarely faced the issue of the validity of a criminal libel statute. But in *Beauharnais v. Illinois* it sustained a group libel statute. The dissent of Justices Black and Douglas in *Beauharnais* would appear to state the appropriate doctrine.[8]

[7] See the discussion of these dangers and the likelihood of their absence in civil libel suits in text following notes 3-5, Ch. V *supra*.

[8] *Beauharnais v. Illinois,* 343 U.S. 250 (1952). For a discussion of the damages to a system of free expression in group libel laws see Alexander Pekelis, *Law and Social Action* (Ithaca, N.Y., Cornell University Press, 1950), pp. 187-193; Note, "Group Libel Laws: Abortive Efforts to Com-

Fair Trial

Freedom of expression may also come into conflict with private interests in the administration of justice. The problem here is principally the extent to which limits should be imposed upon the prosecution and the press in their treatment of dramatic criminal cases. Many such matters are handled in a manner which arouses intense hostility to the accused and makes a fair trial unlikely or unobtainable. The issue is surely a serious one. And it can scarcely be dismissed on the ground that the interest in unlimited utterance requires disregard of specific and grievous injury to the individual.

Using the basic approach already suggested, a satisfactory reconciliation of competing interests here seems feasible within the confines of the First Amendment. Two different aspects of the problem should be distinguished. One is the situation where the communication in issue may adversely affect the jurors, witnesses or other parties. The other arises when the hostile utterance is directed at the court or the general administration of justice. The distinction between the two types of cases is crucial in reaching a satisfactory solution.

In the first situation the impact of the communication, similar to private defamation, has the essential characteristics of "action": in its prejudicial effect the harm tends to be immediate and irremediable.[9] On this premise the principle of reconciliation should be one of accommodating the two interests—freedom of communication and the obtaining of justice—under rules administered by the courts. The limiting rules can be framed with some degree of objectivity, preferably by the legislature. They would include regulations concerning the issuance by the government or the parties of statements relating to confessions,

---

bat Hate Propaganda," *Yale Law Journal,* Vol. 61 (1952), p. 252. On criminal libel see Note, "Constitutionality of the Law of Criminal Libel," *Columbia Law Review,* Vol. 52 (1952), p. 521; John Kelly, "Criminal Libel and Free Speech," *Kansas Law Review,* Vol. 6 (1958), p. 295.

[9] To some extent the harm can be corrected by change of venue, care in the selection and instruction of the jury, and other similar safeguards. The factual assumption being made here, however, is that these devices, especially in an era of modern communication, are deemed inadequate and that other types of control are necessary to preserve the right of the individual.

admissions, opinions of guilt, prospective testimony, credibility of witnesses, and the like; or publication of such matters.[10] The overall standard under the First Amendment should be one that would preserve the right of communication so far as possible but allow the court to protect the rights of the individual in situations demanding it. For such purposes a "reasonable tendency" test is probably too restrictive. The accommodation is perhaps better expressed in terms of a "clear and present danger" test or a "probable danger" test.[11] In any event the court is in a position to administer the standard with reasonable impartiality. The judge's own prestige or position is not under attack. The prosecution and the accused, or the parties in a civil case, represent opposing interests. The court is in the umpire's role, where it can decide with equal regard for both interests at stake.

On the other hand, in the situation where the court or the administration of justice is the object of the adverse expression, different considerations prevail. We are dealing here with the impact of expression upon the governmental organization itself, upon government officials in their professional capacity, not with the impact upon private citizens called upon to participate in the governmental process in the capacity of amateurs. Here the harm feared is not so closely linked to the actual communication but lies more remotely in the influence of the communication on the subsequent conduct of the government itself. The injury is subject to control by regulation dealing directly with the feared harm. Here, also, the court becomes an interested party. It is unlikely, furthermore, that expression which does not affect the jurors, witnesses or parties will seriously prejudice the conduct of the proceeding by the judge. In spite of argument to the contrary, the judge must be presumed to possess a higher degree of fortitude in the face of public pressure than the ordinary juror, witness or party. In any event, a presumption that the judge will not show courage or impartiality in the performance of his duty is hardly a satisfactory ground for restricting freedom of

---

[10] For suggestions along these lines, see Richard C. Donnelly and Ronald Goldfarb, "Contempt By Publication in the United States," *Modern Law Review,* Vol. 24 (1961), pp. 239, 255.

[11] This is not meant to imply a wholesale adoption of the clear and present danger test. See note 21, Ch. IV *supra.* But in this particular context, it appears to provide an adequate standard which can be administered without unduly repressive consequences.

expression. The applicable rule here should be that governing criticism of government generally. The appropriate doctrine, as discussed shortly, would not seem to be one of accommodation but of full protection for the right of expression.

In practice, a reconciliation along these lines would not seriously interfere with freedom of expression. In this area the press has demonstrated both the inclination and the capacity to protect its rights. General social forces tend to favor the side of free expression. Criticism of the judicial process and the administration of law—the primary aspect of the social interest— would remain unimpaired. All in all the balance of forces at work would tend to produce a reasonable accommodation.

The decisions of the Supreme Court have in result not been inconsistent with the position urged. All the cases thus far decided have been of the second variety, involving criticism of the court or the administration of justice. In all, the right of expression has been upheld. Thus far the Court has not faced the issue in cases of the first type.[12]

Privacy

Exercise of the right to express oneself may also come into conflict with those interests of other individuals which may be grouped under the general heading of a right to privacy—this is the right of a person to be free at some point from intrusion by society into his intimate and personal affairs. Protection of this interest is essential to the maintenance of the proper balance between the life of a person as an individual and his life as a member of society. As the nature of modern society unfolds we come to appreciate more and more the feeling of Justice Brandeis that "The right to be let alone [is] the most comprehensive of rights and the right most valued by civilized men." [13]

By what principles should the reconciliation of these two in-

[12] The relevant Supreme Court decisions are *Bridges v. California,* 314 U.S. 252 (1941); *Pennekamp v. Florida,* 328 U.S. 331 (1946); *Craig v. Harney,* 331 U.S. 367 (1947); *Wood v. Georgia,* 370 U.S. 375 (1962). *Cf. Maryland v. Baltimore Radio Show,* 338 U.S. 912 (1950); also *Stroble v. California,* 343 U.S. 181 (1952). See generally Comment, "Free Speech Versus The Fair Trial in the English and American Law of Contempt by Publication," *University of Chicago Law Review,* Vol. 17 (1950), p. 540.

[13] *Olmstead v. United States,* 277 U.S. 438, 478 (1928). Generally on the right to privacy see Charles Warren and Louis Brandeis, "The Right to Privacy," *Harvard Law Review,* Vol. 4 (1890), p. 193.

terests be effected? At first glance the problem looks formidable. A general formula attempting to draw a line between communication on matters of public interest and communication on matters of private interest is unsuitable.[14] But a strict use of the distinction between "expression" and "action," and an application of principles requiring accommodation as to time, place and manner of exercising the right of expression, furnish the basis of satisfactory doctrine. The application of these principles can be illustrated by considering the two main areas in which the problem of reconciliation has thus far arisen.

The first involves undesired publicity. In certain rather specific situations—such as where a photograph has been used without permission for commercial purposes or where a person living in seclusion has been, without justification, publicly identified with long past events of a damaging or disturbing nature—some courts or legislatures have allowed the individual whose privacy has been invaded to recover damages in a private suit.[15] Other circumstances in which a private suit for damages should be permitted could similarly be recognized. The considerations involved are very similar to those governing the problem of private defamation. The impact of the communication presses toward a classification as "action." And so long as the interest of privacy is genuine, the conditions of recovery clearly defined and the remedy left to individual suit, it is most unlikely that the balance will be tipped too far toward restriction of expression.

The second area concerns communication which by its nature disturbs the quiet or repose of an individual or a neighborhood. Examples occur in the use of a sound truck in a residential area at night, or a public meeting in a section of a park set aside for rest or relaxation. In these situations, it should be noted, the restriction upon expression usually takes the form of a public prosecution rather than an individual right to take legal action. The applicable doctrine here should be one of fair accommodation of the two interests—communication and privacy. The restriction can be couched in terms of a limitation on time, geo-

[14] The distinction is not appropriate because communications on matters of public interest may easily interfere with a legitimate right to privacy—*e.g.*, cases involving sound trucks. While the distinction between public and private based on *subject matter* appears to me unworkable, it should not be confused with the distinction earlier adopted between public and private on the basis of the *interests affected* by a communication.

[15] See Harper and James, *Torts*, Vol. 1, § 9.6 n.13 (1956).

graphical area, or decibels, or the allocation of space in the public park system. No element of prohibition or of regulation of the content of the communication is involved. Such restrictions can be reasonably objective, equally applicable to all those wishing to use the mode of communication, and relatively free of administrative abuse. Provided the courts insist affirmatively on a fair accommodation, rather than acquiesce in a merely plausible or even reasonable one, both interests can be satisfactorily reconciled. The Supreme Court's decisions in *Saia* and *Kovacs,* the sound truck cases, leave the problem in some uncertainty, but the results in those cases are not necessarily inconsistent with the views expressed here.[16]

In practical terms of maintaining an effective system of free expression, moreover, these issues yield rather readily to solution. Any society sincerely interested in protecting the right of privacy is hardly likely to be at the same time hostile to the right of free expression. Both interests tend to have the same friends and the same enemies. The chief danger is that the right of privacy will be used as a screen, by those not really interested in either interest, to infringe upon legitimate expression. This danger can be met if the courts actively insist upon a careful definition of a genuine right to privacy and upon a fair accommodation of the two interests.

In summary, the formulation of legal doctrines, under the First Amendment, to reconcile the right to freedom of expression with the private interests of the individual does not appear to pose insuperable problems. In most cases the working rules can be stated with some objectivity. Institutional machinery is geared to deal with these issues on a relatively impartial basis. Social pressures are not so likely to distort the balance in favor of either interest; indeed, if anything, it is the private interest that is more likely to suffer. At this level there are, in short, built-in conditions which tend to preserve an appropriate balance.

Reconciliation With Other Social Interests

MOST OF THE PROBLEMS in defining the scope of freedom of expression under the First Amendment concern the reconciliation

---

[16] *Saia v. New York,* 334 U.S. 558 (1948); *Kovacs v. Cooper,* 336 U.S. 77 (1949). See also *Martin v. Struthers,* 319 U.S. 141 (1943) (upholding right to seek opportunity for communication by ringing doorbells).

of that interest with social interests. These issues are vastly more difficult to resolve than those in the private sphere. In this area the state is generally cast less in the role of impartial umpire and more in the role of interested agent, to a considerable extent engaged in making a decision in its own cause. This is because the social interests which compete, or may appear in the short run to compete, with the interest in freedom of expression are ones the state machinery is specifically designed and organized to protect. Maintenance of the social interest in internal order, external security, and the protection of property interests constitutes the day-to-day job of the governmental apparatus. Protection of freedom of expression is more abstract, more remote, less insistent. Furthermore, advancement of the competing social interest is more likely to be the direct concern of the groups which influence and control the government machinery. And the problem of self-control may be even more difficult in a government bureaucracy than in an individual.

Other similar factors operate in the same direction. Reconciliation of competing social interests raises broader issues, less clearly defined, less easily measured and less manageable than the reconciliation of private interests. The forces in conflict are likewise more impersonal; moral principles of group conduct are not as easily learned or applied as in individual conduct. And it must be remembered that the expression which needs protection is normally that which is the unorthodox, the hated and the feared. Most of the powerful pressures of the majority are likely to be ranged against the interest of free expression.

In short, the self-correcting forces that are at work in the reconciliation of freedom of expression with individual interests do not operate to the same extent where competing social interests are at stake. Here the legal doctrines necessary to maintain the intended balance must be more precisely and firmly formulated, and the judicial institutions charged with their administration more alert and vigorous.

Consensus and Efficiency

In attempting to enunciate specific doctrine we may commence with certain areas where the prior balance struck by the framers of the First Amendment most clearly contemplates unqualified protection of the right to expression. These are where the social interest at issue is the promotion of national unity or consensus, the direction of gradual orderly change, or the maintenance of general efficiency in government operations. The power to restrict freedom of expression in order to promote these social interests is not often explicitly asserted. Nevertheless, such a claim is frequently implicit in much popular, and even legal, thinking on the subject. It is important, therefore, to bring these issues fully into the open. This discussion will also serve as a statement of the general principles governing the approach to the narrower and more openly controversial questions which follow.

Any society must, in order to function and survive, maintain within itself a certain unity. It requires sufficient agreement among its members not only to settle differences according to the rules and without resort to force, but to make the formal rules work in practice. No mechanism for government can by its mere existence hold a society together. This is especially true of a modern industrial community, with the interdependence of its parts and the complexities of its operations. Hence any society must seek to promote consensus among its members, and in this the machinery of the government will necessarily play an important role.

Nevertheless, a democracy may not seek to promote its broad interest in consensus by means of restrictions on expression. If we accept the theory underlying freedom of expression, there is no fundamental conflict between the two interests. It would contradict the basic tenets of a democratic society to say that the greater the freedom of expression, the less the area of agreement among its members. On the contrary, for reasons already stated, a healthy consensus is possible only where freedom of expression flourishes. Such freedom is essential to the whole process of legitimation of social decisions. And suppression not only is ineffective in promoting general agreement or stability, but hinders the process by engendering hostility, resentment, fear and other divisive forces. Furthermore, a principle of suppressing freedom of expression in any situation where the right is found to be outweighed by the general social interest in achieving consensus is administratively unworkable. The principle is not susceptible of any meaningful limitation. The difference between a society governed by such a principle and a totalitarian society becomes one of mere expediency.

The state may use its other powers to promote the social interest in consensus. It may control conduct other than expression; it may establish the economic, political and social conditions in which the necessary agreement is possible; it may engage in programs of education or propaganda, subject to limitations considered later. And institutions other than the state exist or may be devised to achieve the same ends. But if these measures are insufficient to maintain the necessary degree of national unity, the suppression of expression will not solve the problem except by destroying the democratic character of the society.

Society must also concern itself with the dynamics of change. While endeavoring to maintain a proper balance between stability and change, a society must be prepared to accept constant and substantial adjustment to new conditions. If there is one certain aspect of modern life, it is that no modern society can survive for long by merely preserving the status quo. A democratic society therefore has a vital interest in the process of orderly change, that is, in change which is accomplished by methods that are legitimate, at a rate of speed that allows satisfactory adjustment, and in a direction that advances the ultimate goals of the society.

This social interest, however, cannot justify restrictions upon expression. The principle is plain that there can be no interference with freedom of expression on the general ground that it will lead to social change, or change at the wrong rate or in the wrong direction. Here again there is no real issue of reconciling conflicting interests because there is no basic conflict. On the contrary, freedom of expression is one of the chief instruments for achieving orderly change. No objection can be made that the use of expression is an improper method of influencing change, for adjustment through public discussion is the essence of the democratic process. As for the rate of social change, the problem of modern society is more likely to be that the pace is too slow than that it is too rapid; the forces of stability and conformity tend to outweigh the forces of movement. In any event, there is no known technique by which the rate of change can be regulated through restricting freedom of expression without destroying that freedom altogether. The same is true of the direction of change. Under democratic principles this must be determined by the sovereign people themselves, and that decision is possible only by the process of full and free discussion. There are risks in this procedure, as the theory of freedom of expression recognizes, but they are the risks which must be assumed by a democratic system.

There is likewise a social interest in the effective operation of government. This interest is of increasing importance as the functions of government expand and grow more intricate. Exercise of the right to expression may create dissatisfaction with governmental policies, institutions or officials, tend to add difficulties to the formulation or administration of law, or otherwise appear to impede the smooth operation of government. But this general social interest cannot be the basis for limiting expression. Again the conflict is more apparent than real. In the long run, open criticism of the government's operations results in a more responsible, alert and fair administration, and hence in more effective government. And again any criterion of limitation which attempted to balance these two interests could only result in nullifying all freedom of expression.

Claims for the restriction of freedom of expression in order to promote consensus, alter the direction of change, or increase government efficiency have seldom been expressly made before the Supreme Court. The principal instance was in the flag salute cases, which also involved the problem of coercion of belief. The decision of the majority in the *Barnette* case seems plainly correct.[17]

The more difficult problems in reconciling the interest in freedom of expression with other social interests lie within narrower and more specific bounds. These issues, as they have emerged from the experience of our nation over the years and as they confront us today, must now be considered.

Preservation of Internal Order

Maintenance of law and order in a society, along with protection against external dangers, has traditionally constituted the chief purpose for which governments were instituted among men. The developing theory of freedom of expression was therefore necessarily and primarily concerned with the problem of reconciling the new right being asserted with the older interest in

[17] *West Va. State Bd. of Educ. v. Barnette,* 319 U.S. 624 (1943).

preserving internal order. This issue was indeed the main point of controversy in the evolution of the theory. And it may safely be assumed that the framers of the First Amendment, in adopting the solution embodied in that provision, were making a deliberate choice on the basis of prolonged consideration and direct experience. If we are to give weight to this decision, we must accept the basic legal doctrine that expression must be given full protection and only what may reasonably be called action be subject to restriction.

Broadly speaking, the problem is that exercise of the right of expression may cause or tend to cause conduct which violates existing law. The resulting conduct or potential conduct may be violent or nonviolent in character. And it may arise because those to whom the expression is communicated may be persuaded toward unlawful conduct in support of the expression or in opposition to it. But the social interest in maintaining internal order is concerned only with the ensuing unlawful conduct. In this context the expression, in itself and apart from such conduct, is of no social harm. If the theory of freedom of expression means anything, therefore, it requires that social control be directed toward the subsequent action. Hence the appropriate legal doctrine must be derived from the distinction between "expression" and "action."

This conclusion is reinforced by all our experience in attempting to effect a reconciliation by drawing a line at some other point. As already observed in the discussion of other theories of limitation, any formula for establishing a cut-off point between permissible and prohibited "expression" is doomed to failure. Such rules are hopelessly vague and unenforceable by judicial supervision. They can give the lower federal or state courts no adequate guidance. A fortiori, prosecutors, police and other officials charged with maintaining internal order are left largely unrestrained. Even more devastating to freedom of expression, the individual seeking to exercise the right cannot know where he stands. Pressures at the grass roots level, where the freedom is to be exercised, are intense, and the dynamics of administration push to extremes. Only a rule based on distinguishing "expression" from "action" can in practice preserve a system of freedom of expression.

The basic decision made by the framers that adequate protection can be afforded the interest in internal order through sanctions confined to the illegal action itself applies with even greater force to the problem in our times. The powers and resources of modern government, if exercised with skill and vigor, are sufficient for the task. The trend in modern society to greater acceptance of law and legal institutions, public attitudes toward the use of violence and illegal methods, the strength in this country of democratic procedures for resolving conflict, all create a favorable climate. A community which sincerely undertakes to maintain law and order without suppressing expression possesses the powers and techniques to accomplish that task. Where the attempt seems on the verge of failure, the remedy lies in using other measures which will restore a basic consensus rather than in abandoning the system of freedom of expression.

It must be admitted that the problem of defining the area of freedom of expression when it appears to conflict with the social interest in internal order has been one of the most controversial in the whole field of individual rights. Strong objections have been raised that there are certain situations, some firmly established in the law, where the principle of allowing freedom of expression cannot afford adequate protection to the community interest in preserving internal order. It is submitted, however, that most of these difficulties can be resolved by careful formulation of the distinction between "expression" and "action." Thus the use of speech inseparably locked with action should be treated as part of "action." An example is where the words are the equivalent of a spark in a powder keg resulting in instantaneous explosion, as in "fighting words" hurled in face-to-face encounter, or the classic cry of "fire" in the theater. Similarly, sheer threats of immediate physical harm delivered on a person-to-person basis would fall into the category of "action." And "expression" which amounts to a signal for action, such as a command to shoot, can be conceived as by its very nature constituting "action." [18] In short, the line between "expression" and "action" can be drawn to accommodate the main situations in which it has been urged that "absolute" protection cannot be extended to freedom of expression at the expense of maintaining internal order. The crucial principle is that the issue be con-

[18] See *Chaplinsky v. New Hampshire,* 315 U.S. 568 (1942).

ceived and its resolution sought in terms of permitting "expression" and punishing "action."

One particular area which has seemed to some to raise a difficult doctrinal problem is the field of solicitation to crime. The law of solicitation evolved long before First Amendment freedoms were recognized, and the courts have never squarely faced the problem of reconciling the two areas of law. It would seem, however, that the "expression"-"action" dichotomy conveys the basic distinction. The problem is, indeed, no different from that involving the use of speech generally in the commission of crimes of action. Most crimes—certainly those in which more than one person participate—involve the use of speech or other communication. Where the communication is an integral part of a course of criminal action, it is treated as action and receives no protection under the First Amendment. Solicitation to crime is similar conduct, but in a situation where for some reason the contemplated crime does not take place. Solicitation involves a hiring or partnership arrangement, designed to accomplish a specific action in violation of law, where the communication is an essential link in a direct chain leading to criminal action, though the action may have been interrupted. In short, the person charged with solicitation must, in a direct sense, have been a participant in an abortive crime of action. Thus the crime of criminal solicitation may be seen as a particular instance of the more general category of criminal attempts. Here, also, the applicable legal doctrine undertakes to draw the line between "expression" and "action." The fact that issues of this nature rarely arise indicates that establishing the division between free expression and solicitation to crime has not created a serious problem.[19]

The problem of reconciling freedom of expression with internal order has arisen in two main types of situations. One is where the threat to order is local in nature and relatively isolated. This is the problem of maintaining order in meetings, parades,

[19] On solicitation and other "inchoate" crimes, see Herbert Wechsler, Charles A. Jones, and Harold L. Korn, "The Treatment of Inchoate Crimes in the Model Penal Code of the American Law Institute: Attempt, Solicitation and Conspiracy," *Columbia Law Review*, Vol. 61 (1961), pp. 571, 957. For a suggestion of the distinction based on private versus public expression, see the dissent in *Musser v. Utah*, 333 U.S. 95, 98 (1948).

demonstrations and the like. The other is where the anticipated danger affects the country on a broader scale, arises out of organization activity, and may involve a whole movement. This problem is usually considered one of "national security."

Community attempts to deal with the local problem often give rise to the harder cases. The danger of internal disorder may be more immediate and the relationship of "expression" to "action" more direct. The appropriate response of the community, however, should lie in affording adequate police protection. This was the reasoning of the Supreme Court in *Cooper v. Aaron,* where the constitutional right of equal protection was threatened by public disorder. "Thus law and order are not here to be preserved," the Court said, "by depriving the Negro children of their constitutional rights." [20] The principle is similarly applicable to the constitutional right of free expression. Where the problem genuinely exceeds these bounds, the ultimate recourse of the community is in martial law. This involves a substitution of military for civilian procedures, and the normal rules of the democratic process are no longer applicable. The question of when such an emergency may be declared, how long it may be continued, and who may make these decisions are critical issues in any theory of freedom of expression. They cannot, however, be dealt with here.

As to the broader problem of "national security," the doctrine of drawing the line between "expression" and "action" is even more clearly appropriate. The availability of other legislation protecting society against the use of anti-democratic methods makes such a distinction workable. The increased reliance upon an apparatus of secret police, informers, and other paraphernalia of ideological suppression, and the impact of suppression upon the society generally, render adherence to the basic principle more imperative. Certain special problems, however, require comment.

Exercise of the right to expression through the medium of an association may pose greater dangers to internal order than where the expression emanates from unorganized individuals. Indeed, it is only in comparatively recent times that political or

[20] *Cooper v. Aaron,* 358 U.S. 1 (1958). For an elaboration of this proposition see Laurent Frantz, "The First Amendment in the Balance," *Yale Law Journal,* Vol. 71 (1962), pp. 1424, 1437-1438.

other associations have been tolerated at all, even in emerging democratic societies. It is now recognized, however, that the right of association is essential to effective expression, and the greater political and social stability of our society not only enables us to accept but to encourage it. The concept of freedom of expression presently extends to a right of association, that is, a right to form and join organizations for the advancement of particular views and to carry on all the normal activities of such associations.

In general the same principles of reconciliation should apply to associational expression. The line must be drawn between expression and other conduct. But safeguarding the social interest in order may require increased attention to conduct which is in the nature of "preparation" for illegal action. Thus classes in the use of sabotage or street fighting, the wearing of uniforms, or similar paramilitary training would fall within the area of "action" rather than "expression."

Two additional principles of prime significance may be stated with respect to associational expression. One relates to the situation where an organization may be engaging in illegal conduct and at the same time seek to assert a right also to engage in legal expression. In the case of an individual, the answer is clear. He is punishable for illegal conduct but otherwise remains free to exercise his legal right to expression. The same rule should apply to associations. The first principle, therefore, is that where an association engages in both legitimate and illegitimate activity, the two must be separated; the illegal conduct may be prohibited, but the legal activity, including expression, should be permitted. A corollary principle is that illegitimate conduct by certain members of an association ought not to be ground for restricting expression on the part of other members or sympathizers.

The Supreme Court has not, of course, adhered to the doctrines here urged for reconciling freedom of expression with internal order. In the *Feiner* case a majority cut off expression in a local situation at a very early point, allowing an extreme degree of discretion to police officers in suppressing speech.[21] In the Smith Act cases a majority of the Court in the interest of national security employed a watered-down version of the clear

---

[21] *Feiner v. New York,* 340 U.S. 315 (1951). *Cf. Kunz v. New York,* 340 U.S. 290 (1951); *Terminiello v. Chicago,* 337 U.S. 1 (1949).

and present danger test to punish Communist Party members who were found to "advocate principles of action" intended to lead to overthrow of the government by force and violence, as distinguished from "advocating ideas." [22] In the McCarran Act case a majority upheld requirements of disclosure, amounting in practice to the elimination of open activities by the Communist Party, upon the basis of standards which were not even confined to the use or advocacy of force or violence or other illegal action.[23] In all these cases a minority in dissent contended for principles more appropriate for preserving a vital system of free expression.

Safeguarding External Security

Another major social interest with which freedom of expression may sometimes be felt to conflict is the interest of the society in external security. In a broad sense this social interest embraces all relations between the society and other societies or nations. Those aspects of the problem which relate to war and preparation for war, however, have been the subject of most controversy and will be considered first.

In attempting to formulate the legal doctrine by which the interest in freedom of expression must be reconciled with the social interest in carrying on a war or maintaining an effective defense, we start with the general principle already enunciated with respect to internal order—that expression must be protected and only other conduct prohibited. Full and open discussion of matters relating to war and defense are, if anything, more vital to the life of a democracy than any other area. And the reasons for not attempting to draw a line cutting off expression at any point short of overt action are, generally speaking, equally persuasive in this sphere. Accepting this prior balance, it is clear that full freedom of expression must be allowed with respect to such matters as general opposition to a war, criticism of war or defense policies, and discussion of particular measures whether related to direct military or supporting action.

[22] *Dennis v. United States,* 341 U.S. 494 (1951); *Yates v. United States,* 354 U.S. 298 (1957); *Scales v. United States,* 367 U.S. 203 (1961); *Noto v. United States,* 367 U.S. 290 (1961).
[23] *Communist Party v. Subversive Activities Control Bd.,* 367 U.S. 1 (1961).

Nevertheless, in the sphere of war and defense an important factor originating outside the area of free expression must be recognized: military operations cannot be conducted strictly in accordance with democratic principles. A military organization is not constructed along democratic lines and military activity cannot be governed by democratic procedures. To a certain extent, at least, the military sector of a society must function outside the realm of democratic principles, including the principle of freedom of expression. This qualification is in turn qualified by the principle that in a democratic society the military must remain under the ultimate control of civilian authority. Yet at some point the nondemocratic nature of military operations must be recognized; the problem is to fit this sector of society into the basic democratic framework.

Some of the points where conduct in the military sphere falls outside the area of free expression are reasonably clear. Certainly, members of the armed forces, at least when operating in that capacity, can be restricted in their right to open discussion. Similarly, the social interest in external security would justify limitations on the disclosure of military operations in wartime, or certain other forms of military censorship; prohibitions against espionage or the disclosure of military secrets; restrictions on access to military installations; and punishment of direct efforts to create mutiny or insubordination in the armed forces. The problem is to draw the line at that point where the requirements of the military sector end and civilian principles again come into play.[24]

Apart from war and defense, the social interest in external security may extend to other aspects of the conduct of foreign affairs. Here also a new element, likewise beyond the realm of

[24] The Supreme Court's decisions in the World War I period, when First Amendment doctrine was in its infancy, undoubtedly went too far in upholding restrictions on expression. See *Schenck v. United States*, 249 U.S. 47 (1919); *Frohwerk v. United States*, 249 U.S. 204 (1919); *Debs v. United States*, 249 U.S. 211 (1919); *Abrams v. United States*, 250 U.S. 616 (1919); *Schaefer v. United States*, 251 U.S. 466 (1920); *Pierce v. United States*, 252 U.S. 239 (1920); *United States ex rel. Milwaukee Social Democratic Publishing Co. v. Burleson*, 255 U.S. 407 (1921); *Gilbert v. Minnesota*, 254 U.S. 325 (1920). In the World War II period the Court did not squarely pass on the issues. See *Hartzell v. United States*, 322 U.S. 680 (1944); *Keegan v. United States*, 325 U.S. 478 (1945); *Gara v. United States*, 178 F.2d 38 (6th Cir. 1949), *aff'd by an equally divided court*, 340 U.S. 857 (1950).

freedom of expression, enters the picture. We are dealing with the relations of one society or government to another, not with relations between members of a single society or such members and their government. This makes it necessary to consider the means by which the government can maintain control over its relations with foreign nations, for instance in the making and enforcement of international commitments. Moreover, the inhabitants or government of another nation are not part of our society; they are not subject to our laws, institutions, customs or loyalties; and they do not share the rights or obligations of our citizens. Hence the problem of communicating with or receiving communications from other societies may raise novel questions.

In certain situations these factors pose no problems in application of the basic theory. Such considerations would not operate to prevent criticism of the general conduct of foreign affairs. Nor would they limit the general right of members of our society to communicate with members of another nation, to receive communications from such sources, or to travel abroad (apart from limitations based on military requirements or the need to prevent escape from justice). But they would justify a prohibition against espionage or the disclosure of government secrets to foreign governments or interests. And they would warrant limitation on the right of individuals in this country to conduct negotiations with a foreign government, or restrictions on the activities of paid agents of a foreign power. In other situations more difficult problems might arise. The essential point here also is that the legal judgment turns upon defining the proper area of freedom of expression, as embodied in the basic theory and enacted into fundamental law by the First Amendment, and distinguishing these limited sectors of social activity which are dominated by extraneous elements.[25]

[25] The ruling of the majority of the Supreme Court in the McCarran Act registration case, based on a broad construction of "direction, domination and control by a foreign government," pushes the line much too far into the domain of free expression. *Communist Party v. Subversive Activities Control Bd.*, 367 U.S. 1 (1961). But the Court's decision in the Foreign Agents Registration case is not in conflict with the doctrine proposed here. *Viereck v. United States*, 318 U.S. 236 (1943). The Court has not yet passed on issues of constitutional limitation in passport cases. See *Kent v. Dulles*, 357 U.S. 116 (1958); but *cf. Worthy v. Herter*, 270 F.2d 905 (D.C. Cir.), *cert. denied*, 361 U.S. 918 (1959).

Interests Sought to Be Protected by Restrictions on Obscene Publications

There is no clear agreement as to what social interests are sought to be protected by the laws restricting expression on grounds of obscenity. The main justifications advanced for such legislation, however, would seem to fall into the following categories: (1) that the expression has an adverse moral impact, apart from any effect upon overt behavior; (2) that the expression may stimulate or induce subsequent conduct in violation of law; (3) that the expression may produce adverse effects on personality and attitudes which in the long run lead to illegal behavior; (4) that the expression has a shock effect of an emotionally disturbing nature; and (5) that the expression has especially adverse effects, of the sort described in the previous categories, upon children, who are intellectually and emotionally immature.[26]

Most of the factual assumptions underlying these justifications are unsupported by empirical evidence. According to a recent survey, such evidence as is available indicates that expression of an erotic nature does result in "heightened sexual arousal" in some persons under some circumstances, and is for some persons "a distinctly adverse experience." But there is virtually no evidence as to how or whether these responses "affect overt behavior" or "attitudes governing behavior and mental health." [27] The ultimate resolution of the obscenity issue will undoubtedly be influenced by the development of a body of scientific knowledge pertaining to these matters.

The prevailing legal doctrine is that enunciated by the majority of the Supreme Court in the *Roth* case. The principle there stated is (1) "obscenity is not within the area of constitutionally

[26] Recent literature discussing the obscenity problem includes: William B. Lockhart and Robert C. McClure, "Censorship of Obscenity: The Developing Constitutional Standards," *Minnesota Law Review,* Vol. 45 (1960), p. 5; Harry Kalven, "The Metaphysics of the Law of Obscenity," *The Supreme Court Review,* Vol. 1 (1960); J. C. N. Paul and M. L. Schwartz, *Federal Censorship: Obscenity in the Mail* (New York, Free Press of Glencoe, 1961); R. B. Cairns, J. C. N. Paul and J. Wishner, "Sex Censorship: The Assumptions of Anti-Obscenity Laws and the Empirical Evidence," *Minnesota Law Review,* Vol. 46 (1962), p. 1009.

[27] See Cairns, Paul and Wishner, pp. 1031-1034, *supra* note 26, Ch. V.

protected speech"; and (2) the test for determining obscenity is "whether to the average person, applying contemporary community standards, the dominant theme of the material taken as a whole appeals to prurient interest." [28] The rule of the *Roth* case is open to criticism on a number of grounds, among others that the standard of "appeal to prurient interest" is so vague as not to afford any precise line of demarcation. Other efforts to draft a clear formula, distinguishing between protected and unprotected speech in terms of obscenity, have been equally unsuccessful. The practical result of the recent Supreme Court decisions has been, as nearly as it can be reduced to words, that only "hard core pornography" is likely to be found obscene.[29]

If one approaches the problem in the light of the considerations suggested here, it would appear that the first three justifications advanced for the obscenity laws are incompatible with the basic theory of freedom of expression as incorporated in the First Amendment. The fact that expression influences moral beliefs and attitudes, apart from any impact on behavior, is clearly no ground for restriction. Most expression is intended to and does have this result.[30] Similarly, the argument that obscene expression stimulates or induces subsequent illegal conduct, even if true, falls before the fundamental proposition that society must deal with the illegal action directly and may not use restriction of expression as a means of control. Again, many forms of expression would have a similar effect in influencing subsequent conduct. Nor is there anything in the nature of illegal conduct induced by obscene expression which would differentiate it from any other illegal conduct or require application of a different rule. A fortiori, the fact that the expression influences attitudes which in the long run influence behavior is unacceptable as a basis of restriction. Strict adherence to the distinction between "expression" and "action" which underlies the whole theory of freedom of expression is even more important if one takes into consideration the conditions under which obscenity restrictions

---

[28] *Roth v. United States*, 354 U.S. 476, 485, 489 (1957); *cf. Manual Enterprises, Inc. v. Day*, 370 U.S. 478 (1962).

[29] For analysis of the Supreme Court decisions following the *Roth* case, see Lockhart and McClure, *supra* note 26, Ch. V. See also *Manual Enterprises, Inc. v. Day, supra* note 28, Ch. V.

[30] The Supreme Court took this position in *Kingsley Int'l Pictures Corp. v. Regents*, 360 U.S. 684, 688-689 (1959).

would operate. No one has yet conceived a formula for defining "obscenity" which can be applied with any precision, and the abuses of all systems of literary censorship are notorious. No general restriction on expression in terms of "obscenity" can, therefore, be reconciled with the First Amendment.

On the other hand, certain aspects of the "shock effect" of erotic expression present different considerations. Where a shock effect is produced by forcing an "obscene" communication upon a person contrary to his wishes, the issue is somewhat similar to that involved in private defamation. The harm is direct, immediate and not controllable by regulating subsequent action. The conduct can realistically be considered an "assault" on the other person, and hence placed within the category of "action." Issues of this sort arise, of course, only in limited situations, such as where the communication is displayed publicly on a billboard or sent into a private home through the mail. Regulations can be devised to deal with this matter that do not create serious administrative problems. Under the circumstances, restriction of communications of this nature would not be inconsistent with the First Amendment.[31]

Different factors come into play also where the interest at stake is the effect of erotic expression upon children. The world of children is not strictly part of the adult realm of free expression. The factor of immaturity, and perhaps other considerations, impose different rules. Without attempting here to formulate the principles relevant to freedom of expression for children, it suffices to say that regulations of communication addressed to them need not conform to the requirements of the First Amendment in the same way as those applicable to adults. Serious administrative difficulties arise, of course, in attempting to frame restrictions which affect only children and do not impinge upon the rights of others.[32] But to the extent that these practical problems can be solved, the First Amendment would not seem to preclude controls over erotic communication addressed to children.

[31] It might be suggested that the Supreme Court, in limiting the concept of obscenity to "hard core pornography," is in effect employing a "shock effect" test, but one based on general community standards and applicable to willing as well as unwilling recipients.

[32] See *Butler v. Michigan*, 352 U.S. 380 (1957).

Other Social Interests Sought to Be Protected by Direct Restrictions Upon Expression

Apart from the situations already discussed, there would appear to be very few instances where even a plausible argument can be made that protection of a social interest requires a direct limitation on expression. So far as past experience indicates, it is hardly disputed that all such interests can be adequately safeguarded by restrictions on the conduct which is opposed to the interest affected, rather than upon the expression which may create or lead to the offending conduct. Among the isolated situations where such a problem has arisen, the case of the city ordinance which undertakes to prevent littering of the streets by forbidding the distribution of handbills may serve as an illustration. Here it is entirely clear that the remedy for the social evil is a direct prohibition against littering the streets rather than a limitation on circulation of literature. Thus the general legal doctrine ensuring full protection to expression is applicable to other kinds of social interests.[33]

Two types of special cases require brief mention. One concerns those relatively rare situations where expression and the action sought to be regulated are inseparable. The outstanding examples are picketing, which may be both a form of expression and an exercise of economic pressure; and speech by employers which, through implicit threat of economic retaliation, impairs the right of employees to self-organization and collective bargaining. In such situations, the communication being in and of itself coercive, the conduct is appropriately classified as "action" rather than "expression." [34]

The other special situation is where the conflict between expression and the other social interest is essentially one of physical incompatibility, as where a parade or meeting is held on a street or in a park which is also used for other purposes. The problem here is the regulation of the time, place or manner of expression in order to make a proper allocation of limited physical facilities.

[33] See *Lovell v. City of Griffin,* 303 U.S. 444 (1938); *cf. Eastern R.R. Presidents Conference v. Noerr Motor Freight, Inc.,* 365 U.S. 127 (1961).

[34] See, on picketing, the line of cases culminating in *Int'l Bhd. of Teamsters Union v. Vogt,* 354 U.S. 284 (1957); on employer free speech, *NLRB v. Virginia Elec. & Power Co.,* 314 U.S. 469 (1941).

The legal doctrines would be the same as those applicable to other cases of traffic control, discussed below.

Social Interests Sought to Be Protected by Measures Which Also Affect Freedom of Expression

The problems of reconciliation thus far discussed have involved governmental regulations explicitly directed at control of expression. But the expression may be curtailed also by measures which are directed, at least ostensibly, at other forms of activity, but which have a "secondary," "indirect" or "incidental" effect upon expression. Such measures include various types of tax and economic regulations, the imposition of political qualifications for obtaining government employment or other benefits or privileges, the activities of legislative investigating committees, and political restrictions on the rights of aliens. The fact that these forms of government action do not directly prohibit or regulate expression does not mean that they are of less significance in the functioning of a system of free expression. Quite the contrary, in the period since World War II the impact of such measures upon freedom of expression has probably been as serious as, or more serious than, the impact of explicit limitations. Unfortunately, the principles for reconciling the social interest in achieving the goals sought by these measures with the maintenance of free expression have received relatively little attention.

Ever since the *Douds* case, a majority of the Supreme Court has employed the ad hoc balancing test as the formula for solving this problem.[35] For reasons already stated, the test is defective in theory and appears to have failed to afford adequate protection to freedom of expression in practice. Is it possible, then, to frame a more satisfactory interpretation of the First Amendment in this area, one that will be less open-ended and that will permit the courts to function more like judicial institutions?

In attempting to frame such legal doctrine we start again with the basic principle—the prior decision on balancing incorporated in the First Amendment—that the state may not seek to achieve

[35] See Laurent Frantz, "The First Amendment in the Balance," *Yale Law Journal*, Vol. 71 (1962), pp. 1424, 1426.

control over action by regulation of expression. The main problem here, to repeat, is one of defining the area of "expression." In addition, another element must now be considered. By hypothesis the regulation imposed is, taken by itself, a legitimate one, aimed directly at control of "action." The question is its secondary impact upon an admitted area of "expression." This is essentially a problem of determining when the regulation at issue has an effect upon expression which constitutes "abridging" within the meaning of the First Amendment. In other words, the courts must now undertake to define and give content to the concept of "abridging." This judgment, like the judgment in defining "expression," must be made in light of the affirmative theory underlying freedom of expression and the various conditions essential to maintaining a workable system.

Formulation of specific legal doctrine along these lines requires consideration of the separate types of situations in which the issue arises.

TAXATION AND ECONOMIC REGULATION

Regular tax measures, economic regulations, social welfare legislation and similar provisions may, of course, have some effect upon freedom of expression when applied to persons or organizations engaged in various forms of communication. But where the burden is the same as that borne by others engaged in different forms of activity, the similar impact on expression seems clearly insufficient to constitute an "abridging" of freedom of expression. Hence a general corporate tax, wage and hour or collective bargaining legislation, factory laws and the like are as applicable to a corporation engaged in newspaper publishing as to other business organizations.[36] On the other hand, the use of such measures as a sanction to diminish the volume of expression or control its content would clearly be as impermissible an "abridgment" as direct criminal prohibitions. The line may sometimes be difficult to draw, the more so as the scope of the regulation is narrowed.

Two principles for delineating the bounds of "abridging" may be stated. First, as a general proposition the validity of the measure may be tested by the rule that it must be equally ap-

---

[36] See *Associated Press v. NLRB*, 301 U.S. 103 (1937).

plicable to a substantially larger group than that engaged in expression. Thus a special tax on the press alone, or a tax exemption available only to those with particular political views or associations, would not be permitted.[37] Second, neither the substantive nor the procedural provisions of the measure, even though framed in general terms, may place any substantial burden on expression because of their peculiar impact in that area. Thus the enforcement of a tax or corporate registration statute by requiring disclosure of membership in an association, where such disclosure would substantially impair freedom of expression, should be found to violate First Amendment protection.[38]

One special problem in this area should be noted. Since children cannot, at least in some respects, be considered as within the framework of a system of free expression, economic regulations controlling the conduct of children, such as a law regulating the employment of children, which operated to prevent them from distributing literature in the streets, would not necessarily infringe the principles of freedom of expression.[39]

So far as concrete problems of this nature have arisen, the application of these doctrines would appear entirely workable. Indeed, in the results reached, the Supreme Court decisions in this area have been wholly consistent with them.[40]

QUALIFICATIONS FOR BENEFITS OR PRIVILEGES OR HOLDING POSITIONS

One of the major developments of recent years has been the increasing volume of government regulation which requires persons, as a condition to obtaining certain benefits or privileges or holding certain positions, to meet qualifications based on political views or associations. Requirements of this nature have been imposed in many fields, including the right to appear on the ballot, to hold public office, to obtain public employment, to practice law, to be granted various kinds of licenses, to receive welfare benefits, to live in publicly assisted housing, to travel

---

[37] See *Grosjean v. American Press Co.*, 297 U.S. 233 (1936); *Murdock v. Pennsylvania*, 319 U.S. 105 (1943); *Speiser v. Randall*, 357 U.S. 513 (1958); *Cammarano v. United States*, 358 U.S. 498 (1959).

[38] See *NAACP v. Alabama*, 357 U.S. 449 (1958); *Bates v. City of Little Rock*, 361 U.S. 516 (1960).

[39] See *Prince v. Massachusetts*, 321 U.S. 158 (1944).

[40] See cases cited in notes 36-39, Ch. V *supra*.

abroad, and to hold office in a labor organization. The purpose of these restrictions in theory is not to penalize past political expression, but to prevent future conduct by eliminating those who might in the future engage in activities damaging to the social interest involved in the basic regulation. Thus in the field of government employment—an area where requirements of this nature are widespread—the loyalty programs are designed to weed out in advance those persons whose prior expression of political views is thought to indicate a greater likelihood that they would engage in treason, espionage, sabotage or other conduct detrimental to government service.

Reconciliation of the interest in freedom of expression with the social interest sought to be protected by these preventive measures raises issues essentially the same as where direct restriction is used to safeguard the social interest in internal order. Without attempting at this point to examine the concrete issues involved in particular regulations, the general principle may be stated that use of qualifications based upon exercise of the right of expression is wholly incompatible with a system of free expression, and that the other social interests at stake can be adequately protected by prohibition of the conduct rather than the expression. Whether actually intended or not, the imposition of such qualifications operates as a penalty—a severe and pervasive one—upon free expression. The administration of such restrictions—involving searching without limits or logic into every phase of a person's beliefs, opinions and associations; the imputation to individuals of the views of others with whom he associates; the creation of a far-reaching apparatus of investigation and enforcement; the stimulation of an atmosphere of fear and hysteria—is particularly destructive. The use of beliefs, opinions and associations as a guide to future improper conduct, where relevant at all, is of minimal value. Employment of such qualifications, even on a limited scale, seriously "abridges" freedom of expression. Widespread use under conditions of modern life must result in virtual annihilation of any real freedom of expression intended to be protected by the First Amendment.

Two special situations, however, do not fall within the above doctrine. The military sector of our national life, as previously noted, must operate to some degree outside the system of free expression. This may justify certain qualifications for those who have access to important secret military information. And in government employment, a relatively few high posts demanding the exercise of policy discretion may require incumbents who, in order to carry on the functions of the office, must adhere to certain views. To demand the necessary qualifications under these circumstances does not "abridge" the freedom of expression of persons holding other opinions. But these areas should be narrowly and carefully defined.

The Supreme Court does not accept these doctrines, a majority applying the ad hoc balancing test. In this area the First Amendment has afforded small protection to freedom of expression.[41]

LEGISLATIVE INVESTIGATING COMMITTEES

Operations of legislative investigating committees during the last several decades have raised issues which have come to be of the first importance. The social interest here is that the legislature obtain the information necessary to carry out its function of considering and enacting legislation and to perform its other duties. The value of this process of legislative fact-finding cannot be ignored. Yet, in pursuit of that objective, legislative investigating committees have seriously curtailed freedom of expression in the United States. Of this fact there can be no doubt. But the problem of reconciling competing interests in this area has proved to be particularly difficult. The investigating process, by its very nature, does not readily lend itself to limitation. No one can say with certainty how much information is necessary, what line of investigation may lead to valuable information, where the boundaries of relevance lie. Moreover, institutional techniques available for effecting an accommodation between opposing interests are by no means satisfactory. Thus the judiciary is

[41] The leading case, as previously noted, is *American Communications Ass'n v. Douds*, 339 U. S. 382 (1950). See also *Konigsberg v. State Bar*, 366 U.S. 36 (1961); *In re* Anastaplo, 366 U.S. 82 (1961); *Flemming v. Nestor*, 363 U.S. 603 (1960); *Garner v. Board of Pub. Works*, 341 U.S. 716 (1951); *Adler v. Board of Educ.*, 342 U.S. 485 (1952); *Lerner v. Casey*, 357 U.S. 468 (1958); *Nelson v. County of Los Angeles*, 362 U.S. 1 (1960); *Cafeteria & Restaurant Workers Union v. McElroy*, 367 U.S. 886 (1961); *cf. Gerende v. Board of Supervisors*, 341 U.S. 56 (1951); *Wieman v. Updegraff*, 344 U.S. 183 (1952); *Schware v. Board of Bar Examiners*, 353 U.S. 232 (1957); *Shelton v. Tucker*, 364 U.S. 479 (1960); Louisiana *ex rel. Gremillion v. NAACP*, 366 U.S. 293 (1961).

naturally reluctant, and politically at a disadvantage, in attempting to limit legislative action in this area. And under present procedures the witness must guess, at peril of prison if he errs, at what point his right to decline to answer arises.

For these and other reasons the development of principles of reconciliation has been slow and inadequate. The rule presently prevailing in court decisions is that an ad hoc balance must be struck between the interest in freedom of speech and the interest of the legislature in securing the information it seeks. But again this doctrine has plainly not solved the problem. Another principle advanced has been that the legislature should have no authority to expose, for the sake of exposure, without reference to a legislative purpose. But the line here is most difficult to determine, is readily evaded, and is not of much help to courts or witnesses. A third test—that the investigation may not invade the area of expression protected against direct state interference —has run into the claim that it may be necessary to overstep the boundary in order to determine where the boundary is, and has been of limited utility where the protected area of expression is defined in loose terms of clear and present danger or balancing interests.

On the basis of our previous analysis, however, legal doctrines may be formulated which promise some degree of certainty and a reasonable accommodation. In the first place, the process of legislative investigation under certain circumstances clearly constitutes an "abridgment" of freedom of speech. This is obviously true where the inquiry is directed into the opinions, utterances or associations of a hated or highly unpopular minority. The harassment involved in being summoned before a legislative committee, the economic and social sanctions which follow the forced disclosure of views or associational ties, the atmosphere of fear and hysteria engendered by dramatic revelations of the committee, the creation of a permanent bureaucracy devoted to investigating opinions and organizations, and similar factors, seriously impair full and open discussion of controversial issues. The fact that this curtailment of free expression occurs has been widely recognized. The legal conclusion that it constitutes an "abridgment" within the meaning of the First Amendment follows from the considerations set forth above. There may be other circumstances, of course, where a legislative inquiry concerning opinion does not operate as an "abridgment." For example, questions put to the president of a large corporation concerning an address in which he discussed a pending tax proposal would hardly fall within that classification. The problem of differentiating may be troublesome at times, but certainly it is not beyond the capacity of a court to determine.

Secondly, the principle that the government may not seek to achieve its legitimate objectives in the area of "action" through methods abridging "expression" fully applies to legislative inquiries. The prior balance struck by the First Amendment precludes such intrusion. In theory there is no reason why an exception to the basic principle should be made for a legislative committee; indeed such a committee is less likely to represent the public need or desires than when the legislature acts as a whole in passing a statute. In practice, experience tends to show that the fact-finding necessary for legislative purposes can be achieved by voluntary testimony or compulsory testimony more closely related to the area in which the legislature may enact legislation.

Hence similar legal doctrines ought to apply here as in other situations of legislative action having a "secondary" or "indirect" effect upon freedom of expression. Briefly stated they might be:

(1) A legislative committee should not be permitted to inquire into conduct previously defined as "expression" under circumstances where such inquiry would realistically constitute an "abridgment." It may investigate "action," or it may investigate "expression" where no "abridgment" occurs, subject to other rules such as the privilege against self-incrimination. The rule is a workable one if the distinction between "expression" and "action" is maintained. It would follow that a legislative committee should not intrude in an area of "expression" in order to seek leads for an inquiry into conduct within its permitted sphere of investigation.

(2) Expression in the form of associational activity should be protected by doctrines similar to those discussed above in connection with reconciling freedom of expression and internal order. Thus the fact that an association is engaged in certain forms of "action" ought not to permit inquiry into its conduct in the area of "expression." The two forms of conduct should be kept separate. Likewise, the conduct of one member constituting "action" ought not to be ground for investigating the conduct of another member in the field of "expression."

We may, by way of illustration, apply these rules to the most controversial issue in the operation of legislative committees—whether the committee may compel a witness to answer whether he is "a member of the Communist Party." Such an inquiry clearly constitutes an "abridgment." It also invades the area of "expression." For the Communist Party, whatever else it may be doing, engages in various forms of legitimate expression; and the question put, as Dr. Meiklejohn has pointed out, is a "complex" one, embracing many different kinds of conduct, some of which are protected as an exercise of the right to expression.[42] The committee may properly inquire into alleged activities of the witness or the Communist Party which constitute "action," including espionage, sabotage, violence, preparations for violence, and the like. But it should not, by lumping the different forms of conduct together in one question, abridge freedom of expression.

It may be added that the foregoing legal doctrines should be supplemented by certain legislative reforms for improving the institutional structure. These would include such requirements as a definite mandate to the committee from the parent body, certain safeguards for witnesses, and a mode of judicial review which is less risky than a citation for contempt.

Once again the Supreme Court decisions do not adhere to these principles. A majority has held that a state legislative committee may not inquire into the associations of a witness in the Progressive Party. But it has consistently upheld broad inquiries into membership in the Communist Party and into "Communist activities." In general, as a protection to freedom of expression against the conduct of legislative committees, the First Amendment has been of very limited usefulness.[43]

ALIENS

Another area where restrictions on expression have played a prominent role is in the treatment of aliens. Severe limitations

---

[42] Alexander Meiklejohn, "The Barenblatt Opinion," *University of Chicago Law Review,* Vol. 27 (1960), pp. 329, 338-339.

[43] See *Barenblatt v. United States,* 360 U.S. 109 (1959); *Uphaus v. Wyman,* 360 U.S. 72 (1959); *Braden v. United States,* 365 U.S. 431 (1961); *Wilkinson v. United States,* 365 U.S. 399 (1961). *Cf. United States v. Rumely,* 345 U.S. 41 (1953); *Watkins v. United States,* 354 U.S. 178 (1957); *Sweezy v. New Hampshire,* 354 U.S. 234 (1957).

have been imposed upon aliens through laws and regulations dealing with their deportation, naturalization and denaturalization. The social interests sought to be achieved by these restrictions have never been clearly defined. Presumably the objective has been to promote national unity and to prevent violation of law.

The basic theory of freedom of expression would seem clearly to preclude any special restriction upon freedom of expression by aliens. The right of expression extends to all individuals as members of a society, regardless of whether they are born into it, formally accepted as members, or are members by virtue of residence alone. Realization of the social values of free expression requires also that all members of the society have and exercise the right. Actually, noncitizens have made and constantly make vital contributions to our national life. Finally, limitation on aliens in the area of expression necessarily restricts the rights of citizens. Not only does it curtail the right of the citizen to hear, but it seriously deters the citizen from exercising his own right of expression. Reconciliation of competing interests is hence no different in the case of aliens than for any other members of the society.[44]

Government Action Designed to Facilitate Operation of the System

A THEORY OF FREEDOM of expression must deal not only with the powers of the state to restrict the right of expression but also with the obligations of the state to protect it and, in some instances, to encourage it. To use the government itself—the traditional enemy of freedom of expression—as an instrument for promoting freedom of expression and eliminating obstacles to its proper functioning calls for unprecedented imagination and discipline.

The problems arise in four major areas: (1) traffic controls; (2) purification of the democratic process; (3) protection of

---

[44] The Supreme Court has notoriously not followed these principles. See *Galvan v. Press*, 347 U.S. 522 (1954). The principles do not fully apply, of course, to the admission of aliens, since they are not yet members of our society. Here the First Amendment would seem to guarantee no protection. The policy which should be adopted on admission of aliens is another matter.

the free functioning of the system against undue interference from private (nongovernmental) sources; and (4) affirmative measures which the government may take to increase the effective operation of the system by encouraging greater use and diversity of expression.

Traffic Controls

The first problem involves the physical context in which expression takes place. Two types of situations have arisen: those where it is necessary to reconcile the interests of two or more persons or groups who seek to express their views at the same time or place; and those where exercise of the right of expression may conflict with the desire of others to use the same facilities for other forms of activity. Neither situation involves regulation of the content of expression. These are essentially questions of traffic control, and they are resolvable through the development of legal doctrine giving content to the meaning of "abridge."

The first kind of traffic control occurs where two or more groups desire to hold a parade, demonstration or meeting in the same place, or to use the same public buildings or other public facilities for communication. The issue here is not one of reconciling the right to freedom of expression with other social interests, but rather one of devising a method of public control in order to maintain orderly expression and thereby promote freedom of expression. The traditional tests of "absolute" freedom, clear and present danger, or balancing different kinds of social interests are irrelevant. But the substantive principle is clear. It is simply the requirement that the system of control afford equality of treatment as between individuals or groups and allow no discrimination on the basis of the content of the expression. The application of this principle presents real difficulties only where the physical facilities are seriously limited in relation to demand, such as in the field of radio and television. Here the question of equality of treatment may involve complex factors, and the issue of control of content re-enters. The resolution of this problem requires consideration of the specific facts in individual situations and will not be attempted here.

Protection against abuse in the administration of the traffic system may raise troublesome questions. But potentially adequate principles of control are available to the courts. The main ones are (1) that the standards be specifically and objectively formulated, a requirement also enforceable under the rule against vagueness or the rule against excessive delegation of power; (2) that the procedures be fair, enforceable also under doctrines of due process; and (3) that effective judicial supervision be afforded, enforceable under general doctrines of judicial review.

The second form of traffic regulation becomes necessary in situations where a group wishes to engage in some form of communication at a place which will interfere with the normal flow of traffic or the activities of other persons engaged in other affairs; or where a group wishes to use a public building ordinarily devoted to other purposes. The standards just stated are applicable here. But one addition is necessary: the traffic system must provide for a reasonable accommodation of opposing interests. This is, of course, a balancing test. Since resolution of the problem does not involve total foreclosure of either interest, however, but merely adjustments of time and place, it requires consideration of much more precise and limited factors. Hence, in this context, a balancing test seems manageable.

The Supreme Court decisions in this area, while not clearly articulating these principles, have in substance adhered to them.[45]

Purification of the Democratic Process

Problems of reconciliation have likewise arisen where the state seeks to impose restrictions upon expression designed to purify the democratic process by eliminating corruption, fraud, misrepresentation, appeals to hatred and similar forms of expression. The chief restrictions of this nature have been corrupt practices legislation, lobbying legislation, registration and disclosure requirements, and group libel laws. The purpose of such

[45] For application of the principle of nondiscrimination, see *Niemotko v. Maryland,* 340 U.S. 268 (1951); *Fowler v. Rhode Island,* 345 U.S. 67 (1953). On the rule against vagueness, see *Cantwell v. Connecticut,* 310 U.S. 296 (1940); *Kunz v. New York,* 340 U.S. 290 (1951); *Staub v. City of Baxley,* 355 U.S. 313 (1958). On accommodation with those using the same facilities for other purposes, see *Hague v. CIO,* 307 U.S. 496 (1939); *Cox v. New Hampshire,* 312 U.S. 569 (1941). All the above cases, of course, allow judicial review. But in *Poulos v. New Hampshire,* 345 U.S. 395 (1953), a majority of the Court imposed severe limitations upon the practical use of judicial review.

measures, at least in theory, is to promote the healthier and more efficient operation of a system of free expression. And the issue posed, again at least in theory, is not the reconciliation of freedom of expression with another kind of interest but the reconciliation of opposing interests within the system of free expression itself. Yet the problems are far more difficult than those arising in connection with the physical ordering of expression. Here the regulation often seeks to deal with the content of expression and, unless carefully circumscribed, is more likely to impair than promote open discussion.

In the light of prior discussion of the theory and administration of a system of free expression, the following proposals would appear to provide suitable principles of reconciliation:

(1) In general, purification through restrictions on the manner or content of expression is an "abridgment" and hence invalid. This is true for the same reasons that limitations framed in terms of "social value" or "truth" are not generally acceptable criteria. It is the function of the individual, not the government, to sift the true from the false, the relevant from the irrelevant, the rational from the appeal to prejudice. The standards used in purifying regulations are necessarily vague and in practice subject to misuse for partisan purposes. Although there is considerable appeal in the ideal of conducting all expression on a clean, fair and rational level, such an ideal is not attainable in the actual conduct of human affairs. The result of such broad restrictions can only be the suppression of unorthodox, unpopular, or minority expression.

(2) One cannot say that every regulation of the purifying type is inconsistent with a system of free expression. In theory such restrictions may, by limiting the freedom of some, expand the freedom of a greater number. In practice, certain types of restriction have been employed without proving destructive. The basic principle just stated must therefore allow for limited exceptions. But the restriction must be considered an *exception*, with proponents having the burden of showing that it is clearly necessary to correct a grave abuse in the operation of the system; that it is narrowly limited to that end; that it does not limit the content of the expression; that it is in the nature of a regulation, not a prohibition, and does not substantially impair the area of expression controlled; that the objective cannot adequately be

achieved by other means; that the regulation can be specifically formulated in objective terms; that it is reasonably free from administrative abuse; and that it operates equitably, with no undue advantage to any group or point of view.[46]

By way of illustration, it may be said that certain restraints on expenditure of money in political campaigns or in direct contacts with the legislature would qualify as falling within the area of exception. On the other hand, registration or disclosure which substantially interferes with expression, as in the case of unpopular groups whose activities would be curtailed by disclosure, would not qualify for the above enumerated exceptions. Similarly, group libel laws would not meet the test.

Protection of the System Against Interference From Private Sources

The government has, of course, traditionally exercised the function of protecting the right to freedom of expression against interference by other persons through the use of force or violence. No issue under the First Amendment arises; the major problems relate only to matters of enforcement. But to what extent should the government assume the function of protecting the right of expression against pressures which fall short of force or violence? Here the issues become more troublesome.

Clearly, the government cannot and should not undertake to

[46] Regulations which would be justifiable under the above principles were upheld in *Burroughs v. United States,* 290 U.S. 534 (1934); *United States v. Harriss,* 347 U.S. 612 (1954); *Lewis Publishing Co. v. Morgan,* 229 U.S. 288 (1913). A restriction not justifiable under these principles was held invalid in *Talley v. California,* 362 U.S. 60 (1960). Restrictions not justifiable under these principles were upheld in *Beauharnais v. Illinois,* 343 U.S. 250 (1952); *United States v. UAW,* 352 U.S. 567 (1957); *cf. Communist Party v. Subversive Activities Control Bd.,* 367 U.S. 1 (1961).

Fraud or misrepresentation of business character falls into an area outside the system of the freedom of expression. Communications in connection with commercial transactions generally relate to a separate sector of social activity involving the system of property rights rather than free expression. The principles governing commercial speech, and the relations between this sector and the area of free expression, have never been worked out. See, *e.g., Cammarano v. United States,* 358 U.S. 498 (1959). That task is not attempted here. Up to the present, the problem of differentiating between commercial and other communication has not in practice proved to be a serious one.

eliminate all pressures from private sources—economic, social, personal and so on—which may affect the volume, content or manner of expression. The very process of reaching social decisions assumes that such pressures will be constantly at work. In the functioning of our society, however, certain problems have emerged which seem to call for government action. These include such matters as the use of economic pressure by employers, landlords or creditors to prevent the exercise of the right to participate in the elective process; the use of property rights by owners of company towns to interfere with the distribution of literature or similar activity; and the organization of certain types of boycotts by powerful organizations to prevent certain kinds of communication. Where the government undertakes to protect the system of freedom of expression against obstructions of this nature through legislation, no problem under the First Amendment is presented so long as the regulation is addressed to "action" rather than "expression." In the absence of legislation, the First Amendment may properly be invoked to protect freedom of expression if the source of obstruction is the government itself or even a nongovernmental organization possessed of equivalent powers; in such cases the principles previously discussed are applicable.[47]

A special, important and exceedingly complex problem arises, however, in connection with membership rights in voluntary associations. One of the outstanding characteristics of modern democratic society has been the development of private, in the sense of nongovernmental, centers of power. Numerous organizations, such as labor unions, business associations, professional societies and many others, wield increasing power in the economic, political and other spheres of our national life. In many areas the individual alone is helpless to protect or advance his interests and can operate effectively only through an organization. This pluralism is a vital feature of our complex society, but it is beginning to create serious issues for the maintenance of an effective system of free expression.

These private centers of power have come to possess extensive authority over the welfare of their individual members. Moreover, they often generate large and impersonal bureaucracies, which tend to have a life and direction of their own. Frequently

[47] See *Marsh v. Alabama,* 326 U.S. 501 (1946).

such organizations exercise monopolistic or near monopolistic power, as in the case of a labor organization operating under a closed shop arrangement, or a medical association with control over access to hospitals. And very often they are supported or regulated by government, so that they take on even more the character of quasi-public institutions.

The basic problem is to what extent the principles which are applicable to government in its relationships with individuals should apply to these private centers of power in their relationships with individuals; and by what methods and institutions should any such applicable principles be enforced. These questions present novel and perplexing issues.[48]

As the situation has thus far developed, two aspects have come to the fore. First, there are a series of questions involving the right of individuals to join and participate in the affairs of the organization. Should there be limits on the power of the organization to admit, expel or discipline members? What measures, if any, should be adopted to assure that the organization operates in accordance with democratic procedures? What rights should individuals or minority groups have to criticize or oppose the policies and practices of the organization, either from the inside or outside?

A second series of questions revolves around a closely related matter. Many organizations, formed primarily or in part for purposes other than expression, also engage in various forms of political expression. Where economic or other conditions create pressure on individuals to join such organizations, or where the government requires individuals to join or otherwise protects the organization's monopoly, a serious issue arises over the expenditure of organizational funds for political purposes contrary to the wishes of a minority of the membership. Thus far these issues have been presented where a labor organization operating a closed shop, or an integrated bar association, has engaged in political activity. The precise question is whether the government should protect the minority interest in this situation, apart from the matter of assuring democratic procedures, by prohibiting the organization from carrying on the political activity with funds contributed by the dissenters.

---

[48] See also Arthur S. Miller, "The Constitutional Law of the 'Security State,'" *Stanford Law Review,* Vol. 10 (1958), p. 620.

There are dangers from the intrusion of governmental regulation into these or comparable matters. Any form of government control reduces the capacity of the organization to function independently, and particularly to resist the government which has power over it. Once the principle of governmental restriction is accepted for any purpose, it becomes difficult to establish a stopping place. Problems tend to be settled by resort to further public controls, rather than to be left to internal reform. Experience indicates there is little probability of turning back; movement is likely to be all in one direction. Hence we must start with a presumption against the need for government regulation.

However, on occasion, government regulation may be the lesser evil, and we seem to have reached this point already in some situations. The need for government intervention will turn upon various factors, including the importance of the function that the organization performs and the capacity of the group concerned to assure the protection of individual rights through self-regulation. In addition, it will depend upon whether conditions are such that a multiplicity of organizations can exist in the area affected, or whether circumstances drive toward a monopoly. In the former case, there is minimum need for governmental controls; dissidents can withdraw and form their own association. In the latter case such diversity is not possible and the choice may be between regulation or unregulated monopoly. Beyond this the problem is one of finding a satisfactory balance between preservation of the individual or minority right and effective performance of the organization's functions.

Issues under the First Amendment arise in either of two settings. Legislation attempting to deal directly with the problem may be challenged as infringing upon First Amendment rights of association. Or, in the case of organizations subject to some measure of governmental regulation in other matters, a right may be asserted in judicial proceedings by individuals on the theory that sufficient "state action" is involved to bring First Amendment protection into play. In neither case has the application of First Amendment doctrine been clearly formulated.[49]

[49] The major federal legislation of this type—the Labor-Management Reporting and Disclosure Act of 1959, 73 Stat. 519—has not been tested in the Supreme Court. The leading case in which the issue was presented to the courts under a claim of "state action" is *International Ass'n of Machinists v. Street,* 367 U.S. 740 (1961).

In the first type of case—where government regulation aimed at protecting expression is alleged to interfere with rights of free association—two distinctions should be made which would provide the basis for deciding when an "abridging" of freedom of expression occurs. First, it is necessary to distinguish between organizations which are to be considered as operating in the public sector and those which operate in the private sector. A labor organization or medical association possessing quasi-monopolistic powers, or an integrated bar association, by reason of their functions, powers and extent of governmental support would provide the clearest instance of associations falling within the public sector; in contrast, a social or recreational club would most clearly come within the private sector. The line between is shadowy, and would have to be drawn in the light of concrete circumstances.[50] Wherever the line is drawn, the right of association under the First Amendment would preclude governmental regulation of the type here involved in the case of associations in the private sector. Secondly, assuming the organization is in the public sector, the validity of government regulation under the First Amendment would be controlled by the principle that the restriction imposed on association or expression be necessary for protection of the system of freedom of expression; that it not be of such a character as substantially to impair the functioning or frustrate the legitimate objectives of the association; and that it otherwise conform to the principles stated above in connection with government regulation designed as purification of the democratic process.[51]

In the case of claims by individuals against restrictions of expression by "private" organizations, presented on the theory that the group's restriction constitutes "state action," somewhat similar principles would apply. In addition the court is faced with the problem of defining the term "law" as used in the First Amendment. An association classified as in the private sector would not be subject to any First Amendment requirements, no "state action" or "law" being involved. Where the organization operated in the public sector, the issue would turn upon the question whether, in light of the relations between government

[50] For discussion of the problem, in a somewhat different context, see C. Black, Jr., "The Constitution and Public Power," *Yale Review* (Autumn 1962), p. 54.
[51] See text accompanying notes 45-46, Ch. V *supra*.

and the association, the requirements for maintaining an effective system of freedom of expression demand judicial protection of the right asserted. Certainly in this area the courts should proceed slowly. But where government support is substantial and the First Amendment right clear, the courts, in performing their function of giving positive support to the system of free expression, should act to protect the right. The decision of the Supreme Court in the *Street* case, while provoking disagreement as to the manner in which the right should be protected, would appear to have reached a sound conclusion as to the underlying First Amendment question.[52]

The doctrines applicable here are, of course, much looser than where direct governmental curbs on free expression are in issue. But in this context, their generality and flexibility would not appear to involve any danger to the system of freedom of expression, but rather would afford the capacity for development to meet the basic problems presented by the operation of voluntary associations. It seems unlikely that government action in these areas will be carried too far in the foreseeable future. The balance of forces in our society tends rather in the other direction. Certainly an excess of governmental control here has so far not proved to be a serious matter.

Affirmative Measures to Increase the Effective Operation of the System

It is possible here only to point out certain areas in which the problem of governmental encouragement to freedom of expression has arisen, and to suggest tentatively some of the principles which may be applicable in guiding this development.

(1) The most common form of governmental assistance to freedom of expression is the furnishing of facilities for communication. Traditionally streets, parks, commons and similar open public places have been used for meetings, parades and other forms of expression. Clearly there should be a right for any person or group to use such public property, subject only to restrictions of the traffic control type.

The use of public buildings presents a somewhat different

---

[52] *International Ass'n of Machinists v. Street,* 367 U.S. 740 (1961). *Cf. Lathrop v. Donohue,* 367 U.S. 820 (1961).

problem. It cannot be said that private persons or groups have a legal right to use such structures for meetings or similar private purposes. But it is certainly sound policy for the government to make public buildings available for this use. Where this is done, the applicable principle is that the public facility should be open to all on an equal basis; no differentiation based upon the content of the expression is permissible.

At the present time the furnishing of government facilities has not progressed much beyond this point. But suggestions have been made for extension of government participation. Thus it has been proposed that the government furnish funds to be used in election campaigns, that government control and allocate newsprint, or that it take over all broadcasting facilities. Such an expansion of government functions would raise very serious issues. Dependence upon the government to this degree for the facilities of communication clearly poses grave dangers to the whole system of free expression. Moreover, even if techniques were evolved to minimize this danger, extraordinarily difficult problems would arise in attempting to administer the basic principle of equality of treatment to minority groups, to new groups being formed, to individuals not sharing the viewpoint of any group, to "crackpots," and so on.

(2) Development of the mass media of communication in this country raises the most pressing current questions as to the scope of government measures necessary or advisable for maintaining an effective system of free expression. The problem has been clear for some time. More and more control over communication is being centralized in the hands of a small group which owns and operates the mass media. As a result the communication reaching most members of the community conforms to a single pattern; other views are rarely or never heard. Instead of a system of open communication in which all the facts and a diversity of opinion are available in the marketplace of ideas, our system approaches a closed one in which only a single point of view with minor variations can find an outlet.

What can or should be done about this organization of our system of communication? Thus far government action has largely been confined to two areas. One is the use of the antitrust laws as a deterrent to monopoly. Here no serious problem of principle is involved. Insofar as the anti-trust laws encourage diversity of control and variation in expression they clearly promote freedom of expression. Their impact being upon the majority or predominant views, they are scarcely a threat to minority or unpopular expression. In practice, of course, the anti-trust laws have had little effect upon prevailing trends and hence have not contributed much to the solution of the underlying problem.

The other area of governmental action has been the licensing of radio and television stations, made necessary by physical limitations upon the number of wave lengths. Exercise of this function necessarily involves the development of principles governing the choice of stations to be licensed, including principles relating to the measure of government control over the content of the program. But little progress has been made. The need is to formulate reasonably concrete standards, based upon the underlying principle of public service and diversity. Equally important, it is necessary to develop the institutions and techniques for applying the standard and supervising that application.

(3) A third set of questions concerns what has come to be called "the right to know"—the problem of secrecy in government. Here again the issue is clear. Successful operation of a democratic society, and particularly the functioning of a system of free expression, depends upon members of the society having access to the information necessary for making decisions. But more and more of this essential information is being withheld by the government for reasons of military secrecy, foreign policy, or simple face-saving. This is not an area where the courts, applying First Amendment doctrines, can be of much assistance. But the principle which should be followed by the legislature and executive is plain: the maximum amount of information should be disclosed. Implementation of the principle is difficult and little progress has been made in developing techniques for its realization in practice.

Government Participation in Political Expression

THE FUNCTION of government has never been confined to regulating the free play of expression by private individuals or groups. The government itself has always participated in the marketplace of ideas. With the growth of modern industrial society this activity of the government has become ever more pervasive and more significant.

Government activity in the field of expression takes many forms. It includes statements by public officials, publications of all kinds, and the operation of opinion-forming institutions, primarily the system of education. Few limitations have been imposed upon expression by the government, except its own self-restraint, and little thought has been given to the development of principles which should control its action in this field. At this point it is possible only to state certain broad generalizations.

Where the government voice is not the exclusive one in a field, but must compete with expression by private individuals or groups, there is less need of limitation. Thus government statements and publications in most instances enter a marketplace to which nongovernmental sources have access. They are subject to contradiction, modification, or testing against statements or publications by newspapers and similar forms of communication. But where the government expression operates as a monopoly or near monopoly, some principles of limitation may be necessary. Such a situation arises, for example, in the field of education, which is a nearly closed system under the control of the government. Here the possibilities of nongovernmental communication offsetting the government influence are small or nonexistent.

What the principles of limitation should be, and how they can be enforced against the government, raise difficult questions. But it is not impossible to formulate some guiding lines. One such principle may be found in the concept of balanced presentation. Under this principle it would be the obligation of the government to present a fairly balanced exposition of the various relevant points of view and of the alternatives open for action. The developing theory of academic freedom furnishes some basis for expanding and refining such a concept. Another principle is that the government may not engage in political expression where it addresses a captive audience.[53] In the administration and

[53] See *Public Util. Comm'n v. Pollak,* 343 U.S. 451 (1952).

enforcement of such principles, institutional safeguards, including judicial review, would have to be devised or perfected.

Traditional doctrines of freedom of expression do not provide theories of limitation in these areas. But the need for addressing ourselves to these questions and endeavoring to frame the controlling principles is great.

‖ IN THE FIRST PART OF THIS book we have attempted to set forth the various factors upon which any nonverbal interpretation of the First Amendment must rest. Without undertaking to summarize those considerations, we may emphasize two of the major conclusions that emerge. One is that the essence of a system of freedom of expression lies in the distinction between expression and action. The whole theory rests upon the general proposition that expression must be free and unrestrained, that the state may not seek to achieve other social objectives through control of expression, and that the attainment of such objectives can and must be secured through regulation of action. The dynamics of the system require that this line be carefully drawn and strictly adhered to. The acceptance of this general position was the fundamental decision made in adopting the First Amendment, and this balance of values and methods must be recognized in any interpretation of that constitutional guarantee.

The other conclusion is that conditions in a modern democratic society demand that a deliberate, affirmative, and even aggressive effort be made to support the system of free expression. The natural balance of forces in society today tends to be weighted against individual expression. Only through a positive approach, in which law and judicial institutions play a leading role, can an effective system be maintained.

Our second task has been to formulate a basic theory and specific legal doctrines which would take into account the underlying factors. Such a theory must start by accepting the prior judgment embodied in the First Amendment. The issue before the court cannot therefore be a de novo balancing of different social values and objectives involved in each case. Rather the issue must be framed in terms of ascertaining the area of expression which it is the purpose of the First Amendment to protect, the kind of governmental action which constitutes an infringement of that area, and the nature of ostensibly private action which nevertheless carries the imprint of government authority to such an extent that it, too, should be considered an exercise of state power. In more formal language these are questions of defining the key terms of the First Amendment: "freedom of expression," "abridge," and "law." The definitions sought must be functional in character, derived from a consideration of the basic elements which shape and determine an effective system of freedom of expression.

Employing this approach it is possible to spell out in more detail the specific legal doctrines which are applicable to the various types of problems in which a First Amendment issue arises. Our efforts to accomplish this have necessarily been summary in form and tentative in result. The endeavor has been to demonstrate that a comprehensive and consistent theory of the First Amendment, providing a rational basis for explaining apparent exceptions and remedying deficiencies in existing doctrine, is possible. That theory does give force and meaning to the fundamental judgment embraced in the First Amendment and allows the courts to take into account the basic considerations necessary for a realistic solution of the particular problem. At the same time it attempts to provide doctrines at a level of generality, or rather specificity, which permit the courts to perform effectively their functions as judicial institutions.

It is not to be expected that any reader will be wholly satisfied or will agree with all the resolutions proposed for the numerous areas of intense controversy. To this writer, these resolutions appear to follow from the premises developed in the earlier part of this book, premises with which most readers probably would agree. Thus, the task is to see that the doctrines offered and the resolutions suggested herein do, in fact, follow from the principles underlying a viable system of free expression. Disagreement should lead to a rethinking of the logic of the deduction; it should not lead to a rejection of the fundamental postulates underlying the First Amendment. Thus, the various conclusions expressed and proposals for working principles made will certainly need to be elaborated, modified, or perhaps abandoned. But the hope is that they will furnish a rational and acceptable approach for giving significant meaning to the great and vital concept expressed by the First Amendment.

Appendix

|| SELECTIONS FROM SOME OF
the major Supreme Court decisions discussed in the text are set
forth below. Also included are excerpts from the more significant decisions which have come from the Court since the text
was completed. The extracts are intended to reveal in more
elaborate and more concrete form the various attitudes and
theories held by the Court and its individual justices at different
times and under varying circumstances. Much of the material
also makes good reading, of course, as sheer literature or political science.

The cases have been arranged chronologically rather than
grouped by subject matter or doctrine as in the text. Footnotes
and cited cases have in most instances been omitted, without the
excision being specifically indicated. All other omissions are
shown in the usual manner.

Schenck v. United States
249 U.S. 47 (1919)

[Schenck was indicted under the original provisions of the
Espionage Act of 1917 for causing insubordination in the
armed forces of the United States and for obstructing recruiting and enlistment during the war. Schenck, the general
secretary of the Socialist Party, had participated in printing
and mailing 15,000 leaflets, many of which went to men who
had been called for duty by their draft boards. The leaflet
asserted that the draft was unconstitutional and that it constituted "a monstrous wrong against humanity in the interests
of Wall Street's chosen few"; it contained other arguments
and urged recipients to "assert your opposition to the draft."]

MR. JUSTICE HOLMES delivered the opinion of the Court. . . .

We admit that in many places and in ordinary times the defendants in saying all that was said in the circular would have been within their constitutional rights. But the character of every act depends upon the circumstances in which it is done. The most stringent protection of free speech would not protect a man in falsely shouting fire in a theatre and causing a panic. It does not even protect a man from an injunction against uttering words that may have all the effect of force. The question in every case is whether the words used are used in such circumstances and are of such a nature as to create a clear and present danger that they will bring about the substantive evils that Congress has a right to prevent. It is a question of proximity and degree. When a nation is at war many things that might be said in time of peace are such a hindrance to its effort that their utterance will not be endured so long as men fight and that no Court could regard them as protected by any constitutional right. It seems to be admitted that if an actual obstruction of the recruiting service were proved, liability for words that produced that effect might be enforced. The Statute of 1917, in § 4, punishes conspiracies to obstruct as well as actual obstruction. If the act (speaking, or circulating a paper), its tendency and the intent with which it is done, are the same, we perceive no ground for saying that success alone warrants making the act a crime. Indeed that case might be said to dispose of the present contention if the precedent covers all *media concludendi*. But as the right to free speech was not referred to specially, we have thought fit to add a few words.

Abrams v. United States

250 U.S. 616 (1919)

[The defendants were indicted under the 1918 amendments to the Espionage Act for publishing abusive language about the form of government, for publishing language intended to bring the form of government into contempt, for encouraging resistance to the United States in the war, and for inciting curtailment of production of war materials. The charges were based upon two leaflets which the defendants had printed and distributed by throwing them out the window of a building. The majority of the Supreme Court upheld the conviction.]

MR. JUSTICE HOLMES, dissenting. . . .

I never have seen any reason to doubt that the questions of law that alone were before this Court in the cases of *Schenck, Frohwerk* and *Debs,* 249 U.S. 47, 204, 211, were rightly decided. I do not doubt for a moment that by the same reasoning that would justify punishing persuasion to murder, the United States constitutionally may punish speech that produces or is intended to produce a clear and imminent danger that it will bring about forthwith certain substantive evils that the United States constitutionally may seek to prevent. The power undoubtedly is greater in time of war than in time of peace because war opens dangers that do not exist at other times.

But as against dangers peculiar to war, as against others, the principle of the right to free speech is always the same. It is only the present danger of immediate evil or an intent to bring it about that warrants Congress in setting a limit to the expression of opinion where private rights are not concerned. Congress certainly cannot forbid all effort to change the mind of the country. Now nobody can suppose that the surreptitious publishing of a silly leaflet by an unknown man, without more, would present any immediate danger that its opinions would hinder the success of the government arms or have any appreciable tendency to do so. . . .

Persecution for the expression of opinions seems to me perfectly logical. If you have no doubt of your premises or your power and want a certain result with all your heart you naturally express your wishes in law and sweep away all opposition. To allow opposition by speech seems to indicate that you think the speech impotent, as when a man says that he has squared the circle, or that you do not care wholeheartedly for the result, or that you doubt either your power or your premises. But when men have realized that time has upset many fighting faiths, they may come to believe even more than they believe the very foundations of their own conduct that the ultimate good desired is better reached by free trade in ideas—that the best test of truth is the power of the thought to get itself accepted in the competition of the market, and that truth is the only ground upon which their wishes safely can be carried out. That at any rate is the theory of our Constitution. It is an experiment, as all life is an experiment. Every year if not every day we have to wager our salvation upon some prophecy based upon imperfect knowledge. While that experiment is part of our system I think that we should be eternally vigilant against attempts to check the expressions of opinions that we loathe and believe to be fraught with death, unless they so imminently threaten immediate interference with the lawful and pressing purposes of the law that an immediate check is required to save the country. . . . Only the emergency that makes it immediately dangerous to leave the correction of evil counsels to time warrants making any exception to the sweeping command, "Congress shall make no law . . . abridging the freedom of speech."

Gitlow v. New York
268 U.S. 652 (1925)

[Gitlow was indicted under a New York statute for criminal anarchy—advocating overthrow of the government by force and violence—for publishing a pamphlet entitled "The Left Wing Manifesto."]

MR. JUSTICE SANFORD delivered the opinion of the Court. . . .

The statute does not penalize the utterance or publication of abstract "doctrine" or academic discussion having no quality of incitement to any concrete action. It is not aimed against mere historical or philosophical essays. It does not restrain the advocacy of changes in the form of government by constitutional and lawful means. What it prohibits is language advocating, advising or teaching the overthrow of organized government by unlawful means. These words imply urging to action. Advocacy is defined in the Century Dictionary as: "1. The act of pleading for, supporting, or recommending; active espousal." It is not the abstract "doctrine" of overthrowing organized government by unlawful means which is denounced by the statute, but the advocacy of action for the accomplishment of that purpose. . . .

The Manifesto, plainly, is neither the statement of abstract doctrine nor, as suggested by counsel, mere prediction that industrial disturbances and revolutionary mass strikes will result spontaneously in an inevitable process of evolution in the economic system. It advocates and urges in fervent language mass action which shall progressively foment industrial disturbances and through political mass strikes and revolutionary mass action overthrow and destroy organized parliamentary government. It concludes with a call to action in these words: "The proletariat revolution and the Communist reconstruction of society—*the struggle for these*—is now indispensable. . . . The Communist International calls the proletariat of the world to the final struggle!" This is not the expression of philosophical abstraction, the mere prediction of future events; it is the language of direct incitement.

The means advocated for bringing about the destruction of organized parliamentary government, namely, mass industrial revolts usurping the functions of municipal government, political mass strikes directed against the parliamentary state, and revolutionary mass action for its final destruction, necessarily imply the use of force and violence, and in their essential nature are inherently unlawful in a constitutional government of law and order. That the jury were warranted in finding that the Manifesto advocated not merely the abstract doctrine of overthrowing organized government by force, violence and unlawful means, but action to that end, is clear.

For present purposes we may and do assume that freedom of speech and of the press—which are protected by the First Amendment from abridgment by Congress—are among the fundamental personal rights and "liberties" protected by the due process clause of the Fourteenth Amendment from impairment by the States. We do not regard the incidental statement in *Prudential Ins. Co. v. Cheek,* 259 U.S. 530, 543, that the Fourteenth Amendment imposes no restrictions on the States concerning freedom of speech, as determinative of this question.

It is a fundamental principle, long established, that the freedom of speech and of the press which is secured by the Constitution, does not confer an absolute right to speak or publish, without responsibility, whatever one may choose, or an unrestricted and unbridled license that gives immunity for every possible use of language and prevents the punishment of those who abuse this freedom. . . .

That a State in the exercise of its police power may punish those who abuse this freedom by utterances inimical to the public welfare, tending to corrupt public morals, incite to crime, or disturb the public peace, is not open to question. Thus it was held by this Court in the *Fox Case,* that a State may punish publications advocating and encouraging a breach of its criminal laws; and, in the *Gilbert Case,* that a State may punish utterances teaching or advocating that its citizens should not assist the United States in prosecuting or carrying on war with its public enemies.

And, for yet more imperative reasons, a State may punish utterances endangering the foundations of organized government and threatening its overthrow by unlawful means. These imperil its own existence as a constitutional State. Freedom of speech and press, said Story, does not protect disturbances to the public peace or the attempt to subvert the government. It does not protect publications or teachings which tend to subvert or imperil the government or to impede or hinder it in the performance of its governmental duties. It does not protect publications prompting the overthrow of government by force; the punishment of those who publish articles which tend to destroy organized society being essential to the security of freedom and the stability of the State. And a State may penalize utterances which openly advocate the overthrow of the representative and constitutional form of government of the United States and the several States, by violence or other unlawful means. In short this freedom does not deprive a State of the primary and essential right of self preservation; which, so long as human governments endure, they cannot be denied. . . .

By enacting the present statute the State has determined, through its legislative body, that utterances advocating the overthrow of organized government by force, violence and unlawful means, are so inimical to the general welfare and involve such danger of substantive evil that they may be penalized in the exercise of its police power. That determination must be given great weight. Every presumption is to be indulged in favor of the validity of the statute. And the case is to be considered "in the light of the principle that the State is primarily the judge of regulations required in the interest of public safety and welfare;" and that its police "statutes may only be declared unconstitutional where they are arbitrary or unreasonable attempts to exercise authority vested in the State in the public interest." *Great Northern Ry. v. Clara City,* 246 U.S. 434, 439. That utterances inciting to the overthrow of organized government by unlawful means, present a sufficient danger of substantive evil to bring their punishment within the range of legislative discretion, is clear. Such utterances, by their very nature, involve danger to the public peace and to the security of the State. They threaten breaches of the peace and ultimate revolution. And the immediate danger is none the less real and substantial, because the effect of a given utterance cannot be accurately foreseen. The State cannot reasonably be required to measure the danger from every such utterance in the nice balance of a jeweler's scale. A single revolutionary spark may kindle a fire that, smouldering for a time, may burst into a sweeping and destructive conflagration. It cannot be said that the State is acting arbitrarily or unreasonably when in the exercise of its judgment as to the measures necessary to protect the public peace and safety, it seeks to extinguish the spark without waiting until it has enkindled the flame or blazed into the conflagration. It cannot reasonably be required to defer the adoption of measures for its own peace and safety until the revolutionary utterances lead to actual disturbances of the public peace or imminent and immediate danger of its own destruction; but it may, in the exercise of its judgment, suppress the threatened danger in its incipiency. . . .

Whitney v. California

274 U.S. 357 (1927)

[Miss Anita Whitney was indicted under the California Criminal Syndicalism Act for helping to organize a society that advocated use of force and violence to effect political change. Her conviction was upheld by a majority of the Supreme Court. Justices Holmes and Brandeis concurred on narrow procedural grounds, but disagreed with the majority on the free speech issue.]

MR. JUSTICE BRANDEIS, concurring. . . .

The right of free speech, the right to teach and the right of assembly are, of course, fundamental rights. . . . These may not be denied or abridged. But, although the rights of free speech and assembly are fundamental, they are not in their nature absolute. Their exercise is subject to restriction, if the particular restriction proposed is required in order to protect the State from destruction or from serious injury, political, economic or moral. That the necessity which is essential to a valid restriction does not exist unless speech would produce, or is intended to produce, a clear and imminent danger of some substantive evil which the State constitutionally may seek to prevent has been settled. See *Schenck v. United States,* 249 U.S. 47, 52.

It is said to be the function of the legislature to determine whether at a particular time and under the particular circumstances the formation of, or assembly with, a society organized to advocate criminal syndicalism constitutes a clear and present danger of substantive evil; and that by enacting the law here in question the legislature of California determined that question in the affirmative. Compare *Gitlow v. New York,* 268 U.S. 652, 668-671. The legislature must obviously decide, in the first instance, whether a danger exists which calls for a particular protective measure. But where a statute is valid only in case certain conditions exist, the enactment of the statute cannot alone establish the facts which are essential to its validity. Prohibitory legislation has repeatedly been held invalid, because unnecessary, where the denial of liberty involved was that of engaging in a particular business. The power of the courts to strike down an offending law is no less when the interests involved are not property rights, but the fundamental personal rights of free speech and assembly.

This Court has not yet fixed the standard by which to determine when a danger shall be deemed clear; how remote the danger may be and yet be deemed present; and what degree of evil shall be deemed sufficiently substantial to justify resort to abridgment of free speech and assembly as the means of protection. To reach sound conclusions on these matters, we must bear in mind why a State is, ordinarily, denied the power to prohibit dissemination of social, economic and political doctrine which a vast majority of its citizens believes to be false and fraught with evil consequence.

Those who won our independence believed that the final end of the State was to make men free to develop their faculties; and that in its government the deliberative forces should prevail over the arbitrary. They valued liberty both as an end and as a means. They believed liberty to be the secret of happiness and courage to be the secret of liberty. They believed that freedom to think as you will and to speak as you think are means indispensable to the discovery and spread of political truth; that without free speech and assembly discussion would be futile; that with them, discussion affords ordinarily adequate protection against the dissemination of noxious doctrine; that the greatest menace to freedom is an inert people; that public discussion is a political duty; and that this should be a fundamental principle of the American government. They recognized the risks to which all human institutions are subject. But they knew that order cannot be secured merely through fear of punishment for its infraction; that it is hazardous to discourage thought, hope and imagination; that fear breeds repression; that repression breeds hate; that hate menaces stable government; that the path of safety lies in the opportunity to discuss freely supposed grievances and proposed remedies; and that the fitting remedy for evil counsels is good ones. Believing in the power of reason as applied through public discussion, they eschewed silence coerced by law—the argument of force in its worst form. Recognizing the occasional tyrannies of governing majorities, they amended the Constitution so that free speech and assembly should be guaranteed.

Fear of serious injury cannot alone justify suppression of free speech and assembly. Men feared witches and burnt women. It is the function of speech to free men from the bondage of irrational fears. To justify suppression of free speech there must be reasonable ground to fear that serious evil will result if free speech is practiced. There must be reasonable ground to believe that the danger apprehended is imminent. There must be reasonable ground to believe that the evil to be prevented is a serious one. Every denunciation of existing law tends in some measure to increase the probability that there will be violation of it. Condonation of a breach enhances the probability. Expressions of approval add to the probability. Propagation of the criminal state of mind by teaching syndicalism increases it. Advocacy of law-breaking heightens it still further. But even advocacy of violation, however reprehensible morally, is not a justification for denying free speech where the advocacy falls short of incitement and there is nothing to indicate that the advocacy would be immediately acted on. The wide difference between advocacy and incitement, between preparation and attempt, between assembling and conspiracy, must be borne in mind. In order to support a finding of clear and present danger it must be shown either that immediate serious violence was to be expected or was advocated, or that the past conduct furnished reason to believe that such advocacy was then contemplated.

Those who won our independence by revolution were not cowards. They did not fear political change. They did not exalt order at the cost of liberty. To courageous, self-reliant men, with confidence in the power of free and fearless reasoning applied through the processes of popular government, no danger flowing from speech can be deemed clear and present, unless the incidence of the evil apprehended is so imminent that it may befall before there is opportunity for full discussion. If there be time to expose through discussion the falsehoods and fallacies, to avert the evil by the processes of education, the remedy to be applied is more speech, not enforced silence. Only an emergency can justify repression. Such must be the rule if authority is to be reconciled with freedom. Such, in my opinion, is the command of the Constitution. It is therefore always open to Americans to challenge a law abridging free speech and assembly by showing that there was no emergency justifying it.

Moreover, even imminent danger cannot justify resort to prohibition of these functions essential to effective democracy, unless the evil apprehended is relatively serious. Prohibition of free speech and assembly is a measure so stringent that it would be inappropriate as the means for averting a relatively trivial harm to society. A police measure may be unconstitutional merely because the remedy, although effective as means of protection, is unduly harsh or oppressive. Thus, a State might, in the exercise of its police power, make any trespass upon the land of another a crime, regardless of the results or of the intent or purpose of the trespasser. It might, also, punish an attempt, a conspiracy, or an incitement to commit the trespass. But it is hardly conceivable that this Court would hold constitutional a statute which punished as a felony the mere voluntary assembly with a society formed to teach that pedestrians had the moral right to cross unenclosed, unposted, waste lands and to advocate their doing so, even if there was imminent danger that advocacy would lead to a trespass. The fact that speech is likely to result in some violence or in destruction of property is not enough to justify its suppression. There must be the probability of serious injury to the State. Among free men, the deterrents ordinarily to be applied to prevent crime are education and punishment for violations of the law, not abridgment of the rights of free speech and assembly.

Near v. Minnesota

283 U.S. 697 (1931)

[Defendants were enjoined under a Minnesota statute from publishing a newspaper alleged to contain "malicious, scandalous and defamatory" matter.]

MR. CHIEF JUSTICE HUGHES delivered the opinion of the Court. . . .

This statute, for the suppression as a public nuisance of a newspaper or periodical, is unusual, if not unique, and raises questions of grave importance transcending the local interests involved in the particular action. It is no longer open to doubt that the liberty of the press, and of speech, is within the liberty safeguarded by the due process clause of the Fourteenth Amendment from invasion by state action. . . .

If we cut through mere details of procedure, the operation and effect of the statute in substance is that public authorities may bring the owner or publisher of a newspaper or periodical before a judge upon a charge of conducting a business of publishing scandalous and defamatory matter—in particular that the matter consists of charges against public officers of official dereliction—and, unless the owner or publisher is able and disposed to bring competent evidence to satisfy the judge that the charges are true and are published with good motives and for justifiable ends, his newspaper or periodical is suppressed and further publication is made punishable as a contempt. This is of the essence of censorship.

The question is whether a statute authorizing such proceedings in restraint of publication is consistent with the conception of the liberty of the press as historically conceived and guaranteed. In determining the extent of the constitutional protection, it has been generally, if not universally, considered that it is the chief purpose of the guaranty to prevent previous restraints upon publication. The struggle in England, directed against the legislative power of the licenser, resulted in renunciation of the censorship of the press. . .

[It] is recognized that punishment for the abuse of the liberty accorded to the press is essential to the protection of the public, and that the common law rules that subject the libeler to responsibility for the public offense, as well as for the private injury, are not abolished by the protection extended in our constitution. The law of criminal libel rests upon that secure foundation. There is also the conceded authority of courts to punish for contempt when publications directly tend to prevent the proper discharge of judicial functions. In the present case, we have no occasion to inquire as to the permissible scope of subsequent punishment. For whatever wrong the appellant has committed or may commit, by his publications, the State appropriately affords both public and private redress by its libel laws. As has been noted, the statute in question does not deal with punishments; it provides for no punishment, except in case of contempt for violation of the court's order, but for suppression and injunction, that is, for restraint upon publication.

The objection has also been made that the principle as to immunity from previous restraint is stated too broadly, if every such restraint is deemed to be prohibited. That is undoubtedly true; the protection even as to previous restraint is not absolutely unlimited. But the limitation has been recognized only in exceptional cases: "When a nation is at war many things that might be said in time of peace are such a hindrance to its effort that their utterance will not be endured so long as men fight and that no Court could regard them as protected by any constitutional right." *Schenck v. United States*, 249 U.S. 47, 52. No one would question but that a government might prevent actual obstruction to its recruiting service or the publication of the sailing dates of transports or the number and location of troops. On similar grounds, the primary requirements of decency may be enforced against obscene publications. The security of the community life may be protected against incitements to acts of violence and the overthrow by force of orderly government. The constitutional guaranty of free speech does not "protect a man from an injunction against uttering words that may have all the effect of force."

Schenck v. United States. These limitations are not applicable here. Nor are we now concerned with questions as to the extent of authority to prevent publications in order to protect private rights according to the principles governing the exercise of the jurisdiction of courts of equity.

The exceptional nature of its limitations places in a strong light the general conception that liberty of the press, historically considered and taken up by the Federal Constitution, has meant, principally although not exclusively, immunity from previous restraints or censorship. The conception of the liberty of the press in this country had broadened with the exigencies of the colonial period and with the efforts to secure freedom from oppressive administration. That liberty was especially cherished for the immunity it afforded from previous restraint of the publication of censure of public officers and charges of official misconduct. . . .

The fact that for approximately one hundred and fifty years there has been almost an entire absence of attempts to impose previous restraints upon publications relating to the malfeasance of public officers is significant of the deep-seated conviction that such restraints would violate constitutional right. Public officers, whose character and conduct remain open to debate and free discussion in the press, find their remedies for false accusations in actions under libel laws providing for redress and punishment, and not in proceedings to restrain the publication of newspapers and periodicals. The general principle that the constitutional guaranty of the liberty of the press gives immunity from previous restraints has been approved in many decisions under the provisions of state constitutions.

The importance of this immunity has not lessened. While reckless assaults upon public men, and efforts to bring obloquy upon those who are endeavoring faithfully to discharge official duties, exert a baleful influence and deserve the severest condemnation in public opinion, it cannot be said that this abuse is greater, and it is believed to be less, than that which characterized the period in which our institutions took shape. Meanwhile, the administration of government has become more complex, the opportunities for malfeasance and corruption have multiplied, crime has grown to most serious proportions, and the danger of its protection by unfaithful officials and of the impairment of the fundamental security of life and property by criminal alliances and official neglect, emphasizes the primary need of a vigilant and courageous press, especially in great cities. The fact that the liberty of the press may be abused by miscreant purveyors of scandal does not make any the less necessary the immunity of the press from previous restraint in dealing with official misconduct. Subsequent punishment for such abuses as may exist is the appropriate remedy, consistent with constitutional privilege. . . .

The statute in question cannot be justified by reason of the fact that the publisher is permitted to show, before injunction issues, that the matter published is true and is published with good motives and for justifiable ends. If such a statute, authorizing suppression and injunction on such a basis, is constitutionally valid, it would be equally permissible for the legislature to provide that at any time the publisher of any newspaper could be brought before a court, or even an administrative officer (as the constitutional protection may not be regarded as resting on mere procedural details) and required to produce proof of the truth of his publication, or of what he intended to publish, and of his motives, or stand enjoined. If this can be done, the legislature may provide machinery for determining in the complete exercise of its discretion what are justifiable ends and restrain publication accordingly. And it would be but a step to a complete system of censorship. The recognition of authority to impose previous restraint upon publication in order to protect the community against the circulation of charges of misconduct, and especially of official misconduct, necessarily would carry with it the admission of the authority of the censor against which the constitutional barrier was erected. The preliminary freedom, by virtue of the very reason for its existence, does not depend, as this Court has said, on proof of truth.

Equally unavailing is the insistence that the statute is designed to prevent the circulation of scandal which tends to disturb the public peace and to provoke assaults and the commission of crime. Charges of reprehensible conduct, and in particular of official malfeasance, unquestionably create a public scandal, but the theory of the constitutional guaranty is that even a more serious public evil would be caused by authority to prevent publication. "To prohibit the intent to excite those unfavorable sentiments against those who administer the Government, is equivalent to a prohibition of the actual excitement of them; and to prohibit the actual excitement of them is equivalent to a prohibition of discussions having that tendency and effect; which, again, is equivalent to a protection of those who administer the Government, if they should at any time deserve the contempt or hatred of the people, against being exposed to it by free animadversions on their characters and conduct." [James Madison, "Report on the Virginia Resolutions," *Madison's Works,* Vol. IV, p. 549]. . . . The danger of violent reactions becomes greater with effective organization of defiant groups resenting exposure, and, if this consideration warranted legislative interference with the initial freedom of publication, the constitutional protection would be reduced to a mere form of words.

De Jonge v. Oregon

299 U.S. 353 (1937)

[De Jonge was convicted of violating the Oregon Criminal Syndicalism Law by assisting in the conduct of a meeting called under the auspices of the Communist Party.]

Mr. Chief Justice Hughes delivered the opinion of the Court. . . .

It thus appears that, while defendant was a member of the Communist Party, he was not indicted for participating in its organization, or for joining it, or for soliciting members or for distributing its literature. He was not charged with teaching or advocating criminal syndicalism or sabotage or any unlawful acts, either at the meeting or elsewhere. He was accordingly deprived of the benefit of evidence as to the orderly and lawful conduct of the meeting and that it was not called or used for the advocacy of criminal syndicalism or sabotage or any unlawful action. His sole offense as charged, and for which he was convicted and sentenced to imprisonment for seven years, was that he had assisted in the conduct of a public meeting, albeit otherwise lawful, which was held under the auspices of the Communist Party.

The broad reach of the statute as thus applied is plain. While defendant was a member of the Communist Party, that membership was not necessary to conviction on such a charge. A like fate might have attended any speaker, although not a member, who "assisted in the conduct" of the meeting. However innocuous the object of the meeting, however lawful the subjects and tenor of the addresses, however reasonable and timely the discussion, all those assisting in the conduct of the meeting would be subject to imprisonment as felons if the meeting were held by the Communist Party. This manifest result was brought out sharply at this bar by the concessions which the Attorney General made, and could not avoid, in the light of the decision of the state court. Thus if the Communist Party had called a public meeting in Portland to discuss the tariff, or the foreign policy of the Government, or taxation, or relief, or candidacies for the offices of President, members of Congress, Governor, or state legislators, every speaker who assisted in the conduct of the meeting would be equally guilty with the defendant in this case, upon the charge as here defined and sustained. The list of illustrations might be indefinitely extended to every variety of meetings under the auspices of the Communist Party although held for the discussion of political issues or to adopt protests and pass resolutions of an entirely innocent and proper character.

While the States are entitled to protect themselves from the abuse of the privileges of our institutions through an attempted substitution of force and violence in the place of peaceful political action in order to effect revolutionary changes in government, none of our decisions go to the length of sustaining such a curtailment of the right of free speech and assembly as the Oregon statute demands in its present application. . . .

Freedom of speech and of the press are fundamental rights which are safeguarded by the due process clause of the Fourteenth Amendment of the Federal Constitution. The right of peaceable assembly is a right cognate to those of free speech and free press and is equally fundamental. As this Court said in *United States v. Cruikshank,* 92 U.S. 542, 552: "The very idea of a government, republican in form, implies a right on the part of its citizens to meet peaceably for consultation in respect to public affairs and to petition for a redress of grievances." The First Amendment of the Federal Constitution expressly guarantees that right against abridgment by Congress. But explicit mention there does not argue exclusion elsewhere. For the right is one that cannot be denied without violating those fundamental principles of liberty and justice which lie at the base of all civil and political institutions—principles which the Fourteenth Amendment embodies in the general terms of its due process clause.

These rights may be abused by using speech or press or assembly in order to incite to violence and crime. The people through their legislatures may protect themselves against that abuse. But the legislative intervention can find constitutional justification only by dealing with the abuse. The rights themselves must not be curtailed. The greater the importance of safeguarding the community from incitements to the overthrow of our institutions by force and violence, the more imperative is the need to preserve inviolate the constitutional rights of free speech, free press and free assembly in order to maintain the opportunity for free political discussion, to the end that government may be responsive to the will of the people and that changes, if desired, may be obtained by peaceful means. Therein lies the security of the Republic, the very foundation of constitutional government.

It follows from these considerations that, consistently with the Federal Constitution, peaceable assembly for lawful discussion cannot be made a crime. The holding of meetings for peaceable political action cannot be proscribed. Those who assist in the conduct of such meetings cannot be branded as criminals on that score. The question, if the rights of free speech and peaceable assembly are to be preserved, is not as to the auspices under which the meeting is held but as to its purpose; not as to the relations of the speakers, but whether their utterances transcend the bounds of the freedom of speech which the Constitution protects. If the persons assembling have committed crimes elsewhere, if they have formed or are engaged in a conspiracy against the public peace and order, they may be prosecuted for their conspiracy or other violation of valid laws. But it is a different matter when the State, instead of prosecuting them for such offenses, seizes upon mere participation in a peaceable assembly and a lawful public discussion as the basis for a criminal charge.

We are not called upon to review the findings of the state court as to the objectives of the Communist Party. Notwithstanding those objectives, the defendant still enjoyed his personal right of free speech and to take part in a peaceable assembly having a lawful purpose, although called by that Party. The defendant was none the less entitled to discuss the public issues of the day and thus in a lawful manner, without incitement to violence or crime to seek redress of alleged grievances. That was of the essence of his guaranteed personal liberty.

U.S. v. Carolene Products Co.
304 U.S. 144 (1938)

[In the course of an opinion in a case dealing with other issues, Justice Stone appended a footnote, now famous, which has been a prime source of the theory that the Supreme Court should exercise greater strictness in reviewing legislation which restricts individual rights than legislation which affects economic rights.]

Mr. Justice Stone:

There may be narrower scope for operation of the presumption of constitutionality when legislation appears on its face to be within a specific prohibition of the Constitution, such as those of the first ten amendments, which are deemed equally specific when held to be embraced within the Fourteenth. See *Stromberg* v. *California,* 283 U.S. 359, 369-370; *Lovell* v. *Griffin,* 303 U.S. 444, 452.

It is unnecessary to consider now whether legislation which restricts those political processes which can ordinarily be expected to bring about repeal of undesirable legislation, is to be subjected to more exacting judicial scrutiny under the general prohibitions of the Fourteenth Amendment than are most other types of legislation. On restrictions upon the right to vote, see *Nixon* v. *Herndon,* 273 U.S. 536; *Nixon* v. *Condon,* 286 U.S. 73; on restraints upon the dissemination of information, see *Near* v. *Minnesota ex rel. Olson,* 283 U.S. 697, 713-714, 718-720, 722; *Grosjean* v. *American Press Co.,* 297 U.S. 233; *Lovell* v. *Griffin, supra;* on interferences with political organizations, see *Stromberg* v. *California, supra,* 369; *Fiske* v. *Kansas,* 274 U.S. 380; *Whitney* v. *California,* 274 U.S. 357, 373-378; *Herndon* v. *Lowry,* 301 U.S. 242; and see Holmes, J., in *Gitlow* v. *New York,* 268 U.S. 652, 673; as to prohibition of peaceable assembly, see *De Jonge* v. *Oregon,* 299 U.S. 353, 365.

Nor need we enquire whether similar considerations enter into the review of statutes directed at particular religious, *Pierce* v. *Society of Sisters,* 268 U.S. 510, or national, *Meyer* v. *Nebraska,* 262 U.S. 390; *Bartels* v. *Iowa,* 262 U.S. 404; *Farrington* v. *Tokushige,* 273 U.S. 484, or racial minorities, *Nixon* v. *Herndon, supra; Nixon* v. *Condon, supra:* whether prejudice against discrete and insular minorities may be a special condition, which tends seriously to curtail the operation of those political processes ordinarily to be relied upon to protect minorities, and which may call for a correspondingly more searching judicial inquiry. Compare *McCulloch* v. *Maryland,* 4 Wheat. 316, 428; *South Carolina* v. *Barnwell Bros.,* 303 U.S. 177, 184, n. 2, and cases cited.

West Virginia State Board of Education v. Barnette
319 U.S. 624 (1943)

[Children of Jehovah's Witnesses had been expelled from school for refusing to salute the flag, as they were required to do by West Virginia law, on the ground that the salute was contrary to their religious beliefs. In the *Gobitis* case, decided three years before, the Supreme Court had upheld the statute. The *Barnette* case reversed the prior decision.]

MR. JUSTICE JACKSON delivered the opinion of the Court. . . .
Lastly, and this is the very heart of the *Gobitis* opinion, it reasons that "National unity is the basis of national security," that the authorities have "the right to select appropriate means for its attainment," and hence reaches the conclusion that such compulsory measures toward "national unity" are constitutional. Upon the verity of this assumption depends our answer in this case.

National unity as an end which officials may foster by persuasion and example is not in question. The problem is whether under our Constitution compulsion as here employed is a permissible means for its achievement.

Struggles to coerce uniformity of sentiment in support of some end thought essential to their time and country have been waged by many good as well as by evil men. Nationalism is a relatively recent phenomenon but at other times and places the ends have been racial or territorial security, support of a dynasty or regime, and particular plans for saving souls. As first and moderate methods to attain unity have failed, those bent on its accomplishment must resort to an ever-increasing severity. As governmental pressure toward unity becomes greater, so strife becomes more bitter as to whose unity it shall be. Probably no deeper division of our people could proceed from any provocation than from finding it necessary to choose what doctrine and whose program public educational officials shall compel youth to unite in embracing. Ultimate futility of such attempts to compel coherence is the lesson of every such effort from the Roman drive to stamp out Christianity as a disturber of its pagan unity, the Inquisition, as a means to religious and dynastic unity, the Siberian exiles as a means to Russian unity, down to the fast failing efforts of our present totalitarian enemies. Those who begin coercive elimination of dissent soon find themselves exterminating dissenters. Compulsory unification of opinion achieves only the unanimity of the graveyard.

It seems trite but necessary to say that the First Amendment to our Constitution was designed to avoid these ends by avoiding these beginnings. There is no mysticism in the American concept of the State or of the nature or origin of its authority. We set up government by the consent of the governed, and the Bill of Rights denies those in power any legal opportunity to coerce that consent. Authority here is to be controlled by public opinion, not public opinion by authority.

The case is made difficult not because the principles of its decision are obscure but because the flag involved is our own. Nevertheless, we apply the limitations of the Constitution with no fear that freedom to be intellectually and spiritually diverse or even contrary will disintegrate the social organization. To believe that patriotism will not flourish if patriotic ceremonies are voluntary and spontaneous instead of a compulsory routine is to make an unflattering estimate of the appeal of our institutions to free minds. We can have intellectual individualism and the rich cultural diversities that we owe to exceptional minds only at the price of occasional eccentricity and abnormal attitudes. When they are so harmless to others or to the State as those we deal with here, the price is not too great. But freedom to differ is not limited to things that do not matter much. That would be a mere shadow of freedom. The test of its substance is the right to differ as to things that touch the heart of the existing order.

If there is any fixed star in our constitutional constellation, it is that no official, high or petty, can prescribe what shall be orthodox in politics, nationalism, religion, or other matters of opinion or force citizens to confess by word or act their faith therein. If there are any circumstances which permit an exception, they do not now occur to us.

We think the action of the local authorities in compelling the flag salute and pledge transcends constitutional limitations on their power and invades the sphere of intellect and spirit which it is the purpose of the First Amendment to our Constitution to reserve from all official control.

MR. JUSTICE FRANKFURTER, dissenting. . . .

We are told that a flag salute is a doubtful substitute for adequate understanding of our institutions. The states that require such a school exercise do not have to justify it as the only means for promoting good citizenship in children, but merely as one of diverse means for accomplishing a worthy end. We may deem it a foolish measure, but the point is that this Court is not the organ of government to resolve doubts as to whether it will fulfill its purpose. Only if there be no doubt that any reasonable mind could entertain can we deny to the states the right to resolve doubts their way and not ours.

That which to the majority may seem essential for the welfare of the state may offend the consciences of a minority. But, so long as no inroads are made upon the actual exercise of religion by the minority, to deny the political power of the majority to enact laws concerned with civil matters, simply because they may offend the consciences of a minority, really means that the consciences of a minority are more sacred and more enshrined in the Constitution than the consciences of a majority.

We are told that symbolism is a dramatic but primitive way of communicating ideas. Symbolism is inescapable. Even the most sophisticated live by symbols. But it is not for this Court to make psychological judgments as to the effectiveness of a particular symbol in inculcating concededly indispensable feelings, particularly if the state happens to see fit to utilize the symbol that represents our heritage and our hopes. And surely only flippancy could be responsible for the suggestion that constitutional validity of a requirement to salute our flag implies equal validity of a requirement to salute a dictator. The significance of a symbol lies in what it represents. To reject the swastika does not imply rejection of the Cross. And so it bears repetition to say that it mocks reason and denies our whole history to find in the allowance of a requirement to salute our flag on fitting occasions the seeds of sanction for obeisance to a leader. To deny the power to employ educational symbols is to say that the state's educational system may not stimulate the imagination because this may lead to unwise stimulation. . . .

To talk about "clear and present danger" as the touchstone of allowable educational policy by the states whenever school curricula may impinge upon the boundaries of individual conscience, is to take a felicitous phrase out of the context of the particular situation where it arose and for which it was adapted. Mr. Justice Holmes used the phrase "clear and present danger" in a case involving mere speech as a means by which alone to accomplish sedition in time of war. By that phrase he meant merely to indicate that, in view of the protection given to utterance by the First Amendment, in order that mere utterance may not be proscribed, "the words used are used in such circumstances and are of such a nature as to create a clear and present danger that they will bring about the substantive evils that Congress has a right to prevent." *Schenck v. United States,* 249 U.S. 47, 52. The "substantive evils" about which he was speaking were inducement of insubordination in the military and naval forces of the United States and obstruction of enlistment while the country was at war. He was not enunciating a formal rule that there can be no restriction upon speech and, still less, no compulsion where conscience balks, unless imminent danger would thereby be wrought "to our institutions or our government."

The flag salute exercise has no kinship whatever to the oath tests so odious in history. For the oath test was one of the instruments for suppressing heretical beliefs. Saluting the flag suppresses no belief nor curbs it. Children and their parents may believe what they please, avow their belief and practice it. It is not even remotely suggested that the requirement for saluting the flag involves the slightest restriction against the fullest opportunity on the part both of the children and of their parents to disavow as publicly as they choose to do so the meaning that others attach to the gesture of salute. All channels of affirmative free expression are open to both children and parents. Had we before us any act of the state putting the slightest curbs upon such free expression, I should not lag behind any member of this Court in striking down such an invasion of the right to freedom of thought and freedom of speech protected by the Constitution.

Schneiderman v. United States
320 U.S. 118 (1943)

[Schneiderman, a member of the Communist Party and later Secretary of the Party in California, had had his certificate of naturalization revoked upon the ground that at the time of obtaining citizenship he was not "attached to the principles of the Constitution of the United States" as required by the naturalization statute.]

MR. JUSTICE MURPHY delivered the opinion of the Court. . . .
In support of its position that petitioner was not in fact attached to the principles of the Constitution because of his membership in the League and the Party, the Government has directed our attention first to petitioner's testimony that he subscribed to the principles of those organizations, and then to certain alleged Party principles and statements by Party Leaders which are said to be fundamentally at variance with the principles of the Constitution. At this point it is appropriate to mention what will be more fully developed later—that under our traditions beliefs are personal and not a matter of mere association, and that men in adhering to a political party or other organization notoriously do not subscribe unqualifiedly to all of its platforms or asserted principles. Said to be among those Communist principles in 1927 are: the abolition of private property without compensation; the erection of a new proletarian state upon the ruins of the old bourgeois state; the creation of a dictatorship of the proletariat; denial of political rights to others than members of the Party or of the proletariat; and the creation of a world union of soviet republics. Statements that American

democracy "is a fraud" and that the purposes of the Party are "utterly antagonistic to the purposes for which the American democracy, so called, was formed," are stressed.

Those principles and views are not generally accepted—in fact they are distasteful to most of us—and they call for considerable change in our present form of government and society. But we do not think the Government has carried its burden of proving by evidence which does not leave the issue in doubt that petitioner was not in fact attached to the principles of the Constitution and well disposed to the good order and happiness of the United States when he was naturalized in 1927.

The constitutional fathers, fresh from a revolution, did not forge a political strait-jacket for the generations to come. Instead they wrote Article V and the First Amendment, guaranteeing freedom of thought, soon followed. Article V contains procedural provisions for constitutional change by amendment without any present limitation whatsoever except that no State may be deprived of equal representation in the Senate without its consent. This provision and the many important and far-reaching changes made in the Constitution since 1787 refute the idea that attachment to any particular provision or provisions is essential, or that one who advocates radical changes is necessarily not attached to the Constitution. As Justice Holmes said, "Surely it cannot show lack of attachment to the principles of the Constitution that . . . [one] thinks it can be improved." *United States* v. *Schwimmer* [279 U.S. 644] (dissent). Criticism of, and the sincerity of desires to improve, the Constitution should not be judged by conformity to prevailing thought because, "if there is any principle of the Constitution that more imperatively calls for attachment than any other it is the principle of free thought—not free thought for those who agree with us, but freedom for the thought that we hate." *Id.* Whatever attitude we may individually hold toward persons and organizations that believe in or advocate extensive changes in our existing order, it should be our desire and concern at all times to uphold the right of free discussion and free thinking to which we as a people claim primary attachment. To neglect this duty in a proceeding in which we are called upon to judge whether a particular individual has failed to manifest attachment to the Constitution would be ironical indeed.

Thomas v. Collins

323 U.S. 516 (1945)

[A Texas law required a license to solicit members for a labor union. Thomas, an official of the United Automobile Workers Union, went to Texas and held a meeting at which he solicited members for the Union, despite an injunction restraining him from doing so. He was convicted of contempt of court for violating the injunction.]

MR. JUSTICE RUTLEDGE delivered the opinion of the Court. . . .

The case confronts us again with the duty our system places on this Court to say where the individual's freedom ends and the State's power begins. Choice on that border, now as always delicate, is perhaps more so where the usual presumption supporting legislation is balanced by the preferred place given in our scheme to the great, the indispensable democratic freedoms secured by the First Amendment. That priority gives these liberties a sanctity and a sanction not permitting dubious intrusions. And it is the character of the right, not of the limitation, which determines what standard governs the choice. Compare *United States* v. *Carolene Products Co.,* 304 U.S. 144, 152-153.

For these reasons any attempt to restrict those liberties must be justified by clear public interest, threatened not doubtfully or remotely, but by clear and present danger. The rational connection between the remedy provided and the evil to be curbed, which in other contexts might support legislation against attack on due process grounds, will not suffice. These rights rest on firmer foundation. Accordingly, whatever occasion would restrain orderly discussion and persuasion, at appropriate time and place, must have clear support in public danger, actual or impending. Only the gravest abuses, endangering paramount interests, give occasion for permissible limitation. It is therefore in our tradition to allow the widest room for discussion, the narrowest range for its restriction, particularly when this right is exercised in conjunction with peaceable assembly. It was not by accident or coincidence that the rights to freedom in speech and press were coupled in a single guaranty with the rights of the people peaceably to assemble and to petition for redress of grievances. All these, though not identical, are inseparable. They are cognate rights, and therefore are united in the First Article's assurance.

This conjunction of liberties is not peculiar to religious activity and institutions alone. The First Amendment gives freedom of mind the same security as freedom of conscience. Great secular causes, with small ones, are guarded. The grievances for redress of which the right to petition was insured, and with it the right of assembly, are not solely religious or political ones. And the rights of free speech and a free press are not confined to any field of human interest.

The idea is not sound therefore that the First Amendment's safeguards are wholly inapplicable to business or economic activity. And it does not resolve where the line shall be drawn in a particular case merely to urge, as Texas does, that an organization for which the rights of free speech and free assembly are claimed is one "engaged in business activities" or that the individual who leads it in exercising these rights receives compensation for doing so. Nor, on the other hand, is the answer given, whether what is done is an exercise of those rights and the restriction a forbidden impairment, by ignoring the organization's economic function, because those interests of workingmen are involved or because they have the general liberties of the citizen, as appellant would do.

These comparisons are at once too simple, too general, and too inaccurate to be determinative. Where the line shall be placed in a particular application rests, not on such generalities, but on the concrete clash of particular interests and the community's relative evaluation both of them and of how the one will be affected by the specific restriction, the other by its absence. That judgment in the first instance is for the legislative body. But in our system where the line can constitutionally be placed presents a question this Court cannot escape answering independently, whatever the legislative judgment, in the light of our constitutional tradition. And the answer, under that tradition, can be affirmative, to support an intrusion upon this domain, only if grave and impending public danger requires this. . . .

As a matter of principle a requirement of registration in order to make a public speech would seem generally incompatible with an exercise of the rights of free speech and free assembly. Lawful public assemblies, involving no element of grave and immediate danger to an interest the State is entitled to protect, are not instruments of harm which require previous identification of the speakers. And the right either of workmen or of unions under these conditions to assemble and discuss their own affairs is as fully protected by the Constitution as the right of businessmen, farmers, educators, political party members or others to assemble and discuss their affairs and to enlist the support of others. . . .

If the exercise of the rights of free speech and free assembly cannot be made a crime, we do not think this can be accomplished by the device of requiring previous registration as a condition for exercising them and making such a condition the foundation for restraining in advance their exercise and for imposing a penalty for violating such a restraining order. So long as no more is involved than exercise of the rights of free speech and free assembly, it is immune to such a restriction. If one who solicits support for the cause of labor may be required to register as a condition to the exercise of his right to make a public speech, so may he who seeks to rally support for any social, business, religious or political cause. We think a requirement that one must register before he undertakes to make a public speech to enlist support for a lawful movement is quite incompatible with the requirements of the First Amendment.

Once the speaker goes further, however, and engages in conduct which amounts to more than the right of free discussion comprehends, as when he undertakes the collection of funds or securing subscriptions, he enters a realm where a reasonable registration or identification requirement may be imposed. In that context such solicitation would be quite different from the solicitation involved here. It would be free speech plus conduct akin to the activities which were present, and which it was said the State might regulate. . . . That, however, must be done, and the restriction applied, in such a manner as not to intrude upon the rights of free speech and free assembly. In this case the separation was not maintained. If what Thomas did, in soliciting Pat O'Sullivan, was subject to such a restriction, as to which we express no opinion, that act was intertwined with the speech and the general invitation in the penalty which was imposed for violating the restraining order. Since the penalty must be taken to have rested as much on the speech and the general invitation as on the specific one, and the former clearly were immune, the judgment cannot stand.

American Communications Association v. Douds

329 U.S. 382 (1950)

[The question before the Court was the constitutionality of Section 9 (h) of the Taft-Hartley Act. This Section provided that no union could receive the benefits of the National Labor Relations Act unless each officer filed an affidavit "that he is not a member of the Communist Party or affiliated with such party, and that he does not believe in, and is not a member of or supports any organization that believes in or teaches, the overthrow of the United States Government by force or by any illegal or unconstitutional methods."]

MR. CHIEF JUSTICE VINSON delivered the opinion of the Court. . . .

The fact that the statute identifies persons by their political affiliations and beliefs, which are circumstances ordinarily irrelevant to permissible subjects of government action, does not lead to the conclusion that such circumstances are never relevant. . . .

This principle may be illustrated by reference to statutes denying positions of public importance to groups of persons identified by their business affiliations. One federal statute, for example, provides that no partner or employee of a firm primarily engaged in underwriting securities may be a director of a national bank. . . . In this respect, § 9 (h) is not unlike a host of other statutes which prohibit specified groups of persons from holding positions of power and public interest because, in the legislative judgment, they threaten to abuse the trust that is a necessary concomitant of the power of office.

If no more were involved than possible loss of position, the foregoing would dispose of the case. But the more difficult problem here arises because, in drawing lines on the basis of beliefs and political affiliations, though it may be granted that the proscriptions of the statute bear a reasonable relation to the apprehended evil, Congress has undeniably discouraged the lawful exercise of political freedoms as well. Stated otherwise, the problem is this: Communists, we may assume, carry on legitimate political activities. Beliefs are inviolate. *Cantwell v. Connecticut,* 310 U.S. 296, 303 (1940). Congress might reasonably find, however, that Communists, unlike members of other political parties, and persons who believe in overthrow of the Government by force, unlike persons of other beliefs, represent a continuing danger of disruptive political strikes when they hold positions of union leadership. By exerting pressures on unions to deny office to Communists and others identified therein, § 9 (h) undoubtedly lessens the threat to interstate commerce, but it has the further necessary effect of discouraging the exercise of political rights protected by the First Amendment. Men who hold union offices often have little choice but to renounce Communism or give up their offices. Unions which wish to do so are discouraged from electing Communists to office. To the grave and difficult problem thus presented we must now turn our attention.

The unions contend that once it is determined that this is a free speech case, the "clear and present danger" test must apply. See *Schenck v. United States,* 249 U.S. 47 (1919). But they disagree as to how it should be applied. Appellant in No. 10 would require that joining the Communist Party or the expression of belief in overthrow of the Government by force be shown to be a clear and present danger of some substantive evil, since those are the doctrines affected by the statute. Petitioner in No. 13, on the other hand, would require a showing that political strikes, the substantive evil involved, are a clear and present danger to the security of the Nation or threaten widespread industrial unrest.

This confusion suggests that the attempt to apply the term, "clear and present danger," as a mechanical test in every case touching First Amendment freedoms, without regard to the context of its application, mistakes the form in which an idea was cast for the substance of the idea. . . .

[The] question with which we are here faced is not the same one that Justices Holmes and Brandeis found convenient to consider in terms of clear and present danger. Government's interest here is not in preventing the dissemination of Communist doctrine or the holding of particular beliefs because it is feared that unlawful action will result therefrom if free speech is practiced. Its interest is in protecting the free flow of commerce from what Congress considers to be substantial evils of conduct that are not the products of speech at all. Section 9 (h), in other words, does not interfere with speech because Congress fears the consequences of speech; it regulates harmful conduct which Congress has determined is carried on by persons who may be identified by their political affiliations and beliefs. The Board does not contend that political strikes, the substantive evil at which § 9 (h) is aimed, are the present or impending products of advocacy of the doctrines of Communism or the expression of belief in overthrow of the Government by force. On the contrary, it points out that such strikes are called by persons who, so Congress has found, have the will and power to do so *without* advocacy or persuasion that seeks acceptance in the competition of the market. Speech may be fought with speech. Falsehoods and fallacies must be exposed, not suppressed, unless there is not sufficient time to avert the evil consequences of noxious doctrine by argument and education. That is the command of the First Amendment. But force may and must be met with force. Section 9 (h) is designed to protect the public not against what Communists and others identified therein advocate or believe, but against what Congress has concluded they have done and are likely to do again.

The contention of petitioner in No. 13 that this Court must find that political strikes create a clear and present danger to the security of the Nation or of widespread industrial strife in order to sustain § 9 (h) similarly misconceives the purpose that phrase was intended to serve. In that view, not the relative certainty that evil conduct will result from speech in the immediate future, but the extent and gravity of the substantive evil must be measured by the "test" laid down in the *Schenck* case. . . .

But in suggesting that the substantive evil must be serious and substantial, it was never the intention of this Court to lay down an absolutist test measured in terms of danger to the Nation. When the effect of a statute or ordinance upon the exercise of First Amendment freedoms is relatively small and the public interest to be protected is substantial, it is obvious that a rigid test requiring a showing of imminent danger to the security of the Nation is an absurdity. We recently dismissed for want of substantiality an appeal in which a church group contended that its First Amendment rights were violated by a municipal zoning ordinance preventing the building of churches in certain residential areas. And recent cases in this Court involving contempt by publication likewise have no meaning if imminent danger of national peril is the criterion. . . .

When particular conduct is regulated in the interest of public order, and the regulation results in an indirect, conditional, partial abridgment of speech, the duty of the courts is to determine which of these two conflicting interests demands the greater protection under the particular circumstances presented. The high place in which the right to speak, think, and assemble as you will was held by the Framers of the Bill of Rights and is held today by those who value liberty both as a means and an end indicates the solicitude with which we must view any assertion of personal freedoms. We must recognize, moreover, that regulation of "conduct" has all too frequently been employed by public authority as a cloak to hide censorship of unpopular ideas. We have been reminded that "It is not often in this country that we now meet with direct and candid efforts to stop speaking or publication as such. Modern inroads on these rights come from associating the speaking with some other factor which the state may regulate so as to bring the whole within official control." [1]

On the other hand, legitimate attempts to protect the public, not from the remote possible effects of noxious ideologies, but from present excesses of direct, active conduct, are not presumptively bad because they interfere with and, in some of its manifestations, restrain the exercise of First Amendment rights. In essence the problem is one of weighing the probable effects of the statute upon the free exercise of the right of speech and assembly against the congressional determination that political strikes are evils of conduct which cause substantial harm to interstate commerce and that Communists and others identified by § 9 (h) pose continuing threats to that public interest when in positions of union leadership. We must, therefore, undertake

---

[1] MR. JUSTICE JACKSON, concurring in *Thomas v. Collins,* 323 U.S. 516, 547 (1945).

the "delicate and difficult task . . . to weigh the circumstances and to appraise the substantiality of the reasons advanced in support of the regulation of the free enjoyment of the rights." *Schneider v. State,* 308 U.S. 147, 161 (1939).

The "reasons advanced in support of the regulation" are of considerable weight, as even the opponents of § 9 (h) agreed. They are far from being "[m]ere legislative preferences or beliefs respecting matters of public convenience [which] may well support regulation directed at other personal activities, but be insufficient to justify such as diminishes the exercise of rights so vital to the maintenance of democratic institutions." [2] It should be emphasized that Congress, not the courts, is primarily charged with determination of the need for regulation of activities affecting interstate commerce. This Court must, if such regulation unduly infringes personal freedoms, declare the statute invalid under the First Amendment's command that the opportunities for free public discussion be maintained. But insofar as the problem is one of drawing inferences concerning the need for regulation of particular forms of conduct from conflicting evidence, this Court is in no position to substitute its judgment as to the necessity or desirability of the statute for that of Congress. . . .

When compared with ordinances and regulations dealing with littering of the streets or disturbance of householders by itinerant preachers, the relative significance and complexity of the problem of political strikes and how to deal with their leaders becomes at once apparent. It must be remembered that § 9 (h) is not an isolated statute dealing with a subject divorced from the problems of labor peace generally. It is a part of some very complex machinery set up by the Federal Government for the purpose of encouraging the peaceful settlement of labor disputes. Under the statutory scheme, unions which become collective bargaining representatives for groups of employees often represent not only members of the union but nonunion workers or members of other unions as well. Because of the necessity to have strong unions to bargain on equal terms with strong employers, individual employees are required by law to sacrifice rights which, in some cases, are valuable to them. The loss of individual rights for the greater benefit of the group results in a tremendous increase in

[2] *Schneider v. State,* 308 U.S. 147, 161 (1939).

the power of the representative of the group—the union. But power is never without responsibility. And when authority derives in part from Government's thumb on the scales, the exercise of that power by private persons becomes closely akin, in some respects, to its exercise by Government itself.

We do not suggest that labor unions which utilize the facilities of the National Labor Relations Board become Government agencies or may be regulated as such. But it is plain that when Congress clothes the bargaining representative "with powers comparable to those possessed by a legislative body both to create and restrict the rights of those whom it represents," [3] the public interest in the good faith exercise of that power is very great.

What of the effects of § 9 (h) upon the rights of speech and assembly of those proscribed by its terms? The statute does not prevent or punish by criminal sanctions the making of a speech, the affiliation with any organization, or the holding of any belief. But as we have noted, the fact that no direct restraint or punishment is imposed upon speech or assembly does not determine the free speech question. Under some circumstances, indirect "discouragements" undoubtedly have the same coercive effect upon the exercise of First Amendment rights as imprisonment, fines, injunctions or taxes. A requirement that adherents of particular religious faiths or political parties wear identifying armbands, for example, is obviously of this nature.

But we have here no statute which is either frankly aimed at the suppression of dangerous ideas nor one which, although ostensibly aimed at the regulation of conduct, may actually "be made the instrument of arbitrary suppression of free expression of views." *Hague v. Committee for Industrial Organization,* 307 U.S. 496, 516 (1939). There are here involved none of the elements of censorship or prohibition of the dissemination of information that were present in the cases mainly relied upon by those attacking the statute. The "discouragements" of § 9 (h) proceed, not against the groups or beliefs identified therein, but only against the combination of those affiliations or beliefs with occupancy of a position of great power over the economy of the country. Congress has concluded that substantial harm, in the form of direct, positive action, may be expected from that combination. In this legislation, Congress did not restrain the

[3] *Steele v. Louisville & N. R. Co.,* 323 U.S. 192, 202 (1944).

activities of the Communist Party as a political organization; nor did it attempt to stifle beliefs. Section 9 (h) touches only a relative handful of persons, leaving the great majority of persons of the identified affiliations and beliefs completely free from restraint. And it leaves those few who are affected free to maintain their affiliations and beliefs subject only to possible loss of positions which Congress has concluded are being abused to the injury of the public by members of the described groups. . . .

MR. JUSTICE DOUGLAS, MR. JUSTICE CLARK and MR. JUSTICE MINTON took no part in the consideration or decision of these cases.

MR. JUSTICE FRANKFURTER concurring in the Court's opinion except as to Part VII. . . .

In my view Congress has cast its net too indiscriminately in some of the provisions of § 9 (h). To ask avowal that one "does not believe in, and is not a member of or supports any organization that believes in . . . the overthrow of the United States Government . . . by any illegal or unconstitutional methods" is to ask assurances from men regarding matters that open the door too wide to mere speculation or uncertainty. It is asking more than rightfully may be asked of ordinary men to take oath that a method is not "unconstitutional" or "illegal" when constitutionality or legality is frequently determined by this Court by the chance of a single vote. It does not meet the difficulty to suggest that the hazard of a prosecution for perjury is not great since the convictions for perjury must be founded on willful falsity. To suggest that a judge might not be justified in allowing a case to go to a jury, or that a jury would not be justified in convicting, or that, on the possible happening of these events, an appellate court would be compelled to reverse, or, finally, that resort could be had to this Court for review on a petition for certiorari, affords safeguards too tenuous to neutralize the danger. The hazards that were found to be fatal to the legislation under review in *Winters v. New York,* 333 U.S. 507, appear trivial by comparison with what is here involved. . . .

I cannot deem it within the rightful authority of Congress to probe into opinions that involve only an argumentative demonstration of some coincidental parallelism of belief with some of the beliefs of those who direct the policy of the Communist Party, though without any allegiance to it. To require oaths as to matters that open up such possibilities invades the inner life of men whose compassionate thought or doctrinaire hopes may be as far removed from any dangerous kinship with the Communist creed as were those of the founders of the present orthodox political parties in this country.

The offensive provisions of § 9 (h) leave unaffected, however, the valid portions of the section. . . .

MR. JUSTICE JACKSON, concurring and dissenting, each in part.

If the statute before us required labor union officers to forswear membership in the Republican Party, the Democratic Party or the Socialist Party, I suppose all agree that it would be unconstitutional. But why, if it is valid as to the Communist Party?

The answer, for me, is in the decisive differences between the Communist Party and every other party of any importance in the long experience of the United States with party government. In order that today's decision may not be useful as a precedent for suppression of any political opposition compatible with our free institutions, I limit concurrence to grounds and distinctions explicitly set forth herein, without which I should regard this Act as unconstitutional. . . .

From information before its several Committees and from facts of general knowledge, Congress could rationally conclude that, behind its political party façade, the Communist Party is a conspiratorial and revolutionary junta, organized to reach ends and to use methods which are incompatible with our constitutional system. A rough and compressed grouping of this data would permit Congress to draw these important conclusions as to its distinguishing characteristics.

1. *The goal of the Communist Party is to seize powers of government by and for a minority rather than to acquire power through the vote of a free electorate.* . . .

2. *The Communist Party alone among American parties past or present is dominated and controlled by a foreign government.* . . .

3. *Violent and undemocratic means are the calculated and indispensable methods to attain the Communist Party's goal.* . . .

4. *The Communist Party has sought to gain this leverage and hold on the American population by acquiring control of the labor movement.* . . .

5. *Every member of the Communist Party is an agent to execute the Communist program.* . . .

Inferences from membership in such an organization are justifiably different from those to be drawn from membership in the usual type of political party. Individuals who assume such obligations are chargeable, on ordinary conspiracy principles, with responsibility for and participation in all that makes up the Party's program. The conspiracy principle has traditionally been employed to protect society against all "ganging up" or concerted action in violation of its laws. No term passes that this Court does not sustain convictions based on that doctrine for violations of the antitrust laws or other statutes. However, there has recently entered the dialectic of politics a cliché used to condemn application of the conspiracy principle to Communists. "Guilt by association" is an epithet frequently used and little explained, except that it is generally accompanied by another slogan, "guilt is personal." Of course it is; but personal guilt may be incurred by joining a conspiracy. That act of association makes one responsible for the acts of others committed in pursuance of the association. It is wholly a question of the sufficiency of evidence of association to imply conspiracy. There is certainly sufficient evidence that all members owe allegiance to every detail of the Communist Party program and have assumed a duty actively to help execute it, so that Congress could, on familiar conspiracy principles, charge each member with responsibility for the goals and means of the Party. . . .

Congress has, however, required an additional disclaimer, which in my view does encounter serious constitutional objections. A union officer must also swear that "he does not believe in . . . the overthrow of the United States Government by force or by any illegal or unconstitutional methods."

If Congress has power to condition any right or privilege of an American citizen upon disclosure and disavowal of belief on any subject, it is obviously this one. But the serious issue is whether Congress has power to proscribe any opinion or belief which has not manifested itself in any overt act. While the fore-part of the oath requires disclosure and disavowal of relationships which depend on overt acts of membership or affiliation, the afterpart demands revelation and denial of mere beliefs or opinions, even though they may never have matured into any act whatever or even been given utterance. In fact, the oath requires one to form and express a conviction on an abstract proposition which many good citizens, if they have thought of it at all, have considered too academic and remote to bother about.

MR. JUSTICE BLACK, dissenting.

We have said that "Freedom to think is absolute of its own nature; the most tyrannical government is powerless to control the inward workings of the mind." [4] But people can be, and in less democratic countries have been, made to suffer for their admitted or conjectured thoughts. Blackstone recalls that Dionysius is "recorded to have executed a subject, barely for dreaming that he had killed him; which was held for a sufficient proof, that he had thought thereof in his waking hours." [5] Such a result, while too barbaric to be tolerated in our nation, is not illogical if a government can tamper in the realm of thought and penalize "belief" on the ground that it might lead to illegal conduct. Individual freedom and governmental thought-probing cannot live together. As the Court admits even today, under the First Amendment "Beliefs are inviolate."

Today's decision rejects that fundamental principle. The Court admits, as it must, that the "proscriptions" of § 9 (h) of the National Labor Relations Act as amended by the Taft-Hartley Act rest on "beliefs and political affiliations," and that "Congress has undeniably discouraged the lawful exercise of political freedoms" which are "protected by the First Amendment." These inescapable facts should compel a holding that § 9 (h) conflicts with the First Amendment.

Crucial to the Court's contrary holding is the premise that congressional power to regulate trade and traffic includes power to proscribe "beliefs and political affiliations." No case cited by the Court provides the least vestige of support for thus holding that the Commerce Clause restricts the right to think. On the

---

[4] Dissenting opinion in *Jones v. Opelika,* 316 U.S. 584, 618, adopted as the Court's opinion in 319 U.S. 103. See also *Cantwell v. Connecticut,* 310 U.S. 296, 303.

[5] 4 Blackstone, Commentaries 79 (6th ed. Dublin 1775).

contrary, the First Amendment was added after adoption of the Constitution for the express purpose of barring Congress from using previously granted powers to abridge belief or its expression. Freedom to think is inevitably abridged when beliefs are penalized by imposition of civil disabilities.

Since § 9 (h) was passed to exclude certain beliefs from one arena of the national economy, it was quite natural to utilize the test oath as a weapon. History attests the efficacy of that instrument for inflicting penalties and disabilities on obnoxious minorities. It was one of the major devices used against the Huguenots in France, and against "heretics" during the Spanish Inquisition. It helped English rulers identify and outlaw Catholics, Quakers, Baptists, and Congregationalists—groups considered dangerous for political as well as religious reasons. And wherever the test oath was in vogue, spies and informers found rewards far more tempting than truth. Painful awareness of the evils of thought espionage made such oaths "an abomination to the founders of this nation," *In re Summers,* 325 U.S. 561, 576, dissenting opinion. Whether religious, political, or both, test oaths are implacable foes of free thought. By approving their imposition, this Court has injected compromise into a field where the First Amendment forbids compromise.

The Court assures us that today's encroachment on liberty is just a small one, that this particular statutory provision "touches only a relative handful of persons, leaving the great majority of persons of the identified affiliations and beliefs completely free from restraint." But not the least of the virtues of the First Amendment is its protection of each member of the smallest and most unorthodox minority. Centuries of experience testify that laws aimed at one political or religious group, however rational these laws may be in their beginnings, generate hatreds and prejudices which rapidly spread beyond control. Too often it is fear which inspires such passions, and nothing is more reckless or contagious. In the resulting hysteria, popular indignation tars with the same brush all those who have ever been associated with any member of the group under attack or who hold a view which, though supported by revered Americans as essential to democracy, has been adopted by that group for its own purposes.

Under such circumstances, restrictions imposed on proscribed groups are seldom static, even though the rate of expansion may not move in geometric progression from discrimination to arm-band to ghetto and worse. Thus I cannot regard the Court's holding as one which merely bars Communists from holding union office and nothing more. For its reasoning would apply just as forcibly to statutes barring Communists and their suspected sympathizers from election to political office, mere membership in unions, and in fact from getting or holding any jobs whereby they could earn a living. . . .

Today the "political affiliation" happens to be the Communist Party: testimony of an ex-Communist that some Communist union officers had called "political strikes" is held sufficient to uphold a law coercing union members not to elect any Communist as an officer. Under this reasoning, affiliations with other political parties could be proscribed just as validly. Of course there is no practical possibility that either major political party would turn this weapon on the other, even though members of one party were accused of "political lockouts" a few years ago and members of the other are now charged with fostering a "welfare state" alien to our system. But with minor parties the possibility is not wholly fanciful. One, for instance, advocates socialism; another allegedly follows the Communist "line"; still another is repeatedly charged with a desire and purpose to deprive Negroes of equal job opportunities. Under today's opinion Congress could validly bar all members of these parties from officership in unions or industrial corporations; the only showing required would be testimony that some members in such positions had, by attempts to further their party's purposes, unjustifiably fostered industrial strife which hampered interstate commerce. . . .

These experiences underline the wisdom of the basic constitutional precept that penalties should be imposed only for a person's own conduct, not for his beliefs or for the conduct of others with whom he may associate. Guilt should not be imputed solely from association or affiliation with political parties or any other organization, however much we abhor the ideas which they advocate. *Schneiderman v. United States,* 320 U.S. 118, 136-139. Like anyone else, individual Communists who commit overt acts in violation of valid laws can and should be punished. But the postulate of the First Amendment is that our free institutions can be maintained without proscribing or penalizing political belief, speech, press, assembly, or party affiliation. This is a far bolder philosophy than despotic rulers can afford to follow. It is the heart of the system on which our freedom depends.

Fears of alien ideologies have frequently agitated the nation and inspired legislation aimed at suppressing advocacy of those ideologies. At such times the fog of public excitement obscures the ancient landmarks set up in our Bill of Rights. Yet then, of all times, should this Court adhere most closely to the course they mark.

Dennis v. United States
341 U.S. 494 (1951)

[Defendants, members of the executive committee of the Communist Party, were convicted under the Smith Act for conspiring (1) to organize as the Communist Party of the United States a group of persons who teach and advocate the overthrow of the Government by force and violence, and (2) knowingly and willfully to advocate and teach the duty and necessity of overthrowing the Government by force and violence.]

MR. CHIEF JUSTICE VINSON announced the judgment of the Court and an opinion in which MR. JUSTICE REED, MR. JUSTICE BURTON and MR. JUSTICE MINTON join. . . .

The obvious purpose of the statute is to protect existing Government, not from change by peaceable, lawful and constitutional means, but from change by violence, revolution and terrorism. That it is within the *power* of the Congress to protect the Government of the United States from armed rebellion is a proposition which requires little discussion. Whatever theoretical merit there may be to the argument that there is a "right" to rebellion against dictatorial governments is without force where the existing structure of the government provides for peaceful and orderly change. We reject any principle of governmental helplessness in the face of preparation for revolution, which principle, carried to its logical conclusion, must lead to anarchy. No one could conceive that it is not within the power of Congress to prohibit acts intended to overthrow the Government by force and violence. The question with which we are concerned here is not whether Congress has such *power,* but whether the *means* which it has employed conflict with the First and Fifth Amendments to the Constitution.

One of the bases for the contention that the means which Congress has employed are invalid takes the form of an attack on the face of the statute on the grounds that by its terms it prohibits academic discussion of the merits of Marxism-Leninism, that it stifles ideas and is contrary to all concepts of a free speech and a free press. Although we do not agree that the language itself has that significance, we must bear in mind that it is the duty of the federal courts to interpret federal legislation in a manner not inconsistent with the demands of the Constitution. . . .

The very language of the Smith Act negates the interpretation which petitioners would have us impose on that Act. It is directed at advocacy, not discussion. Thus, the trial judge properly charged the jury that they could not convict if they found that petitioners did "no more than pursue peaceful studies and discussions or teachings and advocacy in the realm of ideas." He further charged that it was not unlawful "to conduct in an American college and university a course explaining the philosophical theories set forth in the books which have been placed in evidence." Such a charge is in strict accord with the statutory language, and illustrates the meaning to be placed on those words. Congress did not intend to eradicate the free discussion of political theories, to destroy the traditional rights of Americans to discuss and evaluate ideas without fear of governmental sanction. Rather Congress was concerned with the very kind of activity in which the evidence showed these petitioners engaged.

But although the statute is not directed at the hypothetical cases which petitioners have conjured, its application in this case has resulted in convictions for the teaching and advocacy of the overthrow of the Government by force and violence, which, even though coupled with the intent to accomplish that overthrow, contains an element of speech. For this reason, we must pay special heed to the demands of the First Amendment marking out the boundaries of speech. . . .

In this case we are squarely presented with the application of the "clear and present danger" test, and must decide what that phrase imports. We first note that many of the cases in which this Court has reversed convictions by use of this or similar tests have been based on the fact that the interest which the State was attempting to protect was itself too insubstantial to warrant restriction of speech. . . . Overthrow of the Government by force and violence is certainly a substantial enough interest for the Government to limit speech. Indeed, this is the ultimate value of any society, for if a society cannot protect its very structure, from armed internal attack, it must follow that no subordinate value can be protected. If, then, this interest may be protected, the literal problem which is presented is what has been meant by the use of the phrase "clear and present danger" of the utterances bringing about the evil within the power of Congress to punish.

Obviously, the words cannot mean that before the Government may act, it must wait until the *putsch* is about to be executed, the plans have been laid and the signal is awaited. If Government is aware that a group aiming at its overthrow is attempting to indoctrinate its members and to commit them to a course whereby they will strike when the leaders feel the circumstances permit, action by the Government is required. The argument that there is no need for Government to concern itself, for Government is strong, it possesses ample powers to put down a rebellion, it may defeat the revolution with ease needs no answer. For that is not the question. Certainly an attempt to overthrow the Government by force, even though doomed from the outset because of inadequate numbers or power of the revolutionists, is a sufficient evil for Congress to prevent. The damage which such attempts create both physically and politically to a nation makes it impossible to measure the validity in terms of the probability of success, or the immediacy of a successful attempt. In the instant case the trial judge charged the jury that they could not convict unless they found the petitioners intended to overthrow the Government "as speedily as circumstances would permit." This does not mean, and could not properly mean, that they would not strike until there was certainty of success. What was meant was that the revolutionists would strike when they thought the time was ripe. We must therefore reject the contention that success or probability of success is the criterion.

The situation with which Justices Holmes and Brandeis were concerned in *Gitlow* was a comparatively isolated event, bearing little relation in their minds to any substantial threat to the safety of the community. . . . They were not confronted with any situation comparable to the instant one—the development of an apparatus designed and dedicated to the overthrow of the Government, in the context of world crisis after crisis.

Chief Judge Learned Hand, writing for the majority below, interpreted the phrase as follows: "In each case [courts] must ask whether the gravity of the 'evil,' discounted by its improbability, justifies such invasion of free speech as is necessary to avoid the danger." 183 F.2d at 212. We adopt this statement of the rule. As articulated by Chief Judge Hand, it is as succinct and inclusive as any other we might devise at this time. It takes into consideration those factors which we deem relevant, and relates their significances. More we cannot expect from words.

Likewise, we are in accord with the court below, which affirmed the trial court's finding that the requisite danger existed. The mere fact that from the period 1945 to 1948 petitioners' activities did not result in an attempt to overthrow the Government by force and violence is of course no answer to the fact that there was a group that was ready to make the attempt. The formation by petitioners of such a highly organized conspiracy, with rigidly disciplined members subject to call when the leaders, these petitioners, felt that the time had come for action, coupled with the inflammable nature of world conditions, similar uprisings in other countries, and the touch-and-go nature of our relations with countries with whom petitioners were in the very least ideologically attuned, convince us that their convictions were justified on this score. And this analysis disposes of the contention that a conspiracy to advocate, as distinguished from the advocacy itself, cannot be constitutionally restrained, because it comprises only the preparation. It is the existence of the conspiracy which creates the danger. If the ingredients of the reaction are present, we cannot bind the Government to wait until the catalyst is added.

MR. JUSTICE FRANKFURTER, concurring in affirmance of the judgment. . . .

Few questions of comparable import have come before this Court in recent years. The appellants maintain that they have a right to advocate a political theory, so long, at least, as their advocacy does not create an immediate danger of obvious magnitude to the very existence of our present scheme of society. On the other hand, the Government asserts the right to safeguard the security of the Nation by such a measure as the Smith Act. Our judgment is thus solicited on a conflict of interests of the utmost concern to the well-being of the country. This conflict of interests cannot be resolved by a dogmatic preference for one or the other, nor by a sonorous formula which is in fact only a euphemistic disguise for an unresolved conflict. If adjudication is to be a rational process we cannot escape a candid examination of the conflicting claims with full recognition that both are supported by weighty title-deeds. . . .

In all fairness, the argument cannot be met by reinterpreting the Court's frequent use of "clear" and "present" to mean an entertainable "probability." In giving this meaning to the phrase "clear and present danger," the Court of Appeals was fastidiously confining the rhetoric of opinions to the exact scope of what was decided by them. We have greater responsibility for having given constitutional support, over repeated protests, to uncritical libertarian generalities. . . .

The defendants have been convicted of conspiring to organize a party of persons who advocate the overthrow of the Government by force and violence. The jury has found that the object of the conspiracy is advocacy as "a rule or principle of action," "by language reasonably and ordinarily calculated to incite persons to such action," and with the intent to cause the overthrow "as speedily as circumstances would permit."

On any scale of values which we have hitherto recognized, speech of this sort ranks low. . . .

These general considerations underlie decision of the case before us.

On the one hand is the interest in security. The Communist Party was not designed by these defendants as an ordinary political party. For the circumstances of its organization, its aims and methods, and the relation of the defendants to its organization and aims we are concluded by the jury's verdict. The jury found that the Party rejects the basic premise of our political system—that change is to be brought about by nonviolent constitutional process. The jury found that the Party advocates the theory that there is a duty and necessity to overthrow the Government by force and violence. It found that the Party entertains and promotes this view, not as a prophetic insight or as a bit of unworldly speculation, but as a program for winning adherents and as a policy to be translated into action.

In finding that the defendants violated the statute, we may not treat as established fact that the Communist Party in this country is of significant size, well-organized, well-disciplined, conditioned to embark on unlawful activity when given the command. But in determining whether application of the statute to the defendants is within the constitutional powers of Congress, we are not limited to the facts found by the jury. We must view such a question in the light of whatever is relevant to a legislative judgment. We may take judicial notice that the Communist doctrines which these defendants have conspired to advocate are in the ascendency in powerful nations who cannot be acquitted of unfriendliness to the institutions of this country. We may take account of evidence brought forward at this trial and elsewhere, much of which has long been common knowledge. In sum, it would amply justify a legislature in concluding that recruitment of additional members for the Party would create a substantial danger to national security. . . .

On the other hand is the interest in free speech. The right to exert all governmental powers in aid of maintaining our institutions and resisting their physical overthrow does not include intolerance of opinions and speech that cannot do harm although opposed and perhaps alien to dominant, traditional opinion. The treatment of its minorities, especially their legal position, is among the most searching tests of the level of civilization attained by a society. It is better for those who have almost unlimited power of government in their hands to err on the side of freedom. We have enjoyed so much freedom for so long that we are perhaps in danger of forgetting how much blood it cost to establish the Bill of Rights.

Of course no government can recognize a "right" of revolution, or a "right" to incite revolution if the incitement has no other purpose or effect. But speech is seldom restricted to a single purpose, and its effects may be manifold. A public interest is not wanting in granting freedom to speak their minds even to those who advocate the overthrow of the Government by force. For, as the evidence in this case abundantly illustrates, coupled with such advocacy is criticism of defects in our society. Criticism is the spur to reform; and Burke's admonition that a healthy society must reform in order to conserve has not lost its force. Astute observers have remarked that one of the characteristics of the American Republic is indifference to fundamental criticism. Bryce, The American Commonwealth, c. 84. It is a commonplace that there may be a grain of truth in the most uncouth doctrine, however false and repellent the balance may be. Suppressing advocates of overthrow inevitably will also silence critics who do not advocate overthrow but fear that their criticism may be so construed. No matter how clear we may be that the defendants now before us are preparing to overthrow the Government at the propitious moment, it is self-delusion to think that we can punish them for their advocacy without adding to the risks run by loyal citizens who honestly believe in some of the reforms these defendants advance. It is a sobering fact that in sustaining the conviction before us we can hardly escape restriction on the interchange of ideas.

We must not overlook the value of that interchange. Freedom of expression is the well-spring of our civilization—the civilization we seek to maintain and further by recognizing the right of Congress to put some limitation upon expression. Such are the paradoxes of life. For social development of trial and error, the fullest possible opportunity for the free play of the human mind is an indispensable prerequisite. The history of civilization is in considerable measure the displacement of error which once held sway as official truth by beliefs which in turn have yielded to other truths. Therefore the liberty of man to search for truth ought not to be fettered, no matter what orthodoxies he may challenge. Liberty of thought soon shrivels without freedom of expression. Nor can truth be pursued in an atmosphere hostile to the endeavor or under dangers which are hazarded only by heroes. . . .

It is not for us to decide how we would adjust the clash of interests which this case presents were the primary responsibility for reconciling it ours. Congress has determined that the danger created by advocacy of overthrow justifies the ensuing restriction on freedom of speech. The determination was made after due deliberation, and the seriousness of the congressional purpose is attested by the volume of legislation passed to effectuate the same ends. . . .

Civil liberties draw at best only limited strength from legal guaranties. Preoccupation by our people with the constitutionality, instead of with the wisdom of legislation or of executive action, is preoccupation with a false value. Even those who would most freely use the judicial brake on the democratic process by invalidating legislation that goes deeply against their grain, acknowledge, at least by paying lip service, that constitutionality does not exact a sense of proportion or the sanity of humor or an absence of fear. Focusing attention on constitutionality tends to make constitutionality synonymous with wisdom. When legislation touches freedom of thought and freedom of speech, such a tendency is a formidable enemy of the free spirit. Much that should be rejected as illiberal, because repressive and envenoming, may well be not unconstitutional. The ultimate reliance for the deepest needs of civilization must be found outside their vindication in court of law; apart from all else, judges, howsoever they may seek to discipline themselves against it, unconsciously are too apt to be moved by the deep undercurrents of public feeling. A persistent, positive translation of the liberating faith into the feelings and thoughts and actions of men and women is the real protection against attempts to strait-jacket the human mind. Such temptations will have their way, if fear and hatred are not exorcised. The mark of a truly civilized man is confidence in the strength and security derived from the inquiring mind. We may be grateful for such honest comforts as it supports, but we must be unafraid of its uncertitudes. Without open minds there can be no open society. And if society be not open the spirit of man is mutilated and becomes enslaved.

MR. JUSTICE JACKSON, concurring. . . .

The "clear and present danger" test was an innovation by Mr. Justice Holmes in the *Schenck* case, reiterated and refined by him and Mr. Justice Brandeis in later cases, all arising before the era of World War II revealed the subtlety and efficacy of modernized revolutionary techniques used by totalitarian parties. In these cases, they were faced with convictions under so-called criminal syndicalism statutes aimed at anarchists but which, loosely construed, had been applied to punish socialism, pacifism, and left-wing ideologies, the charges often resting on far-fetched inferences which, if true, would establish only technical or trivial violations. They proposed "clear and present danger" as a test for the sufficiency of evidence in particular cases.

I would save it, unmodified, for application as a "rule of reason" in the kind of case for which it was devised. When the issue is criminality of a hot-headed speech on a street corner, or circulation of a few incendiary pamphlets, or parading by some zealots behind a red flag, or refusal by a handful of school children to salute our flag, it is not beyond the capacity of judicial process to gather, comprehend, and weigh the necessary materials for decision whether it is a clear and present danger of substantive evil or a harmless letting off of steam. It is not a prophecy, for the danger in such cases has matured by the time of trial or it was never present. . . .

I think reason is lacking for applying that test to this case.

If we must decide that this Act and its application are constitutional only if we are convinced that petitioner's conduct creates a "clear and present danger" of violent overthrow, we must appraise imponderables, including international and national phenomena which baffle the best informed foreign offices and our most experienced politicians. We would have to foresee and predict the effectiveness of Communist propaganda, opportunities for infiltration, whether, and when, a time will come that they consider propitious for action, and whether and how fast our existing government will deteriorate. And we would have to speculate as to whether an approaching Communist *coup* would not be anticipated by a nationalistic fascist movement. No doctrine can be sound whose application requires us to make a prophecy of that sort in the guise of a legal decision. The judicial process simply is not adequate to a trial of such far-flung issues. The answers given would reflect our own political predilections and nothing more. . . .

What really is under review here is a conviction of conspiracy, after a trial for conspiracy, on an indictment charging conspiracy, brought under a statute outlawing conspiracy. . . .

The Constitution does not make conspiracy a civil right. The Court has never before done so, and I think it should not do so now. Conspiracies of labor unions, trade associations, and news agencies have been condemned, although accomplished, evidenced and carried out, like the conspiracy here, chiefly by letter-writing, meetings, speeches and organization. Indeed, this Court seems, particularly in cases where the conspiracy has economic ends, to be applying its doctrines with increasing severity. While I consider criminal conspiracy a dragnet device capable of perversion into an instrument of injustice in the hands of a partisan or complacent judiciary, it has an established place in our system of law, and no reason appears for applying it only to concerted action claimed to disturb interstate commerce and withholding it from those claimed to undermine our whole Government.

MR. JUSTICE BLACK, dissenting. . . .

At the outset I want to emphasize what the crime involved in this case is, and what it is not. These petitioners were not charged with an attempt to overthrow the Government. They were not charged with overt acts of any kind designed to overthrow the Government. They were not even charged with saying anything or with writing anything designed to overthrow the Government. The charge was that they agreed to assemble and to talk and to publish certain ideas at a later date: The indictment is that they conspired to organize the Communist Party and to use speech or newspapers and other publications in the future to teach and advocate the forcible overthrow of the Government. No matter how it is worded, this is a virulent form of prior censorship of speech and press, which I believe the First Amendment forbids. I would hold § 3 of the Smith Act authorizing this prior restraint unconstitutional on its face and as applied.

But let us assume, contrary to all constitutional ideas of fair criminal procedure, that petitioners although not indicted for the crime of actual advocacy, may be punished for it. Even on this radical assumption, the other opinions in this case show that the only way to affirm these convictions is to repudiate directly or indirectly the established "clear and present danger" rule. This the Court does in a way which greatly restricts the protections afforded by the First Amendment. The opinions for affirmance indicate that the chief reason for jettisoning the rule is the expressed fear that advocacy of Communist doctrine endangers the safety of the Republic. Undoubtedly, a governmental policy of unfettered communication of ideas does entail dangers. To the Founders of this Nation, however, the benefits derived from free expression were worth the risk. They embodied this philosophy in the First Amendment's command that "Congress shall make no law abridging . . . the freedom of speech, or of the press. . . ." I have always believed that the First Amendment is the keystone of our Government, that the freedoms it guarantees provide the best insurance against destruction of all freedom. At least as to speech in the realm of public matters, I believe that the "clear and present danger" test does not "mark the furthermost constitutional boundaries of protected expression" but does "no more than recognize a minimum compulsion of the Bill of Rights." *Bridges v. California,* 314 U.S. 252, 263.

So long as this Court exercises the power of judicial review of legislation, I cannot agree that the First Amendment permits us to sustain laws suppressing freedom of speech and press on the basis of Congress' or our own notions of mere "reasonableness." Such a doctrine waters down the First Amendment so that it amounts to little more than an admonition to Congress. The Amendment as so construed is not likely to protect any but those "safe" or orthodox views which rarely need its protection. . . .

Public opinion being what it now is, few will protest the conviction of these Communist petitioners. There is hope, however, that in calmer times, when present pressures, passions and fears subside, this or some later Court will restore the First Amendment liberties to the high preferred place where they belong in a free society.

MR. JUSTICE DOUGLAS, dissenting.

If this were a case where those who claimed protection under the First Amendment were teaching the techniques of sabotage, the assassination of the President, the filching of documents from public files, the planting of bombs, the art of street warfare, and the like, I would have no doubts. The freedom to speak is not absolute; the teaching of methods of terror and other seditious conduct should be beyond the pale along with obscenity and immorality. This case was argued as if those were the facts. The argument imported much seditious conduct into the record. That is easy and it has popular appeal, for the activities of Communists in plotting and scheming against the free world are common knowledge. But the fact is that no such evidence was introduced at the trial. There is a statute which makes a seditious conspiracy unlawful. Petitioners, however, were not charged with a "conspiracy to overthrow" the Government. They were charged with a conspiracy to form a party and groups and assemblies of people who teach and advocate the overthrow of our Government by force or violence and with a conspiracy to advocate and teach its overthrow by force and violence. It may well be that indoctrination in the techniques of terror to destroy the Government would be indictable under either statute. But the teaching which is condemned here is of a different character.

So far as the present record is concerned, what petitioners did was to organize people to teach and themselves teach the Marxist-Leninist doctrine contained chiefly in four books: Stalin, Foundations of Leninism (1924); Marx and Engels, Manifesto of the Communist Party (1848); Lenin, The State and Revolution (1917); History of the Communist Party of the Soviet Union (B.) (1939).

Those books are to Soviet Communism what Mein Kampf was to Nazism. If they are understood, the ugliness of Communism is revealed, its deceit and cunning are exposed, the nature of its activities becomes apparent, and the chances of its success less likely. That is not, of course, the reason why petitioners chose these books for their classrooms. They are fervent Communists to whom these volumes are gospel. They preached the creed with the hope that some day it would be acted upon.

The opinion of the Court does not outlaw these texts nor condemn them to the fire, as the Communists do literature offensive to their creed. But if the books themselves are not outlawed, if they can lawfully remain on library shelves, by what reasoning does their use in a classroom become a crime? It would not be a crime under the Act to introduce these books to a class, though that would be teaching what the creed of violent overthrow of the government is. The Act, as construed, requires the element of intent—that those who teach the creed believe in it. The crime then depends not on what is taught but on who the teacher is. That is to make freedom of speech turn not on *what is said,* but on the *intent* with which it is said. Once we start down that road we enter territory dangerous to the liberties of every citizen. . . .

Free speech has occupied an exalted position because of the

high service it has given our society. Its protection is essential to the very existence of a democracy. The airing of ideas releases pressures which otherwise might become destructive. When ideas compete in the market for acceptance, full and free discussion exposes the false and they gain few adherents. Full and free discussion even of ideas we hate encourages the testing of our own prejudices and preconceptions. Full and free discussion keeps a society from becoming stagnant and unprepared for the stresses and strains that work to tear all civilizations apart.

Full and free discussion has indeed been the first article of our faith. We have founded our political system on it. It has been the safeguard of every religious, political, philosophical, economic, and racial group amongst us. We have counted on it to keep us from embracing what is cheap and false; we have trusted the common sense of our people to choose the doctrine true to our genius and to reject the rest. This has been the one single outstanding tenet that has made our institutions the symbol of freedom and equality. We have deemed it more costly to liberty to suppress a despised minority than to let them vent their spleen. We have above all else feared the political censor. We have wanted a land where our people can be exposed to all the diverse creeds and cultures of the world.

There comes a time when even speech loses its constitutional immunity. Speech innocuous one year may at another time fan such destructive flames that it must be halted in the interests of the safety of the Republic. That is the meaning of the clear and present danger test. When conditions are so critical that there will be no time to avoid the evil that the speech threatens, it is time to call a halt. Otherwise, free speech which is the strength of the Nation will be the cause of its destruction. . . .

The nature of Communism as a force on the world scene would, of course, be relevant to the issue of clear and present danger of petitioners' advocacy within the United States. But the primary consideration is the strength and tactical position of petitioners and their converts in this country. On that there is no evidence in the record. If we are to take judicial notice of the threat of Communists within the nation, it should not be difficult to conclude that *as a political party* they are of little consequence. Communists in this country have never made a respectable or serious showing in any election. I would doubt that there is a village, let alone a city or county or state which the Communists could carry. Communism in the world scene is no bogeyman; but Communism as a political faction or party in this country plainly is. Communism has been so thoroughly exposed in this country that it has been crippled as a political force. Free speech has destroyed it as an effective political party. It is inconceivable that those who went up and down this country preaching the doctrine of revolution which petitioners espouse would have any success. In days of trouble and confusion when bread lines were long, when the unemployed walked the streets, when people were starving, the advocates of a short-cut by revolution might have a chance to gain adherents. But today there are no such conditions. The country is not in despair; the people know Soviet Communism; the doctrine of Soviet revolution is exposed in all of its ugliness and the American people want none of it.

How it can be said that there is a clear and present danger that this advocacy will succeed is, therefore, a mystery. Some nations less resilient than the United States, where illiteracy is high and where democratic traditions are only budding, might have to take drastic steps and jail these men for merely speaking their creed. But in America they are miserable merchants of unwanted ideas; their wares remain unsold. The fact that their ideas are abhorrent does not make them powerful.

The political impotence of the Communists in this country does not, of course, dispose of the problem. Their numbers; their positions in industry and government; the extent to which they have in fact infiltrated the police, the armed services, transportation, stevedoring, power plants, munitions works, and other critical places—these facts all bear on the likelihood that their advocacy of the Soviet theory of revolution will endanger the Republic. But the record is silent on these facts. If we are to proceed on the basis of judicial notice, it is impossible for me to say that the Communists in this country are so potent or so strategically deployed that they must be suppressed for their speech. I could not so hold unless I were willing to conclude that the activities in recent years of committees of Congress, of the Attorney General, of labor unions, of state legislatures, and of Loyalty Boards were so futile as to leave the country on the edge of grave peril. To believe that petitioners and their following are placed in such critical positions as to endanger the Nation is to believe the incredible. It is safe to say that the followers of the creed of Soviet Communism are known to the F. B. I.; that in case of war with Russia they will be picked up overnight as were all prospective saboteurs at the commencement of World War II; that the invisible army of petitioners is the best known, the most beset, and the least thriving of any fifth column in history. Only those held by fear and panic could think otherwise.

Adler v. Board of Education
342 U.S. 485 (1952)

[The case involved the constitutionality of New York's Feinberg law, passed in 1949. The Feinberg law provides that the Board of Regents shall make a listing of organizations which it finds advocate, advise, teach or embrace the doctrine that government should be overthrown by force or violence or any other unlawful means; and shall provide that membership in such an organization constitutes prima facie evidence for disqualification from holding any position in the New York school system.]

MR. JUSTICE MINTON delivered the opinion of the Court. . . .

It is first argued that the Feinberg Law and the rules promulgated thereunder constitute an abridgment of the freedom of speech and assembly of persons employed or seeking employment in the public schools of the State of New York.

It is clear that such persons have the right under our law to assemble, speak, think and believe as they will. It is equally clear that they have no right to work for the State in the school system on their own terms. They may work for the school system upon the reasonable terms laid down by the proper authorities of New York. If they do not choose to work on such terms, they are at liberty to retain their beliefs and associations and go elsewhere. Has the State thus deprived them of any right to free speech or assembly? We think not. Such persons are or may be denied, under the statutes in question, the privilege of working for the school system of the State of New York because, first, of their advocacy of the overthrow of the government by force or violence, or, secondly, by unexplained membership in an organization found by the school authorities, after notice and hearing, to teach and advocate the overthrow of the government by force or violence, and known by such persons to have such purpose.

The constitutionality of the first proposition is not questioned here. *Gitlow v. New York,* 268 U.S. 652, 667-672, construing § 161 of the New York Penal Law.

As to the second, it is rather subtly suggested that we should not follow our recent decision in *Garner v. Los Angeles Board,* 341 U.S. 716. We there said:

> "We think that a municipal employer is not disabled because it is an agency of the State from inquiring of its employees as to matters that may prove relevant to their fitness and suitability for the public service. Past conduct may well relate to present fitness; past loyalty may have a reasonable relationship to present and future trust. Both are commonly inquired into in determining fitness for both high and low positions in private industry and are not less relevant in public employment." 341 U.S., at p. 720.

We adhere to that case. A teacher works in a sensitive area in a schoolroom. There he shapes the attitude of young minds towards the society in which they live. In this, the state has a vital concern. It must preserve the integrity of the schools. That the school authorities have the right and the duty to screen the officials, teachers, and employees as to their fitness to maintain the integrity of the schools as a part of ordered society, cannot be doubted. One's associates, past and present, as well as one's conduct, may properly be considered in determining fitness and loyalty. From time immemorial, one's reputation has been determined in part by the company he keeps. In the employment of officials and teachers of the school system, the state may very properly inquire into the company they keep, and we know of no rule, constitutional or otherwise, that prevents the state, when determining the fitness and loyalty of such persons, from considering the organizations and persons with whom they associate.

If, under the procedure set up in the New York law, a person is found to be unfit and is disqualified from employment in the public school system because of membership in a listed organization, he is not thereby denied the right of free speech and assembly. His freedom of choice between membership in the organization and employment in the school system might be limited, but not his freedom of speech or assembly, except in the remote sense that limitation is inherent in every choice. Certainly such limitation is not one the state may not make in the exercise of its police power to protect the schools from pollution and thereby to defend its own existence.

MR. JUSTICE BLACK, dissenting.

While I fully agree with the dissent of MR. JUSTICE DOUGLAS, the importance of this holding prompts me to add these thoughts.

This is another of those rapidly multiplying legislative enactments which make it dangerous—this time for school teachers—to think or say anything except what a transient majority happen to approve at the moment. Basically these laws rest on the belief that government should supervise and limit the flow of ideas into the minds of men. The tendency of such governmental policy is to mould people into a common intellectual pattern. Quite a different governmental policy rests on the belief that government should leave the mind and spirit of man absolutely free. Such a governmental policy encourages varied intellectual outlooks in the belief that the best views will prevail. This policy of freedom is in my judgment embodied in the First Amendment and made applicable to the states by the Fourteenth. Because of this policy public officials cannot be constitutionally vested with powers to select the ideas people can think about, censor the public views they can express, or choose the persons or groups people can associate with. Public officials with such powers are not public servants; they are public masters.

I dissent from the Court's judgment sustaining this law which effectively penalizes school teachers for their thoughts and their associates.

[Mr. Justice Frankfurter dissented on the ground that the issues were not ripe for constitutional review and that the plaintiffs lacked standing to sue.]

MR. JUSTICE DOUGLAS, with whom MR. JUSTICE BLACK concurs, dissenting.

I have not been able to accept the recent doctrine that a citizen who enters the public service can be forced to sacrifice his civil rights. I cannot for example find in our constitutional scheme the power of a state to place its employees in the category of second-class citizens by denying them freedom of thought and expression. The Constitution guarantees freedom of thought and expression to everyone in our society. All are entitled to it; and none needs it more than the teacher.

The public school is in most respects the cradle of our democracy. The increasing role of the public school is seized upon by proponents of the type of legislation represented by New York's Feinberg law as proof of the importance and need for keeping the school free of "subversive influences." But that is to misconceive the effect of this type of legislation. Indeed the impact of this kind of censorship on the public school system illustrates the high purpose of the First Amendment in freeing speech and thought from censorship.

The present law proceeds on a principle repugnant to our society—guilt by association. A teacher is disqualified because of her membership in an organization found to be "subversive." The finding as to the "subversive" character of the organization is made in a proceeding to which the teacher is not a party and in which it is not clear that she may even be heard. To be sure, she may have a hearing when charges of disloyalty are leveled against her. But in that hearing the finding as to the "subversive" character of the organization apparently may not be reopened in order to allow her to show the truth of the matter. The irrebuttable charge that the organization is "subversive" therefore hangs as an ominous cloud over her own hearing. The mere fact of membership in the organization raises a prima facie case of her own guilt. She may, it is said, show her innocence. But innocence in this case turns on knowledge; and when the witch hunt is on, one who must rely on ignorance leans on a feeble reed.

The very threat of such a procedure is certain to raise havoc with academic freedom. Youthful indiscretions, mistaken causes, misguided enthusiasms—all long forgotten—become the ghosts of a harrowing present. Any organization committed to a liberal cause, any group organized to revolt against an hysterical trend, any committee launched to sponsor an unpopular program becomes suspect. These are the organizations into which Communists often infiltrate. Their presence infects the whole, even though the project was not conceived in sin. A teacher caught in that mesh is almost certain to stand condemned. Fearing condemnation, she will tend to shrink from any association that stirs controversy. In that manner freedom of expression will be stifled.

But that is only part of it. Once a teacher's connection with a listed organization is shown, her views become subject to scrutiny to determine whether her membership in the organization is innocent or, if she was formerly a member, whether she has *bona fide* abandoned her membership.

The law inevitably turns the school system into a spying project. Regular loyalty reports on the teachers must be made out. The principals become detectives; the students, the parents, the community become informers. Ears are cocked for tell-tale signs of disloyalty. The prejudices of the community come into play in searching out the disloyal. This is not the usual type of supervision which checks a teacher's competency; it is a system which searches for hidden meanings in a teacher's utterances.

What was the significance of the reference of the art teacher to socialism? Why was the history teacher so openly hostile to Franco Spain? Who heard overtones of revolution in the English teacher's discussion of the Grapes of Wrath? What was behind the praise of Soviet progress in metallurgy in the chemistry class? Was it not "subversive" for the teacher to cast doubt on the wisdom of the venture in Korea?

What happens under this law is typical of what happens in a police state. Teachers are under constant surveillance; their pasts are combed for signs of disloyalty; their utterances are watched for clues to dangerous thoughts. A pall is cast over the classrooms. There can be no real academic freedom in that environment. Where suspicion fills the air and holds scholars in line for fear of their jobs, there can be no exercise of the free intellect. Supineness and dogmatism take the place of inquiry. A "party line"—as dangerous as the "party line" of the communists—lays hold. It is the "party line" of the orthodox view, of the conventional thought, of the accepted approach. A problem can no longer be pursued with impunity to its edges. Fear stalks the classroom. The teacher is no longer a stimulant to adventurous thinking; she becomes instead a pipe line for safe and sound information. A deadening dogma takes the place of free inquiry. Instruction tends to become sterile; pursuit of knowledge is discouraged; discussion often leaves off where it should begin.

This, I think, is what happens when a censor looks over a teacher's shoulder. This system of spying and surveillance with its accompanying reports and trials cannot go hand in hand with academic freedom. It produces standardized thought, not the pursuit of truth. Yet it was the pursuit of truth which the First Amendment was designed to protect. A system which directly or inevitably has that effect is alien to our system and should be struck down. Its survival is a real threat to our way of life. We need be bold and adventuresome in our thinking to survive. A school system producing students trained as robots threatens to rob a generation of the versatility that has been perhaps our greatest distinction. The Framers knew the danger of dogmatism; they also knew the strength that comes when the mind is free, when ideas may be pursued wherever they lead. We forget these teachings of the First Amendment when we sustain this law.

Of course the school systems of the country need not become cells for Communist activities; and the classrooms need not become forums for propagandizing the Marxist creed. But the guilt of the teacher should turn on overt acts. So long as she is a law-abiding citizen, so long as her performance within the public school system meets professional standards, her private life, her political philosophy, her social creed should not be the cause of reprisals against her.

Watkins v. United States
354 U.S. 178 (1957)

[Watkins was convicted of contempt of Congress for refusing to answer questions before the House Committee on Un-American Activities as to whether certain persons known to him had been members of the Communist Party.]

MR. CHIEF JUSTICE WARREN delivered the opinion of the Court. . . .

A far more difficult task evolved from the claim by witnesses that the committees' interrogations were infringements upon the freedoms of the First Amendment. Clearly, an investigation is subject to the command that the Congress shall make no law abridging freedom of speech or press or assembly. While it is true that there is no statute to be reviewed, and that an investigation is not a law, nevertheless an investigation is part of law-making.

It is justified solely as an adjunct to the legislative process. The First Amendment may be invoked against infringement of the protected freedoms by law or by law-making.

Abuses of the investigative process may imperceptibly lead to abridgment of protected freedoms. The mere summoning of a witness and compelling him to testify, against his will, about his beliefs, expressions or associations is a measure of governmental interference. And when those forced revelations concern matters that are unorthodox, unpopular, or even hateful to the general public, the reaction in the life of the witness may be disastrous. This effect is even more harsh when it is past beliefs, expressions or associations that are disclosed and judged by current standards rather than those contemporary with the matters exposed. Nor does the witness alone suffer the consequences. Those who are identified by witnesses and thereby placed in the same glare of publicity are equally subject to public stigma, scorn and obloquy. Beyond that, there is the more subtle and immeasurable effect upon those who tend to adhere to the most orthodox and uncontroversial views and associations in order to avoid a similar fate at some future time. That this impact is partly the result of nongovernmental activity by private persons cannot relieve the investigators of their responsibility for initiating the reaction. . . .

Accommodation of the congressional need for particular information with the individual and personal interest in privacy is an arduous and delicate task for any court. We do not underestimate the difficulties that would attend such an undertaking. It is manifest that despite the adverse effects which follow upon compelled disclosure of private matters, not all such inquiries are barred. *Kilbourn v. Thompson* teaches that such an investigation into individual affairs is invalid if unrelated to any legislative purpose. That is beyond the powers conferred upon the Congress in the Constitution. *United States v. Rumely* makes it plain that the mere semblance of legislative purpose would not justify an inquiry in the face of the Bill of Rights. The critical element is the existence of, and the weight to be ascribed to, the interest of the Congress in demanding disclosures from an unwilling witness. We cannot simply assume, however, that every congressional investigation is justified by a public need that overbalances any private rights affected. To do so would be to abdicate the responsibility placed by the Constitution upon the judiciary to insure that the Congress does not unjustifiably encroach upon an individual's right to privacy nor abridge his liberty of speech, press, religion or assembly.

National Association for the Advancement of Colored People v. Alabama
357 U.S. 449 (1958)

[The question presented was whether Alabama could enforce its laws, providing that out-of-state corporations must register before carrying on any activities within the State, by requiring the N.A.A.C.P. to disclose to the State's Attorney General the names and addresses of all its members and agents in Alabama.]

MR. JUSTICE HARLAN delivered the opinion of the Court. . . .
We thus reach petitioner's claim that the production order in the state litigation trespasses upon fundamental freedoms protected by the Due Process Clause of the Fourteenth Amendment. Petitioner argues that in view of the facts and circumstances shown in the record, the effect of compelled disclosure of the membership lists will be to abridge the rights of its rank-and-file members to engage in lawful association in support of their common beliefs. It contends that governmental action which, although not directly suppressing association, nevertheless carries this consequence, can be justified only upon some overriding valid interest of the State.

Effective advocacy of both public and private points of view, particularly controversial ones, is undeniably enhanced by group association, as this Court has more than once recognized by remarking upon the close nexus between the freedoms of speech and assembly. It is beyond debate that freedom to engage in association for the advancement of beliefs and ideas is an inseparable aspect of the "liberty" assured by the Due Process Clause of the Fourteenth Amendment, which embraces freedom of speech. Of course, it is immaterial whether the beliefs sought to be advanced by association pertain to political, economic, religious or cultural matters, and state action which may have the effect of curtailing the freedom to associate is subject to the closest scrutiny.

The fact that Alabama, so far as is relevant to the validity of the contempt judgment presently under review, has taken no direct action to restrict the right of petitioner's members to associate freely, does not end inquiry into the effect of the production order. In the domain of these indispensable liberties, whether of speech, press, or association, the decisions of this Court recognize that abridgment of such rights, even though unintended, may inevitably follow from varied forms of governmental action. Thus in *Douds,* the Court stressed that the legislation there challenged, which on its face sought to regulate labor unions and to secure stability in interstate commerce, would have the practical effect "of discouraging" the exercise of constitutionally protected political rights, 339 U.S., at 393, and it upheld the statute only after concluding that the reasons advanced for its enactment were constitutionally sufficient to justify its possible deterrent effect upon such freedoms. Similar recognition of possible unconstitutional intimidation of the free exercise of the right to advocate underlay this Court's narrow construction of the authority of a congressional committee investigating lobbying and of an Act regulating lobbying, although in neither case was there an effort to suppress speech. The governmental action challenged may appear to be totally unrelated to protected liberties. Statutes imposing taxes upon rather than prohibiting particular activity have been struck down when perceived to have the consequence of unduly curtailing the liberty of freedom of press assured under the Fourteenth Amendment.

It is hardly a novel perception that compelled disclosure of affiliation with groups engaged in advocacy may constitute as effective a restraint on freedom of association as the forms of governmental action in the cases above were thought likely to produce upon the particular constitutional rights there involved. This Court has recognized the vital relationship between freedom to associate and privacy in one's associations. When referring to the varied forms of governmental action which might interfere with freedom of assembly, it said in *American Communications Assn. v. Douds,* at 402: "A requirement that adherents of particular religious faiths or political parties wear identifying armbands, for example, is obviously of this nature." Compelled disclosure of membership in an organization engaged in advocacy of particular beliefs is of the same order. Inviolability of privacy in group association may in many circumstances be indispensable to preservation of freedom of association, particularly where a group espouses dissident beliefs.

We think that the production order, in the respects here drawn in question, must be regarded as entailing the likelihood of a substantial restraint upon the exercise by petitioner's members of their right to freedom of association. Petitioner has made an uncontroverted showing that on past occasions revelation of the identity of its rank-and-file members has exposed these members to economic reprisal, loss of employment, threat of physical coercion, and other manifestations of public hostility. Under these circumstances, we think it apparent that compelled disclosure of petitioner's Alabama membership is likely to affect adversely the ability of petitioner and its members to pursue their collective effort to foster beliefs which they admittedly have the right to advocate, in that it may induce members to withdraw from the Association and dissuade others from joining it because of fear of exposure of their beliefs shown through their associations and of the consequences of this exposure.

It is not sufficient to answer, as the State does here, that whatever repressive effect compulsory disclosure of names of petitioner's members may have upon participation by Alabama citizens in petitioner's activities follows not from *state* action but from *private* community pressures. The crucial factor is the interplay of governmental and private action, for it is only after the initial exertion of state power represented by the production order that private action takes hold.

We turn to the final question whether Alabama has demonstrated an interest in obtaining the disclosures it seeks from petitioner which is sufficient to justify the deterrent effect which we have concluded these disclosures may well have on the free exercise by petitioner's members of their constitutionally protected right of association. . . .

We hold that the immunity from state scrutiny of membership lists which the Association claims on behalf of its members is here so related to the right of the members to pursue their lawful private interest privately and to associate freely with others in so doing as to come within the protection of the Fourteenth Amendment. And we conclude that Alabama has fallen short of showing a controlling justification for the deterrent effect on the free enjoyment of the right to associate which disclosure of membership lists is likely to have. Accordingly, the judgment of civil contempt and the $100,000 fine which resulted from petitioner's refusal to comply with the production order in this respect must fall.

Barenblatt v. United States
360 U.S. 109 (1959)

[Barenblatt, formerly a graduate student and teaching fellow at the University of Michigan, refused to answer questions of the House Committee on Un-American Activities with respect to whether he was then or ever had been a member of the Communist Party. He was convicted of contempt of Congress.]

MR. JUSTICE HARLAN delivered the opinion of the Court. . . .

Our function, at this point, is purely one of constitutional adjudication in the particular case and upon the particular record before us, not to pass judgment upon the general wisdom or efficacy of the activities of this Committee in a vexing and complicated field.

The precise constitutional issue confronting us is whether the Subcommittee's inquiry into petitioner's past or present membership in the Communist Party transgressed the provisions of the First Amendment, which of course reach and limit congressional investigations.

The Court's past cases establish sure guides to decision. Undeniably, the First Amendment in some circumstances protects an individual from being compelled to disclose his associational relationships. However, the protections of the First Amendment, unlike a proper claim of the privilege against self-incrimination under the Fifth Amendment, do not afford a witness the right to resist inquiry in all circumstances. Where First Amendment rights are asserted to bar governmental interrogation resolution of the issue always involves a balancing by the courts of the competing private and public interests at stake in the particular circumstances shown. These principles were recognized in the *Watkins* case, where, in speaking of the First Amendment in relation to congressional inquiries, we said (at p. 198): "It is manifest that despite the adverse effects which follow upon compelled disclosure of private matters, not all such inquiries are barred. . . . The critical element is the existence of, and the weight to be ascribed to, the interest of the Congress in demanding disclosures from an unwilling witness." More recently in *National Association for the Advancement of Colored People* v. *Alabama,* 357 U.S. 449, 463-466, we applied the same principles in judging state action claimed to infringe rights of association assured by the Due Process Clause of the Fourteenth Amendment, and stated that the " 'subordinating interest of the State must be compelling' " in order to overcome the individual constitutional rights at stake. In light of these principles we now consider petitioner's First Amendment claims.

The first question is whether this investigation was related to a valid legislative purpose, for Congress may not constitutionally require an individual to disclose his political relationships or other private affairs except in relation to such a purpose.

That Congress has wide power to legislate in the field of Communist activity in this Country, and to conduct appropriate investigations in aid thereof, is hardly debatable. The existence of such power has never been questioned by this Court, and it is sufficient to say, without particularization, that Congress has enacted or considered in this field a wide range of legislative measures, not a few of which have stemmed from recommendations of the very Committee whose actions have been drawn in question here. In the last analysis this power rests on the right of self-preservation, "the ultimate value of any society," *Dennis* v. *United States,* 341 U.S. 494, 509. Justification for its exercise in turn rests on the long and widely accepted view that the tenets of the Communist Party include the ultimate overthrow of the Government of the United States by force and violence, a view which has been given formal expression by the Congress.

On these premises, this Court in its constitutional adjudications has consistently refused to view the Communist Party as an ordinary political party, and has upheld federal legislation aimed at the Communist problem which in a different context would certainly have raised constitutional issues of the gravest character. On the same premises this Court has upheld under the Fourteenth Amendment state legislation requiring those occupying or seeking public office to disclaim knowing membership in any organization advocating overthrow of the Government by force and violence, which legislation none can avoid seeing was aimed at membership in the Communist Party. Similarly, in other areas, this Court has recognized the close nexus between the Communist Party and violent overthrow of government. See *Dennis* v. *United States, supra; American Communications Assn.* v. *Douds, supra.* To suggest that because the Communist Party may also sponsor peaceable political reforms the constitutional issues before us should now be judged as if that Party were just an ordinary political party from the standpoint of national security, is to ask this Court to blind itself to world affairs which have determined the whole course of our national policy since the close of World War II, affairs to which Judge Learned Hand gave vivid expression in his opinion in *United States* v. *Dennis,* 183 F. 2d 201, 213, and to the vast burdens which these conditions have entailed for the entire Nation. . . .

In our opinion this position rests on a too constricted view of the nature of the investigatory process, and is not supported by a fair assessment of the record before us. An investigation of advocacy of or preparation for overthrow certainly embraces the right to identify a witness as a member of the Communist Party, and to inquire into the various manifestations of the Party's tenets. The strict requirements of a prosecution under the Smith Act are not the measure of the permissible scope of a congressional investigation into "overthrow," for of necessity the investigatory process must proceed step by step. Nor can it fairly be concluded that this investigation was directed at controlling what is being taught at our universities rather than at overthrow. The statement of the Subcommittee Chairman at the opening of the investigation evinces no such intention, and so far as this record reveals nothing thereafter transpired which would justify our holding that the thrust of the investigation later changed. The record discloses considerable testimony concerning the foreign domination and revolutionary purposes and efforts of the Communist Party. That there was also testimony on the abstract philosophical level does not detract from the dominant theme of this investigation—Communist infiltration furthering the alleged ultimate purpose of overthrow. And certainly the conclusion would not be justified that the questioning of petitioner would have exceeded permissible bounds had he not shut off the Subcommittee at the threshold. . . .

Finally, the record is barren of other factors which in themselves might sometimes lead to the conclusion that the individual interests at stake were not subordinate to those of the state. There is no indication in this record that the Subcommittee was attempting to pillory witnesses. Nor did petitioner's appearance as a witness follow from indiscriminate dragnet procedures, lacking in probable cause for belief that he possessed information which might be helpful to the Subcommittee. And the relevancy of the questions put to him by the Subcommittee is not open to doubt.

We conclude that the balance between the individual and the governmental interests here at stake must be struck in favor of the latter, and that therefore the provisions of the First Amendment have not been offended.

MR. JUSTICE BLACK, with whom THE CHIEF JUSTICE [WARREN] and MR. JUSTICE DOUGLAS concur, dissenting. . . .

The First Amendment says in no equivocal language that Congress shall pass no law abridging freedom of speech, press, assembly or petition. The activities of this Committee, authorized by Congress, do precisely that, through exposure, obloquy and public scorn. The Court does not really deny this fact but relies on a combination of three reasons for permitting the infringement: (A) The notion that despite the First Amendment's command Congress can abridge speech and association if this Court decides that the governmental interest in abridging speech is greater than an individual's interest in exercising that freedom, (B) the Government's right to "preserve itself," (C) the fact that the Committee is only after Communists or suspected Communists in this investigation.

(A) I do not agree that laws directly abridging First Amendment freedoms can be justified by a congressional or judicial balancing process. There are, of course, cases suggesting that a law which primarily regulates conduct but which might also indirectly affect speech can be upheld if the effect on speech is minor in relation to the need for control of the conduct. With these cases I agree. Typical of them are *Cantwell* v. *Connecticut,* 310 U.S. 296, and *Schneider* v. *Irvington,* 308 U.S. 147. Both of these involved the right of a city to control its streets. . . .

But we did not in *Schneider,* any more than in *Cantwell,* even remotely suggest that a law directly aimed at curtailing speech and political persuasion could be saved through a balancing process. Neither these cases, nor any others, can be read as allowing legislative bodies to pass laws abridging freedom of speech, press and association merely because of hostility to views peacefully expressed in a place where the speaker had a right to be. Rule XI, on its face and as here applied, since it attempts inquiry into beliefs, not action—ideas and associates, not conduct—does just that.

To apply the Court's balancing test under such circumstances is to read the First Amendment to say "Congress shall pass no law abridging freedom of speech, press, assembly and petition, unless Congress and the Supreme Court reach the joint conclusion that on balance the interest of the Government in stifling these freedoms is greater than the interest of the people in having them exercised." This is closely akin to the notion that neither the First Amendment nor any other provision of the Bill of Rights should be enforced unless the Court believes it is *reasonable* to do so. Not only does this violate the genius of our *written* Constitution, but it runs expressly counter to the injunction to Court and Congress made by Madison when he introduced the Bill of Rights. "If they [the first ten amendments] are incorporated into the Constitution, independent tribunals of justice will consider themselves in a peculiar manner the guardians of those rights; they will be an impenetrable bulwark against *every* assumption of power in the Legislative or Executive; they will be naturally led to resist *every* encroachment upon rights expressly stipulated for in the Constitution by the declaration of rights." [*Annals of Congress,* Vol. 1 (1789), p. 439; italics supplied]. Unless we return to this view of our judicial function, unless we once again accept the notion that the Bill of Rights means what it says and that this Court must enforce that meaning, I am of the opinion that our great charter of liberty will be more honored in the breach than in the observance. . . .

(B) Moreover, I cannot agree with the Court's notion that First Amendment freedoms must be abridged in order to "preserve" our country. That notion rests on the unarticulated premise that this Nation's security hangs upon its power to punish people because of what they think, speak or write about, or because of those with whom they associate for political purposes. The Government, in its brief, virtually admits this position when it speaks of the "communication of unlawful ideas." I challenge this premise, and deny that ideas can be proscribed under our Constitution. I agree that despotic governments cannot exist without stifling the voice of opposition to their oppressive practices. The First Amendment means to me, however, that the only constitutional way our Government can preserve itself is to leave its people the fullest possible freedom to praise, criticize or discuss, as they see fit, all governmental policies and to suggest, if they desire, that even its most fundamental postulates are bad and should be changed; "Therein lies the security of the Republic, the very foundation of constitutional government." On that premise this land was created, and on that premise it has grown to greatness. Our Constitution assumes that the common sense of the people and their attachment to our country will enable them, after free discussion, to withstand ideas that are wrong. To say that our patriotism must be protected against false ideas by means other than these is, I think, to make a baseless charge. Unless we can rely on these qualities —if, in short, we begin to punish speech—we cannot honestly proclaim ourselves to be a free Nation and we have lost what the Founders of this land risked their lives and their sacred honor to defend.

(C) The Court implies, however, that the ordinary rules and requirements of the Constitution do not apply because the Committee is merely after Communists and they do not constitute a political party but only a criminal gang. "[T]he long and widely accepted view," the Court says, is "that the tenets of the Communist Party include the ultimate overthrow of the Government of the United States by force and violence." This justifies the investigation undertaken. By accepting this charge and allowing it to support treatment of the Communist Party and its members which would violate the Constitution if applied to other groups, the Court, in effect, declares that Party outlawed. It has been only a few years since there was a practically unanimous feeling throughout the country and in our courts that this could not be done in our free land. Of course it has always been recognized that members of the Party who, either individually or in combination, commit acts in violation of valid laws can be prosecuted. But the Party as a whole and innocent members of it could not be attainted merely because it had some illegal aims and because some of its members were law-breakers. . . .

[No] matter how often or how quickly we repeat the claim that the Communist Party is not a political party, we cannot outlaw it, as a group, without endangering the liberty of all of us. The reason is not hard to find, for mixed among those aims of communism which are illegal are perfectly normal political and social goals. And muddled with its revolutionary tenets is a drive to achieve power through the ballot, if it can be done. These things necessarily make it a political party whatever other, illegal, aims it may have. Significantly until recently the Communist Party was on the ballot in many States. When that was so, many Communists undoubtedly hoped to accomplish its lawful goals through support of Communist candidates. Even now some such may still remain. To attribute to them, and to those who have left the Party, the taint of the group is to ignore both our traditions that guilt like belief is "personal and not a matter of mere association" and the obvious fact that "men adhering to a political party or other organization notoriously do not subscribe unqualifiedly to all of its platforms or asserted principles." *Schneiderman* v. *United States,* 320 U.S. 118, 136.

The fact is that once we allow any group which has some political aims or ideas to be driven from the ballot and from the battle for men's minds because some of its members are bad and some of its tenets are illegal, no group is safe. Today we deal with Communists or suspected Communists. In 1920, instead, the New York Assembly suspended duly elected legislators on the ground that, being Socialists, they were disloyal to the country's principles. In the 1830's the Masons were hunted as outlaws and subversives, and abolitionists were considered revolutionaries of the most dangerous kind in both North and South. Earlier still, at the time of the universally unlamented alien and sedition laws, Thomas Jefferson's party was attacked and its members were derisively called "Jacobins." Fisher Ames described the party as a "French faction" guilty of "subversion" and "officered, regimented and formed to subordination." Its members, he claimed, intended to "take arms against the laws as soon as they dare." History should teach us then, that in times of high emotional excitement minority parties and groups which advocate extremely unpopular social or governmental innovations will always be typed as criminal gangs and attempts will always be made to drive them out. It was knowledge of this fact, and of its great dangers, that caused the Founders of our land to enact the First Amendment as a guarantee that neither Congress nor the people would do anything to hinder or destroy the capacity of individuals and groups to seek converts and votes for any cause, however radical or unpalatable their principles might seem under the accepted notions of the time. Whatever the States were left free to do, the First Amendment sought to leave Congress devoid of any kind or quality of power to direct any type of national laws against the freedom of individuals to think what they please, advocate whatever policy they choose, and join with others to bring about the social, religious, political and governmental changes which seem best to them. Today's holding, in my judgment, marks another major step in the progressively increasing retreat from the safeguards of the First Amendment. . . .

Ultimately all the questions in this case really boil down to one—whether we as a people will try fearfully and futilely to preserve democracy by adopting totalitarian methods, or whether in accordance with our traditions and our Constitution we will have the confidence and courage to be free.

Konigsberg v. State Bar of California
366 U.S. 36 (1961)

[Konigsberg, having passed the California bar examinations, applied to the Committee of Bar Examiners for a certificate that he was qualified for admission to the bar. In hearings before the Committee, Konigsberg asserted that he did not believe in violent overthrow of government but refused to answer questions as to present or past membership in the Communist Party. The Committee refused to certify him on the ground that he had failed to meet the burden of proving that he was of "good moral character" and did not advocate overthrow of the government by force, violence or other unconstitutional means.]

MR. JUSTICE HARLAN delivered the opinion of the Court. . . .

[We] reject the view that freedom of speech and association, as protected by the First and Fourteenth Amendments, are "absolutes," not only in the undoubted sense that where the constitutional protection exists it must prevail, but also in the sense that the scope of that protection must be gathered solely from a literal reading of the First Amendment.[1] Throughout its history this Court has consistently recognized at least two ways in which constitutionally protected freedom of speech is narrower than an unlimited license to talk. On the one hand, certain forms of speech, or speech in certain contexts, has been considered outside the scope of constitutional protection. On the other hand, general regulatory statutes, not intended to control the content of speech but incidentally limiting its unfettered exercise, have not been regarded as the type of law the First or Fourteenth Amendment forbade Congress or the States to pass, when they have been found justified by subordinating valid governmental interests, a prerequisite to constitutionality which has necessarily involved a weighing of the governmental interest involved. It is in the latter class of cases that this Court has always placed rules compelling disclosure of prior association as an incident of the informed exercise of a valid governmental function. Whenever, in such a context, these constitutional protections are asserted against the exercise of valid governmental powers a reconciliation must be effected, and that perforce requires an appropriate weighing of the respective interests involved. With more particular reference to the present

---

[1] That view, which of course cannot be reconciled with the law relating to libel, slander, misrepresentation, obscenity, perjury, false advertising, solicitation of crime, complicity by encouragement, conspiracy, and the like, is said to be compelled by the fact that the commands of the First Amendment are stated in unqualified terms: "Congress shall make no law . . . abridging the freedom of speech, or of the press; or the right of the people peaceably to assembly . . . ." But as Mr. Justice Holmes once said: "[T]he provisions of the Constitution are not mathematical formulas having their essence in their form; they are organic living institutions transplanted from English soil. Their significance is vital not formal; it is to be gathered not simply by taking the words and a dictionary, but by considering their origin and the line of their growth." *Gompers* v. *United States,* 233 U.S. 604, 610. In this connection also compare the equally unqualified command of the Second Amendment: "the right of the people to keep and bear arms shall not be infringed." And see *United States* v. *Miller,* 307 U.S. 174.

context of a state decision as to character qualifications, it is difficult, indeed, to imagine a view of the constitutional protections of speech and association which would automatically and without consideration of the extent of the deterrence of speech and association and of the importance of the state function, exclude all reference to prior speech or association on such issues as character, purpose, credibility, or intent. On the basis of these considerations we now judge petitioner's contentions in the present case. . . .

[We] regard the State's interest in having lawyers who are devoted to the law in its broadest sense, including not only its substantive provisions, but also its procedures for orderly change, as clearly sufficient to outweigh the minimal effect upon free association occasioned by compulsory disclosure in the circumstances here presented.

MR. JUSTICE BLACK, with whom THE CHIEF JUSTICE [WARREN] and MR. JUSTICE DOUGLAS concur, dissenting. . . .

The recognition that California has subjected "speech and association to the deterrence of subsequent disclosure" is, under the First Amendment, sufficient in itself to render the action of the State unconstitutional unless one subscribes to the doctrine that permits constitutionally protected rights to be "balanced" away whenever a majority of this Court thinks that a State might have interest sufficient to justify abridgment of those freedoms. As I have indicated many time before, I do not subscribe to that doctrine for I believe that the First Amendment's unequivocal command that there shall be no abridgment of the rights of free speech and assembly shows that the men who drafted our Bill of Rights did all the "balancing" that was to be done in this field. The history of the First Amendment is too well known to require repeating here except to say that it certainly cannot be denied that the very object of adopting the First Amendment, as well as the other provisions of the Bill of Rights, was to put the freedoms protected there completely out of the area of any congressional control that may be attempted through the exercise of precisely those powers that are now being used to "balance" the Bill of Rights out of existence. Of course, the First Amendment originally applied only to the Federal Government and did not apply to the States. But what was originally true only of

Congress is now no less true with respect to the governments of the States, unless a majority of this Court wants to overrule a large number of cases in which it has been held unequivocally that the Fourteenth Amendment made the First Amendment's provisions controlling upon the States.

The Court attempts to justify its refusal to apply the plain mandate of the First Amendment in part by reference to the so-called "clear and present danger test" forcefully used by Mr. Justice Holmes and Mr. Justice Brandeis, not to narrow but to broaden the then prevailing interpretation of First Amendment freedoms. I think very little can be found in anything they ever said that would provide support for the "balancing test" presently in use. Indeed, the idea of "balancing" away First Amendment freedoms appears to me to be wholly inconsistent with the view, strongly espoused by Justice Holmes and Brandeis, that the best test of truth is the power of the thought to get itself accepted in the competition of the market. The "clear and present danger test" was urged as consistent with this view in that it protected speech in all cases except those in which danger was so imminent that there was no time for rational discussion. The "balancing test," on the other hand, rests upon the notion that some ideas are so dangerous that Government need not restrict itself to contrary arguments as a means of opposing them even where there is ample time to do so. Thus here, where there is not a semblance of a "clear and present danger," and where there is more than ample time in which to combat by discussion any idea which may be involved, the majority permits the State of California to adopt measures calculated to suppress the advocacy of views about governmental affairs.

I recognize, of course, that the "clear and present danger test," though itself a great advance toward individual liberty over some previous notions of the protections afforded by the First Amendment, does not go as far as my own views as to the protection that should be accorded these freedoms. I agree with Justices Holmes and Brandeis, however, that a primary purpose of the First Amendment was to insure that all ideas would be allowed to enter the "competition of the market." But I fear that the creation of "tests" by which speech is left unprotected under certain circumstances is a standing invitation to abridge it. This is nowhere more clearly indicated than by the sudden transformation of the "clear and present danger test" in *Dennis*

v. *United States*. In that case, this Court accepted Judge Learned Hand's "restatement" of the "clear and present danger test": "In each case [courts] must ask whether the gravity of the 'evil,' discounted by its improbability, justifies such invasion of free speech as is necessary to avoid the danger." After the "clear and present danger test" was diluted and weakened by being recast in terms of this "balancing" formula, there seems to me to be much room to doubt that Justices Holmes and Brandeis would even have recognized their test. And the reliance upon that weakened "test" by the majority here, without even so much as an attempt to find either a "clear" or a "present" danger, is only another persuasive reason for rejecting all such "tests" and enforcing the First Amendment according to its terms.

The Court suggests that a "literal reading of the First Amendment" would be totally unreasonable because it would invalidate many widely accepted laws. I do not know to what extent this is true. I do not believe, for example, that it would invalidate laws resting upon the premise that where speech is an integral part of unlawful conduct that is going on at the time, the speech can be used to illustrate, emphasize and establish the unlawful conduct. On the other hand, it certainly would invalidate all laws that abridge the right of the people to discuss matters of religious or public interest, in the broadest meaning of those terms, for it is clear that a desire to protect this right was the primary purpose of the First Amendment. Some people have argued, with much force, that the freedoms guaranteed by the First Amendment are limited to somewhat broad areas like those. But I believe this Nation's security and tranquility can best be served by giving the First Amendment the same broad construction that all Bill of Rights guarantees deserve. . . .

Whatever may be the wisdom, however, of an approach that would reject exceptions to the plain language of the First Amendment based upon such things as "libel," "obscenity" or "fighting words," such is not the issue in this case. For the majority does not, and surely would not, contend that the kind of speech involved in this case—wholly related as it is to conflicting ideas about governmental affairs and policies—falls outside the protection of the First Amendment, however narrowly that Amendment may be interpreted. So the only issue presently before us is whether speech that must be well within the protection of the Amendment should be given complete protection or whether it is entitled only to such protection as is consistent in the minds of a majority of this Court with whatever interest the Government may be asserting to justify its abridgment. The Court, by stating unequivocally that there are no "absolutes" under the First Amendment, necessarily takes the position that even speech that is admittedly protected by the First Amendment is subject to the "balancing test" and that therefore no kind of speech is to be protected if the Government can assert an interest of sufficient weight to induce this Court to uphold its abridgment. In my judgment, such a sweeping denial of the existence of any inalienable right to speak undermines the very foundation upon which the First Amendment, the Bill of Rights, and, indeed, our entire structure of government rest. The Founders of this Nation attempted to set up a limited government which left certain rights in the people—rights that could not be taken away without amendment of the basic charter of government. The majority's "balancing test" tells us that this is not so. It tells us that no right to think, speak or publish exists in the people that cannot be taken away if the Government finds it sufficiently imperative or expedient to do so. Thus, the "balancing test" turns our "Government of the people, by the people and for the people" into a government over the people.

I cannot believe that this Court would adhere to the "balancing test" to the limit of its logic. Since that "test" denies that any speech, publication or petition has an "absolute" right to protection under the First Amendment, strict adherence to it would necessarily mean that there would be only a conditional right, not a complete right, for any American to express his views to his neighbors—or for his neighbors to hear those views. In other words, not even a candidate for public office, high or low, would have an "absolute" right to speak in behalf of his candidacy, no newspaper would have an "absolute" right to print its opinion on public governmental affairs, and the American people would have no "absolute" right to hear such discussions. All of these rights would be dependent upon the accuracy of the scales upon which this Court weighs the respective interests of the Government and the people. It therefore seems to me that the Court's "absolute" statement that there are no "absolutes" under the First Amendment must be an exaggeration of its own views.

These examples also serve to illustrate the difference between the sort of "balancing" that the majority has been doing and the sort of "balancing" that was intended when that concept was first accepted as a method for insuring the complete protection of First Amendment freedoms even against purely incidental or inadvertent consequences. The term came into use chiefly as a result of cases in which the power of municipalities to keep their streets open for normal traffic was attacked by groups wishing to use those streets for religious or political purposes. When those cases came before this Court, we did not treat the issue posed by them as one primarily involving First Amendment rights. Recognizing instead that public streets are avenues of travel which must be kept open for that purpose, we upheld various city ordinances designed to prevent unnecessary noises and congestions that disrupt the normal and necessary flow of traffic. In doing so, however, we recognized that the enforcement of even these ordinances, which attempted no regulation at all of the content of speech and which were neither openly nor surreptitiously aimed at speech, could bring about an "incidental" abridgment of speech. So we went on to point out that even ordinances directed at and regulating only conduct might be invalidated if, after "weighing" the reasons for regulating the particular conduct, we found them insufficient to justify diminishing "the exercise of rights so vital to the maintenance of democratic institutions" as those of the First Amendment.

But those cases never intimated that we would uphold as constitutional an ordinance which purported to rest upon the power of a city to regulate traffic but which was aimed at speech or attempted to regulate the content of speech. None of them held, nor could they constitutionally have held, that a person rightfully walking or riding along the streets and talking in a normal way could have his views controlled, licensed or penalized in any way by the city—for that would be a direct abridgment of speech itself. Those cases have only begun to take on that meaning by being relied upon, again and again as they are here, to justify the application of the "balancing test" to governmental action that is aimed at speech and depends for its application upon the content of speech. Thus, those cases have been used to support decisions upholding such obviously antispeech actions on the part of government as those involved in *American Communications Assn.* v. *Douds* and *Dennis* v. *United*

States. And the use being made of those cases here must be considered as falling squarely within that class.

The Court seeks to bring this case under the authority of the street-regulation cases and to defend its use of the "balancing test" on the ground that California is attempting only to exercise its permissible power to regulate its Bar and that any effect its action may have upon speech is purely "incidental." But I cannot agree that the questions asked Konigsberg with regard to his suspected membership in the Communist Party had nothing more than an "incidental" effect upon his freedom of speech and association. Why does the Committee of Bar Examiners ask a bar applicant whether he is or has been a member of the Communist Party? The avowed purpose of such questioning is to permit the Committee to deny applicants admission to the Bar if they "advocate" forcible overthrow of the Government. Indeed, that is precisely the ground upon which the majority is here upholding the Committee's right to ask Konigsberg these questions. I realize that there has been considerable talk, even in the opinions of this Court, to the effect that "advocacy" is not "speech." But with the highest respect for those who believe that there is such a distinction, I cannot agree with it. For this reason, I think the conclusion is inescapable that this case presents the question of the constitutionality of action by the State of California designed to control the content of speech. As such, it is a "direct," and not an "incidental" abridgment of speech. Indeed, if the characterization "incidental" were appropriate here, it would be difficult to imagine what would constitute a "direct" abridgment of speech. The use of the "balancing test" under these circumstances thus permits California directly to abridge speech in explicit contradiction to the plain mandate of the First Amendment.

Scales v. United States
367 U.S. 203 (1961)

[Scales was convicted of being a member of an organization (the Communist Party) which advocated overthrow of the Government by force or violence, in violation of the Smith Act.]

MR. JUSTICE HARLAN delivered the opinion of the Court. . . .

Little remains to be said concerning the claim that the statute infringes First Amendment freedoms. It was settled in *Dennis* that the advocacy with which we are here concerned is not constitutionally protected speech, and it was further established that a combination to promote such advocacy, albeit under the aegis of what purports to be a political party, is not such association as is protected by the First Amendment. We can discern no reason why membership, when it constitutes a purposeful form of complicity in a group engaging in this same forbidden advocacy, should receive any greater degree of protection from the guarantees of that Amendment.

If it is said that the mere existence of such an enactment tends to inhibit the exercise of constitutionally protected rights, in that it engenders an unhealthy fear that one may find himself unwittingly embroiled in criminal liability, the answer surely is that the statute provides that a defendant must be proven to have knowledge of the proscribed advocacy before he may be convicted. It is, of course, true that quasi-political parties or other groups that may embrace both legal and illegal aims differ from a technical conspiracy, which is defined by its criminal purpose, so that *all* knowing association with the conspiracy is a proper subject for criminal proscription as far as First Amendment liberties are concerned. If there were a similar blanket prohibition of association with a group having both legal and illegal aims, there would indeed be a real danger that legitimate political expression or association would be impaired, but the membership clause, as here construed, does not cut deeper into the freedom of association than is necessary to deal with "the substantive evils that Congress has a right to prevent." *Schenck* v. *United States,* 249 U.S. 47, 52. The clause does not make criminal all association with an organization which has been shown to engage in illegal advocacy. There must be clear proof that a defendant "specifically intend[s] to accomplish [the aims of the organization] by resort to violence." *Noto* v. *United States* [367 U.S. 290, 299]. Thus the member for whom the organization is a vehicle for the advancement of legitimate aims and policies does not fall within the ban of the statute: he lacks the requisite specific intent "to bring about the overthrow of the government as speedily as circumstances would permit." Such a person may be foolish, deluded, or perhaps merely optimistic, but he is not by this statute made a criminal.

We conclude that petitioner's constitutional challenge must be overruled.

MR. JUSTICE DOUGLAS, dissenting.

When we allow petitioner to be sentenced to prison for six years for being a "member" of the Communist Party, we make a sharp break with traditional concepts of First Amendment rights and make serious Mark Twain's lighthearted comment that "It is by the goodness of God that in our country we have those three unspeakably precious things: freedom of speech, freedom of conscience, and the prudence never to practice either of them." . . .

The case is not saved by showing that petitioner was an active member. None of the activity constitutes a crime. The record contains evidence that Scales was the Chairman of the North and South Carolina Districts of the Communist Party. He recruited new members into the Party, and promoted the advanced education of selected young Party members in the theory of communism to be undertaken at secret schools. He was a director of one such school. He explained the principles of the Party to an FBI agent who posed as someone interested in joining the Party, and furnished him literature, including articles which criticized in vivid language the American "aggression" in Korea and described American "atrocities" committed on Korean citizens. He once remarked that the Party was setting up underground means of communication, and in 1951 he himself "went underground." At the school of which Scales was director, students were told (by someone else) that one of the Party's weaknesses was in failing to place people in key industrial positions. One witness told of a meeting arranged by Scales at which the staff of the school urged him to remain in his position in an industrial plant rather than return to college. In Scales' presence, students at the school were once shown how to kill a person with a pencil, a device which, it was said, might come in handy on a picket line. Other evidence showed Scales to have made several statements or distributed literature containing implicating passages. Among them were comments to the effect that the Party line was that the Negroes in the South and the working classes should be used to foment a violent revolution; that a Communist government could not be voted into power in this country because the Government controlled communication media, newspapers, the military, and the educational systems, and that force was the only way to achieve the revolution; that if a depression were to come the Communist America would be closer at hand than predicted by William Z. Foster; that the revolution would come within a generation; that it would be easier in the United States than in Russia to effectuate the revolution because of assistance and advice from Russian Communists. Petitioner at different times said or distributed literature which said that the goals of communism could only be achieved by violent revolution that would have to start internally with the working classes.

Not one single illegal act is charged to petitioner. That is why the essence of the crime covered by the indictment is merely belief—belief in the proletarian revolution, belief in Communist creed. . . .

Of course, government can move against those who take up arms against it. Of course, the constituted authority has the right of self-preservation. But we deal in this prosecution of Scales only with the legality of ideas and beliefs, not with overt acts. The Court speaks of the prevention of "dangerous behavior" by punishing those "who work to bring about that behavior." That formula returns man to the dark days when government determined what behavior was "dangerous" and then policed the dissidents for tell-tale signs of advocacy. . . .

In recent years we have been departing, I think, from the theory of government expressed in the First Amendment. We have too often been "balancing" the right of speech and association against other values in society to see if we, the judges, feel that a particular need is more important than those guaranteed by the Bill of Rights.

[Justice Black also dissented on First Amendment grounds, and Chief Justice Warren and Justice Brennan dissented on grounds of statutory construction.]

Communist Party v. Subversive Activities Control Board
367 U.S. 1 (1961)

[Acting under the Internal Security Act (the McCarran Act), the Subversive Activities Control Board found the Communist Party to be a "Communist-action organization" and ordered it to register with the Attorney General. Registration required a listing of the names and addresses of all officers and members, an accounting of all moneys received and expended, a listing of all printing presses and printing devices owned or controlled by the organization or its members, and the giving of other information.]

MR. JUSTICE FRANKFURTER delivered the opinion of the Court. . . .

It is argued that if Congress may constitutionally enact legislation requiring the Communist Party to register, to list its members, to file financial statements, and to identify its printing presses, Congress may impose similar requirements upon any group which pursues unpopular political objectives or which expresses an unpopular political ideology. Nothing which we decide here remotely carries such an implication. The Subversive Activities Control Act applies only to *foreign-dominated* organizations which work primarily to advance the objectives of a world movement controlled by the government of a *foreign* country. See §§ 3 (3), 2 (4). It applies only to organizations directed, dominated, or controlled by a *particular* foreign country, the leader of a movement which, Congress has found, is "in its origins, its development, and its present practice, . . . a world-wide revolutionary movement whose purpose it is, by treachery, deceit, infiltration into other groups . . . , espionage, sabotage, terrorism, and any other means deemed necessary, to establish a Communist totalitarian dictatorship in the countries throughout the world through the medium of a world-wide Communist organization." § 2 (1). This is the full purported reach of the statute, and its fullest effect. There is no attempt here to impose stifling obligations upon the proponents of a particular political creed as such, or even to check the importation of particular political ideas from abroad for propagation here. The Act compels the registration of organized groups which have been made the instruments of a long-continued, systematic, disciplined activity directed by a foreign power and purposing to overthrow existing government in this country. Organizations are subject to it only when shown, after administrative hearing subject to judicial review, to be dominated by the foreign power or its organs and to operate primarily to advance its purposes. That a portion of the evidence upon which such a showing is made may consist in the expression of political views by the organization does not alter the character of the Act or of the incidents to which it attaches. Such expressions are relevant only as probative of foreign control and of the purposes to which the organization's actions are directed. The Board, in the present proceeding, so understood the Act. The registration requirement of § 7, on its face and as here applied, does not violate the First Amendment.

MR. JUSTICE DOUGLAS, dissenting [on grounds that the statute violated the privilege against self-incrimination, but agreeing with the majority that there was no violation of the First Amendment] . . . .

From those precedents I would hopefully deduce two principles. First, no individual may be required to register before he makes a speech, for the First Amendment rights are not subject to any prior restraint. Second, a group engaged in lawful conduct may not be required to file with the Government a list of its members, no matter how unpopular it may be. For the disclosure of membership lists may cause harassment of members and seriously hamper their exercise of First Amendment rights. The more unpopular the group, the greater the likelihood of harassment. In logic then it might seem that the Communist Party, being at the low tide of popularity, might make out a better case of harassment than almost any other group on the contemporary scene.

We have, however, as I have said, findings that the Communist Party of the United States is "a disciplined organization" operating in this Nation "under Soviet Union control" with the aim of installing "a Soviet style dictatorship" here. These findings establish that more than debate, discourse, argumentation, propaganda, and other aspects of free speech and association are involved. An additional element enters, *viz.,* espionage, business activities, or the formation of cells for subversion, as well as the use of speech, press, and association by a foreign power to produce on this continent a Soviet satellite.

Picketing is free speech *plus,* and hence can be restricted in all instances and banned in some. Registration of those who disseminate propaganda of foreign origin has been thought to fall in the same category as barring speech in places that will create traffic conditions or provoke breaches of the peace. Though the activities themselves are under the First Amendment, the manner of their exercise or their collateral aspects fall without it.

Like reasons underlie our decisions which sustain laws that require various groups to register before engaging in specified activities. Thus lobbyists who receive fees for attempting to influence the passage or defeat of legislation in Congress may be required to register. Criminal sanctions for failure to report and to disclose all contributions made to political parties are permitted. Publishers of newspapers desiring reduced postal rates have long been required to file with the Postmaster General and with the local post office certain data concerning ownership and circulation; and those disclosure requirements have been sustained. In short, the exercise of First Amendment rights often involves business or commercial implications which Congress in its wisdom may desire to be disclosed, just as it did in strictly financial matters under the Public Utility Holding Company Act of 1935.

If lobbyists can be required to register, if political parties can be required to make disclosure of the sources of their funds, if the owners of newspapers and periodicals must disclose their affiliates, so may a group operating under the control of a foreign power.

The Bill of Rights was designed to give fullest play to the exchange and dissemination of ideas that touch the politics, culture, and other aspects of our life. When an organization is used by a foreign power to make advances here, questions of security are raised beyond the ken of disputation and debate between the people resident here. Espionage, business activities, formation of cells for subversion, as well as the exercise of First

Amendments rights, are then used to pry open our society and make intrusion of a foreign power easy. These machinations of a foreign power add additional elements to free speech just as marching up and down adds something to picketing that goes beyond free speech.

These are the reasons why, in my view, the bare requirement that the Communist Party register and disclose the names of its officers and directors is in line with the most exacting adjudications touching First Amendment activities.

[Chief Justice Warren and Justice Brennan also dissented, but not on First Amendment grounds.]

MR. JUSTICE BLACK, dissenting. . . .

I think also that this outlawry of the Communist Party and imprisonment of its members violate the First Amendment. The question under that Amendment is whether Congress has power to outlaw an association, group or party either on the ground that it advocates a policy of violent overthrow of the existing Government at some time in the distant future or on the ground that it is ideologically subservient to some foreign country. In my judgment, neither of these factors justifies an invasion of rights protected by the First Amendment. Talk about the desirability of revolution has a long and honorable history, not only in other parts of the world, but also in our own country. This kind of talk, like any other, can be used at the wrong time and for the wrong purpose. But, under our system of Government, the remedy for this danger must be the same remedy that is applied to the danger that comes from any other erroneous talk—education and contrary argument. If that remedy is not sufficient, the only meaning of free speech must be that the revolutionary ideas will be allowed to prevail.[1]

This conclusion is not affected by the fact that those advocating a policy of revolution are in sympathy with a foreign government. If there is one thing certain about the First Amendment it is that this Amendment was designed to guarantee the freest interchange of ideas about all public matters and that, of

---

[1] *Cf. Gitlow* v. *New York,* 268 U.S. 652, 673: "If in the long run the beliefs expressed in proletarian dictatorship are destined to be accepted by the dominant forces of the community, the only meaning of free speech is that they should be given their chance and have their way." (Holmes, J., dissenting.)

course, means the interchange of *all* ideas, however such ideas may be viewed in other countries and whatever change in the existing structure of government it may be hoped that these ideas will bring about. Now, when this country is trying to spread the high ideals of democracy all over the world—ideals that are revolutionary in many countries—seems to be a particularly inappropriate time to stifle First Amendment freedoms in this country. The same arguments that are used to justify the outlawry of Communist ideas here could be used to justify an outlawry of the ideas of democracy in other countries. . . .

The truth is that this statutory outlawry of the Communist Party is not at all novel when considered in the perspective of history. Quite the contrary, it represents nothing more than the adoption by this country, in part at least, of one of the two conflicting views that have emerged from a long-standing and widespread dispute among political philosophers as to what kind of Government will best serve the welfare of the people. That view is that Governments should have almost unlimited powers. The other view is that governmental power should be very strictly limited. Both the Smith Act and the Subversive Activities Control Act are based upon the view that officials of the Government should have power to suppress and crush by force critics and criticisms of governmental officials and their policies. The contrary view, which Congress necessarily rejected in passing these laws, is that current public officials should never be granted power to use governmental force to keep people from hearing, speaking or publishing such criticisms of Government or from assembling together to petition their Government to make changes in governmental policies, however basic the majority may deem these policies to be.

It is my belief that our Constitution with its Bill of Rights was expressly intended to make our Government one of strictly limited powers. The Founders were intimately familiar with the restrictions upon liberty which inevitably flow from a Government of unlimited powers. By and large, they had found this experience a painful one. Many of them were descended from families that had left England and had come to this country in order to escape laws that could send them to jail or penalize them in various ways for criticizing laws and policies which they thought bore too heavily and unfairly upon them. Others had personally felt the brunt of such repressive measures. Only after they won the Revolutionary War did these people have an opportunity to set up a Government to their liking. To that end they finally settled upon the Constitution, which very clearly adopted the policy of limiting the powers of the Federal Government. Even then the people of this country were not completely satisfied. They demanded more precise and unequivocal limitations upon the powers of Government and obtained the Bill of Rights, the central provisions of which were the First Amendment guarantees of complete religious and political freedom. . . .

I am ready to admit that strong arguments can be made for saying that Governments in general should have power to suppress the freedoms of speech, press, petition and assembly. There arguments are particularly strong in countries where the existing Government does not represent the will of the people because history shows that people have a way of not being willing to bear oppressive grievances without protest. Such protests, when bottomed upon facts, lead almost inevitably to an irresistible popular demand for either a redress of those grievances or a change in the Government. It is plain that there are Governments in the world today that desperately need to suppress such protests for they probably could not survive a week or even a day if they were deprived of the power to use their informers to intimidate, their jails to imprison and their firing squads to shoot their critics. In countries of that kind, repressive measures like the Smith Act and the Subversive Activities Control Act are absolutely necessary to protect the ruling tyrants from the spread of information about their misdeeds. But in a democracy like ours, such laws are not only unnecessary but also constitute a baseless insult to the patriotism of our people.

I believe with the Framers of the First Amendment that the internal security of a nation like ours does not and cannot be made to depend upon the use of force by Government to make all the beliefs and opinions of the people fit into a common mold on any single subject. Such enforced conformity of thought would tend only to deprive our people of the bold spirit of adventure and progress which has brought this Nation to its present greatness. The creation of public opinion by groups, organizations, societies, clubs, and parties has been and is a necessary part of our democratic society. Such groups, like the Sons of Liberty and the American Corresponding Societies, played a large part in creating sentiment in this country that led the people of the Colonies to want a nation of their own. The Father of the Constitution—James Madison—said, in speaking of the Sedition Act aimed at crushing the Jeffersonian Party, that had that law been in effect during the period before the Revolution, the United States might well have continued to be "miserable colonies, groaning under a foreign yoke."

In my judgment, this country's internal security can better be served by depending upon the affection of the people than by attempting to instill them with fear and dread of the power of Government. The Communist Party has never been more than a small group in this country. And its numbers had been dwindling even before the Government began its campaign to destroy the Party by force of law. This was because a vast majority of the American people were against the Party's policies and over-whelmingly rejected its candidates year after year. That is the true American way of securing this Nation against dangerous ideas. Of course that is not the way to protect the Nation against *actions* of violence and treason. The Founders drew a distinction in our Constitution which we would be wise to follow. They gave the Government the fullest power to prosecute overt actions in violation of valid laws but withheld any power to punish people for nothing more than advocacy of their views.

I am compelled to say in closing that I fear that all the argu-ments and urgings the Communists and their sympathizers can use in trying to convert Americans to an ideology wholly foreign to our habits and our instincts are far less dangerous to the security of this Nation than laws which embark us upon a policy of repression by the outlawry of minority parties because they advocate radical changes in the structure of Government. This widespread program for punishing ideas on the ground that they might impair the internal security of the Nation not only sadly fails to protect that security but also diverts our energies and thoughts from the many far more more important problems that face us as a Nation in this troubled world.

I would reverse this case and leave the Communists free to advocate their beliefs in proletarian dictatorship publicly and openly among the people of this country with full confidence that the people will remain loyal to any democratic Government truly dedicated to freedom and justice—the kind of Government which some of us still think of as being "the last best hope of earth."

New York Times Co. v. Sullivan
376 U.S. 254 (1964)

[In 1960 the *New York Times* published a full-page advertisement, signed by the "Committee to Defend Martin Luther King and the Struggle for Freedom in the South" and endorsed by several score individuals, recounting certain events in the civil rights struggle in Montgomery, Alabama, and appealing for funds. One of the City Commissioners of Montgomery brought a libel suit against four Negro signers of the advertisement and the *New York Times*. A jury in Montgomery awarded him damages of $500,000.]

MR. JUSTICE BRENNAN delivered the opinion of the Court. . . . Under Alabama law as applied in this case, a publication is "libelous per se" if the words "tend to injure a person . . . in his reputation" or to "bring [him] into public contempt"; the trial court stated that the standard was met if the words are such as to "injure him in his public office, or impute misconduct to him in his office, or want of official integrity, or want of fidelity to a public trust. . . ." The jury must find that the words were published "of and concerning" the plaintiff, but where the plaintiff is a public official his place in the governmental hierarchy is sufficient evidence to support a finding that his reputation has been affected by statements that reflect upon the agency of which he is in charge. Once "libel per se" has been established, the defendant has no defense as to stated facts unless he can persuade the jury that they were true in all their particulars. His privilege of "fair comment" for expressions of opinion depends on the truth of the facts upon which the comment is based. Unless he can discharge the burden of proving truth, general damages are presumed, and may be awarded without proof of pecuniary injury. A showing of actual malice is apparently a prerequisite to recovery of punitive damages, and the defendant may in any event forestall a punitive award by a retraction meeting the statutory requirements. Good motives and belief in truth do not negate an inference of malice, but are relevant only in mitigation of punitive damages if the jury chooses to accord them weight.

The question before us is whether this rule of liability, as applied to an action brought by a public official against critics of his official conduct, abridges the freedom of speech and of the press that is guaranteed by the First and Fourteenth Amendments.

Respondent relies heavily, as did the Alabama courts, on statements of this Court to the effect that the Constitution does not protect libelous publications. Those statements do not foreclose our inquiry here. None of the cases sustained the use of libel laws to impose sanctions upon expression critical of the official conduct of public officials. . . .

[We] consider this case against the background of a profound national commitment to the principle that debate on public issues should be uninhibited, robust, and wide-open, and that it may well include vehement, caustic, and sometimes unpleasantly sharp attacks on government and public officials. The present advertisement, as an expression of grievance and protest on one of the major public issues of our time, would seem clearly to qualify for the constitutional protection. The question is whether it forfeits that protection by the falsity of some of its factual statements and by its alleged defamation of respondent.

Authoritative interpretations of the First Amendment guarantees have consistently refused to recognize an exception for any test of truth—whether administered by judges, juries, or administrative officials—and especially one that puts the burden of proving truth on the speaker. The constitutional protection does not turn upon "the truth, popularity, or social utility of the ideas and beliefs which are offered." *N.A.A.C.P.* v. *Button,* 371 U.S. 415, 445. As Madison said, "Some degree of abuse is inseparable from the proper use of every thing; and in no instance is this more true than in that of the press." 4 Elliot's Debates on the Federal Constitution (1876), p. 571. In *Cantwell* v. *Connecticut,* 310 U.S. 296, 310, the Court declared:

> "In the realm of religious faith, and in that of political belief, sharp differences arise. In both fields the tenets of one man may seem the rankest error to his neighbor. To persuade others to his own point of view, the pleader, as we know, at times, resorts to exaggeration, to vilification of men who have been, or are, prominent in church or state,

and even to false statement. But the people of this nation have ordained in the light of history, that, in spite of the probability of excesses and abuses, these liberties are, in the long view, essential to enlightened opinion and right conduct on the part of the citizens of a democracy."

That erroneous statement is inevitable in free debate, and that it must be protected if the freedoms of expression are to have the "breathing space" that they "need . . . to survive," *N.A.A.C.P.* v. *Button,* 371 U.S. 415, 433, was also recognized [in other cases]. . . .

Injury to official reputation affords no more warrant for repressing speech that would otherwise be free than does factual error. Where judicial officers are involved, this Court has held that concern for the dignity and reputation of the courts does not justify the punishment as criminal contempt of criticism of the judge or his decision. This is true even though the utterance contains "half-truths" and "misinformation." Such repression can be justified, if at all, only by a clear and present danger of the obstruction of justice. If judges are to be treated as "men of fortitude, able to thrive in a hardy climate," *Craig* v. *Harney,* 331 U.S., at 376, surely the same must be true of other government officials, such as elected city commissioners. Criticism of their official conduct does not lose its constitutional protection merely because it is effective criticism and hence diminishes their official reputations.

If neither factual error nor defamatory content suffices to remove the constitutional shield from criticism of official conduct, the combination of the two elements is no less inadequate. This is the lesson to be drawn from the great controversy over the Sedition Act of 1798, 1 Stat. 596, which first crystallized a national awareness of the central meaning of the First Amendment. . . .

A rule compelling the critic of official conduct to guarantee the truth of all his factual assertions—and to do so on pain of libel judgments virtually unlimited in amount—leads to . . . "self-censorship." Allowance of the defense of truth, with the burden of proving it on the defendant, does not mean that only false speech will be deterred. Even courts accepting this defense as an adequate safeguard have recognized the difficulties of adducing legal proofs that the alleged libel was true in all its factual particulars. Under such a rule, would-be critics of official conduct may be deterred from voicing their criticism, even though it is believed to be true and even though it is in fact true, because of doubt whether it can be proved in court or fear of the expense of having to do so. They tend to make only statements which "steer far wider of the unlawful zone." *Speiser* v. *Randall,* 357 U.S., at 526. The rule thus dampens the vigor and limits the variety of public debate. It is inconsistent with the First and Fourteenth Amendments.

The constitutional guarantees require, we think, a federal rule that prohibits a public official from recovering damages for a defamatory falsehood relating to his official conduct unless he proves that the statement was made with "actual malice"—that is, with knowledge that it was false or with reckless disregard of whether it was false or not.

MR. JUSTICE BLACK, with whom MR. JUSTICE DOUGLAS joins, concurring.

I concur in reversing this half-million-dollar judgment against the New York Times Company and the four individual defendants. In reversing the Court holds that "the Constitution delimits a State's power to award damages for libel in actions brought by public officials against critics of their official conduct." I base my vote to reverse on the belief that the First and Fourteenth Amendments not merely "delimit" a State's power to award damages to "public officials against critics of their official conduct" but completely prohibit a State from exercising such a power. The Court goes on to hold that a State can subject such critics to damages if "actual malice" can be proved against them. "Malice," even as defined by the Court, is an elusive, abstract concept, hard to prove and hard to disprove. The requirement that malice be proved provides at best an evanescent protection for the right critically to discuss public affairs and certainly does not measure up to the sturdy safeguard embodied in the First Amendment. Unlike the Court, therefore, I vote to reverse exclusively on the ground that the Times and the individual defendants had an absolute, unconditional constitutional right to publish in the Times advertisement their criticisms of the Montgomery agencies and officials. . . .

In my opinion the Federal Constitution has dealt with this

deadly danger to the press in the only way possible without leaving the free press open to destruction—by granting the press an absolute immunity for criticism of the way public officials do their public duty. Stopgap measures like those the Court adopts are in my judgment not enough. This record certainly does not indicate that any different verdict would have been rendered here whatever the Court had charged the jury about "malice," "truth," "good motives," "justifiable ends," or any other legal formulas which in theory would protect the press. Nor does the record indicate that any of these legalistic words would have caused the courts below to set aside or to reduce the half-million-dollar verdict in any amount. . . .

To punish the exercise of this right to discuss public affairs or to penalize it through libel judgments is to abridge or shut off discussion of the very kind most needed. This Nation, I suspect, can live in peace without libel suits based on public discussions of public affairs and public officials. But I doubt that a country can live in freedom where its people can be made to suffer physically or financially for criticizing their government, its actions, or its officials. "For a representative democracy ceases to exist the moment that the public functionaries are by any means absolved from their responsibility to their constituents; and this happens whenever the constituent can be restrained in any manner from speaking, writing, or publishing his opinions upon any public measure, or upon the conduct of those who may advise or execute it." [1] An unconditional right to say what one pleases about public affairs is what I consider to be the minimum guarantee of the First Amendment.

I regret that the Court has stopped short of this holding indispensable to preserve our free press from destruction.

MR. JUSTICE GOLDBERG, with whom MR. JUSTICE DOUGLAS joins, concurring in the result. . . .

In my view, the First and Fourteenth Amendments to the Constitution afford to the citizen and to the press an absolute, unconditional privilege to criticize official conduct despite the harm which may flow from excesses and abuses. The prized American right "to speak one's mind," cf. *Bridges* v. *California*,

[1] 1 Tucker, *Blackstone's Commentaries* (1803), 297 (editor's appendix).

314 U.S. 252, 270, about public officials and affairs needs "breathing space to survive," *N.A.A.C.P.* v. *Button,* 371 U.S. 415, 433. The right should not depend upon a probing by the jury of the motivation of the citizen or press. The theory of our Constitution is that every citizen may speak his mind and every newspaper express its view on matters of public concern and may not be barred from speaking or publishing because those in control of government think that what is said or written is unwise, unfair, false, or malicious. In a democratic society, one who assumes to act for the citizens in an executive, legislative, or judicial capacity must expect that his official acts will be commented upon and criticized. Such criticism cannot, in my opinion, be muzzled or deterred by the courts at the instance of public officials under the label of libel.

It has been recognized that "prosecutions for libel on government have [no] place in the American system of jurisprudence." *City of Chicago* v. *Tribune Co.,* 307 Ill. 595, 601, 139 N. E. 86, 88. I fully agree. Government, however, is not an abstraction; it is made up of individuals—of governors responsible to the governed. In a democratic society where men are free by ballots to remove those in power, any statement critical of governmental action is necessarily "of and concerning" the governors and any statement critical of the governors' official conduct is necessarily "of and concerning" the government. If the rule that libel on government has no place in our Constitution is to have real meaning, then libel on the official conduct of the governors likewise can have no place in our Constitution. . . .

This is not to say that the Constitution protects defamatory statements directed against the private conduct of a public official or private citizen. Freedom of press and of speech insures that government will respond to the will of the people and that changes may be obtained by peaceful means. Purely private defamation has little to do with the political ends of a self-governing society. The imposition of liability for private defamation does not abridge the freedom of public speech or any other freedom protected by the First Amendment. This, of course, cannot be said "where public officials are concerned or where public matters are involved. . . . [O]ne main function of the First Amendment is to ensure ample opportunity for the people to determine and resolve public issues. Where public matters are involved, the doubts should be resolved in favor of freedom of expression rather than against it." Douglas, The Right of the People (1958), p. 41. . . .

If liability can attach to political criticism because it damages the reputation of a public official as a public official, then no critical citizen can safely utter anything but faint praise about the government or its officials. The vigorous criticism by press and citizen of the conduct of the government of the day by the officials of the day will soon yield to silence if officials in control of government agencies, instead of answering criticisms, can resort to friendly juries to forestall criticism of their official conduct.

The conclusion that the Constitution affords the citizen and the press an absolute privilege for criticism of official conduct does not leave the public official without defenses against unsubstantiated opinions or deliberate misstatements. "Under our system of government, counterargument and education are the weapons available to expose these matters, not abridgment . . . of free speech. . . ." *Wood* v. *Georgia,* 370 U.S. 375, 389. The public official certainly has equal if not greater access than most private citizens to media of communication. In any event, despite the possibility that some excesses and abuses may go unremedied, we must recognize that "the people of this nation have ordained in the light of history, that, in spite of the probability of excesses and abuses, [certain] liberties are, in the long view, essential to enlightened opinion and right conduct on the part of the citizens of a democracy." *Cantwell* v. *Connecticut,* 310 U.S. 296, 310. As Mr. Justice Brandeis correctly observed, "sunlight is the most powerful of all disinfectants."

Baggett v. Bullitt
377 U.S. 360 (1964)

[A group of faculty, staff and students at the University of Washington brought suit to test the constitutionality of two oaths required of all State employees.]

MR. JUSTICE WHITE delivered the opinion of the Court. . . .
The oath required by the 1955 statute suffers from similar infirmities [as in the earlier *Cramp* case]. A teacher must swear

that he is not a subversive person: that he is not one who commits an act or who advises, teaches, abets or advocates by any means another person to commit or aid in the commission of any act intended to overthrow or alter, or to assist the overthrow or alteration, of the constitutional form of government by revolution, force or violence. A subversive organization is defined as one which engages in or assists activities intended to alter or overthrow the Government by force or violence or which has as a purpose the commission of such acts. The Communist Party is declared in the statute to be a subversive organization, that is, it is presumed that the Party does and will engage in activities intended to overthrow the Government. Persons required to swear they understand this oath may quite reasonably conclude that any person who aids the Communist Party or teaches or advises known members of the Party is a subversive person because such teaching or advice may now or at some future date aid the activities of the Party. Teaching and advising are clearly acts, and one cannot confidently assert that his counsel, aid, influence or support which adds to the resources, rights and knowledge of the Communist Party or its members does not aid the Party in its activities, activities which the statute tells us are all in furtherance of the stated purpose of overthrowing the Government by revolution, force, or violence. The questions put by the Court in *Cramp* may with equal force be asked here. Does the statute reach endorsement or support for Communist candidates for office? Does it reach a lawyer who represents the Communist Party or its members or a journalist who defends constitutional rights of the Communist Party or its members or anyone who supports any cause which is likewise supported by Communists or the Communist Party? The susceptibility of the statutory language to require forswearing of an undefined variety of "guiltless knowing behavior" is what the Court condemned in *Cramp*. This statute, like the one at issue in *Cramp,* is unconstitutionally vague.

The Washington statute suffers from additional difficulties on vagueness grounds. A person is subversive not only if he himself commits the specified acts but if he abets or advises another in aiding a third person to commit an act which will assist yet a fourth person in the overthrow or alteration of constitutional government. The Washington Supreme Court has said that knowledge is to be read into every provision and we accept this construction. But what is it that the Washington professor must "know"? Must he know that his aid or teaching will be used by another and that the person aided has the requisite guilty intent or is it sufficient that he know that his aid or teaching would or might be useful to others in the commission of acts intended to overthrow the Government? Is it subversive activity, for example, to attend and participate in international conventions of mathematicians and exchange views with scholars from Communist countries? What about the editor of a scholarly journal who analyzes and criticizes the manuscripts of Communist scholars submitted for publication? Is selecting outstanding scholars from Communist countries as visiting professors and advising, teaching, or consulting with them at the University of Washington a subversive activity if such scholars are known to be Communists, or regardless of their affiliations, regularly teach students who are members of the Communist Party, which by statutory definition is subversive and dedicated to the overthrow of the Government?

The Washington oath goes beyond overthrow or alteration by force or violence. It extends to alteration by "revolution" which, unless wholly redundant and its ordinary meaning distorted, includes any rapid or fundamental change. Would, therefore, any organization or any person supporting, advocating or teaching peaceful but far-reaching constitutional amendments be engaged in subversive activity? Could one support the repeal of the Twenty-second Amendment or participation by this country in a world government?

We also conclude that the 1931 oath offends due process because of vagueness. The oath exacts a promise that the affiant will, by precept and example, promote respect for the flag and the institutions of the United States and the State of Washington. The range of activities which are or might be deemed inconsistent with the required promise is very wide indeed. The teacher who refused to salute the flag or advocated refusal because of religious beliefs might well be accused of breaching his promise. Even criticism of the design or color scheme of the state flag or unfavorable comparison of it with that of a sister State or foreign country could be deemed disrespectful and therefore violative of the oath. And what are "institutions" for the purposes of this oath? Is it every "practice, law, custom, etc., which is a material and persistent element in the life or culture of an organized social group" or every "established society or corporation," every "establishment, esp[ecially] one of a public character"? [1] The oath may prevent a professor from criticizing his state judicial system or the Supreme Court or the institution of judicial review. Or it might be deemed to proscribe advocating the abolition, for example, of the Civil Rights Commission, the House Committee on Un-American Activities, or foreign aid.

It is likewise difficult to ascertain what might be done without transgressing the promise to "promote . . . undivided allegiance to the government of the United States." It would not be unreasonable for the serious-minded oathtaker to conclude that he should dispense with lectures voicing far-reaching criticism of any old or new policy followed by the Government of the United States. He could find it questionable under this language to ally himself with any interest group dedicated to opposing any current public policy or law of the Federal Government, for if he did, he might well be accused of placing loyalty to the group above allegiance to the United States.

Indulging every presumption of a narrow construction of the provisions of the 1931 oath, consistent, however, with a proper respect for the English language, we cannot say that this oath provides an ascertainable standard of conduct or that it does not require more than a State may command under the guarantees of the First and Fourteenth Amendments.

As in *Cramp* v. *Board of Public Instruction,* "[t]he vice of unconstitutional vagueness is further aggravated where, as here, the statute in question operates to inhibit the exercise of individual freedoms affirmatively protected by the Constitution." 368 U.S. 278, 287. We are dealing with indefinite statutes whose terms, even narrowly construed, abut upon sensitive areas of basic First Amendment freedoms. The uncertain meanings of the oaths require the oath-taker—teachers and public servants—to "steer far wider of the unlawful zone," *Speiser* v. *Randall,* 357 U.S. 513, 526, than if the boundaries of the forbidden areas were clearly marked. Those with a conscientious regard for what they solemnly swear or affirm, sensitive to the perils posed by the oath's indefinite language, avoid the risk of loss of employment, and perhaps profession, only by restricting their conduct to that

[1] Webster's New Int. Dictionary (2d ed.), at 1288.

which is unquestionably safe. Free speech may not be so inhibited.

MR. JUSTICE CLARK, whom MR. JUSTICE HARLAN joins, dissenting. . . .

First, *Cramp* is not apposite. The majority has failed to recognize that the statute in *Cramp* required an oath of much broader scope than the one in the instant case: *Cramp* involved an oath "that I have not and will not lend my aid, support, advice, counsel or influence to the Communist Party. . . ." That oath was replete with defects not present in the Washington oath. . . . These factors which caused the Court to find the *Cramp* oath unconstitutionally vague are clearly not present in the Washington oath. Washington's oath proscribes only the commission of an *act* of overthrow or alteration of the constitutional form of government by revolution, force or violence; or advising, teaching, abetting or advocating by any means another person to commit or aid in the commission of any act intended to overthrow or alter or to assist the overthrow or alteration of the constitutional form of government by revolution, force or violence. The defects noted by the Court when it passed on the *Cramp* oath have been cured in the Washington statute. . . .

It is, of course, absurd to say that, under the words of the Washington Act, a professor risks violation when he teaches German, English, history or any other subject included in the curriculum for a college degree, to a class in which a Communist Party member might sit. To so interpret the language of the Act is to extract more sunbeams from cucumbers than did Gulliver's mad scientist. And to conjure up such ridiculous questions, the answers to which we all know or should know are in the negative, is to build up a whimsical and farcical straw man which is not only grim but Grimm.

Cox v. Louisiana
379 U.S. 536, 539 (1965)

[Cox, a minister, led a group of about 2000 students on a march from the state capitol building in Baton Rouge to the court house in a demonstration against segregation and the arrest of fellow students the day before. Cox was convicted of violating two statutes, one prohibiting the obstruction of public passages, and the other punishing picketing near a court house.]

MR. JUSTICE GOLDBERG delivered the opinion of the Court. . . .

In upholding appellant's conviction under this statute, the Louisiana Supreme Court thus construed the statute so as to apply to public assemblies which do not have as their specific purpose the obstruction of traffic. There is no doubt from the record in this case that this far sidewalk was obstructed, and thus, as so construed, appellant violated the statute.

Appellant, however, contends that as so construed and applied in this case, the statute is an unconstitutional infringement on freedom of speech and assembly. This contention on the facts here presented raises an issue with which this Court has dealt in many decisions, that is, the right of a State or municipality to regulate the use of city streets and other facilities to assure the safety and convenience of the people in their use and the concomitant right of the people of free speech and assembly.

From these decisions certain clear principles emerge. The rights of free speech and assembly, while fundamental in our democratic society, still do not mean that everyone with opinions or beliefs to express may address a group at any public place and at any time. The constitutional guarantee of liberty implies the existence of an organized society maintaining public order, without which liberty itself would be lost in the excesses of anarchy. The control of travel on the streets is a clear example of governmental responsibility to insure this necessary order. A restriction in that relation, designed to promote the public convenience in the interest of all, and not susceptible to abuses of discriminatory application, cannot be disregarded by the attempted exercise of some civil right which, in other circumstances, would be entitled to protection. One would not be justified in ignoring the familiar red light because this was thought to be a means of social protest. Nor could one, contrary to traffic regulations, insist upon a street meeting in the middle of Times Square at the rush hour as a form of freedom of speech or assembly. Governmental authorities have the duty and responsibility to keep their streets open and available for movement. A group of demonstrators could not insist upon the right to cordon off a street, or entrance to a public or private building, and allow no one to pass who did not agree to listen to their exhortations.

We emphatically reject the notion urged by appellant that the First and Fourteenth Amendments afford the same kind of freedom to those who would communicate ideas by conduct such as patrolling, marching, and picketing on streets and highways, as these amendments afford to those who communicate ideas by pure speech. We reaffirm the statement of the Court in *Giboney* v. *Empire Storage & Ice Co.* [336 U.S. at 502], that "it has never been deemed an abridgment of freedom of speech or press to make a course of conduct illegal merely because the conduct was in part initiated, evidenced, or carried out by means of language, either spoken, written, or printed."

We have no occasion in this case to consider the constitutionality of the uniform, consistent, and nondiscriminatory application of a statute forbidding all access to streets and other public facilities for parades and meetings. Although the statute here involved on its face precludes all street assemblies and parades, it has not been so applied and enforced by the Baton Rouge authorities. City officials who testified for the State clearly indicated that certain meetings and parades are permitted in Baton Rouge, even though they have the effect of obstructing traffic, provided prior approval is obtained. . . .

The situation is thus the same as if the statute itself expressly provided that there could only be peaceful parades or demonstrations in the unbridled discretion of the local officials. The pervasive restraint on freedom of discussion by the practice of the authorities under the statute is not any less effective than a statute expressly permitting such selective enforcement. A long line of cases in this Court makes it clear that a State or municipality cannot "require all who wish to disseminate ideas to present them first to police authorities for their consideration and approval, with a discretion in the police to say some ideas may, while others may not, be . . . disseminate[d]. . . ." *Schneider* v. *State* [308 U.S. at 164].

This Court has recognized that the lodging of such broad discretion in a public official allows him to determine which expressions of view will be permitted and which will not. This thus sanctions a device for the suppression of the communication of ideas and permits the official to act as a censor. Also inherent in such a system allowing parades or meetings only with the prior permission of an official is the obvious danger to the right of a person or group not to be denied equal protection of the laws. It is clearly unconstitutional to enable a public official to determine which expressions of view will be permitted and which will not or to engage in invidious discrimination among persons or groups either by use of a statute providing a system of broad discretionary licensing power or, as in this case, the equivalent of such a system by selective enforcement of an extremely broad prohibitory statute.

It is, of course, undisputed that appropriate, limited discretion, under properly drawn statutes or ordinances, concerning the time, place, duration, or manner of use of the streets for public assemblies may be vested in administrative officials, provided that such limited discretion is "exercised with 'uniformity of method of treatment upon the facts of each application, free from improper or inappropriate considerations and from unfair discrimination' . . . [and with] a 'systematic, consistent and just order of treatment, with reference to the convenience of public use of the highways. . . .' " *Cox* v. *New Hampshire* [312 U.S. at 576].

But here it is clear that the practice in Baton Rouge allowing unfettered discretion in local officials in the regulation of the use of the streets for peaceful parades and meetings is an unwarranted abridgment of appellant's freedom of speech and assembly secured to him by the First Amendment, as applied to the States by the Fourteenth Amendment. It follows, therefore, that appellant's conviction for violating the statute as so applied and enforced must be reversed.

[Mr. Justice Goldberg then takes up the picketing statute.]

This statute, unlike the two previously considered, is a precise, narrowly drawn regulatory statute which proscribes certain specific behavior. It prohibits a particular type of conduct, namely, picketing and parading, in a few specified locations, in or near courthouses.

There can be no question that a State has a legitimate interest in protecting its judicial system from the pressures which picketing near a courthouse might create. . . .

Nor does such a statute infringe upon the constitutionally protected rights of free speech and free assembly. The conduct which is the subject of this statute—picketing and parading—is subject to regulation even though intertwined with expression and association. The examples are many of the application by this Court of the principle that certain forms of conduct mixed with speech may be regulated or prohibited. The most classic of these was pointed out long ago by Mr. Justice Holmes: "The most stringent protection of free speech would not protect a man in falsely shouting fire in a theatre and causing a panic." *Schenck* v. *United States,* 249 U.S. 47, 52. A man may be punished for encouraging the commission of a crime, *Fox* v. *Washington,* 236 U.S. 273, or for uttering "fighting words," *Chaplinsky* v. *New Hampshire,* 315 U.S. 568. This principle has been applied to picketing and parading in labor disputes. . . .

We are not concerned here with such a pure form of expression as newspaper comment or a telegram by a citizen to a public official. We deal in this case not with free speech alone, but with expression mixed with particular conduct. . . .

We hold that this statute on its face is a valid law dealing with conduct subject to regulation so as to vindicate important interests of society and that the fact that free speech is intermingled with such conduct does not bring with it constitutional protection.

[Mr. Justice Goldberg then went on to reverse the conviction on the ground that the police had given permission for the picketing.]

MR. JUSTICE BLACK, concurring [on the obstruction statute] and dissenting [on the picketing statute].

. . . I have no doubt about the general power of Louisiana to bar all picketing on its streets and highways. Standing, patrolling, or marching back and forth on streets is conduct, not speech, and as conduct can be regulated or prohibited. But by specifically permitting picketing for the publication of labor union views, Louisiana is attempting to pick and choose among the views it is willing to have discussed on its streets. It thus is trying to prescribe by law what matters of public interest people whom it allows to assemble on its streets may and may not discuss. This seems to me to be censorship in a most odious form, unconstitutional under the First and Fourteenth Amendments. And to deny this appellant and his group use of the streets because of their views against racial discrimination, while allowing other groups to use the streets to voice opinions on other subjects, also amounts, I think, to an invidious discrimination forbidden by the Equal Protection Clause of the Fourteenth Amendment. Moreover, as the Court points out, city officials despite this statute apparently have permitted favored groups other than labor unions to block the streets with their gatherings. For these reasons I concur in reversing the conviction based on this law. . . .

This statute [the picketing statute], like the federal one which it closely resembles, was enacted to protect courts and court officials from the intimidation and dangers that inhere in huge gatherings at courthouse doors and jail doors to protest arrests and to influence court officials in performing their duties. The very purpose of a court system is to adjudicate controversies, both criminal and civil, in the calmness and solemnity of the courtroom according to legal procedures. Justice cannot be rightly administered, nor are the lives and safety of prisoners secure, where throngs of people clamor against the processes of justice right outside the courthouse or jailhouse doors. The streets are not now and never have been the proper place to administer justice. Use of the streets for such purposes has always proved disastrous to individual liberty in the long run, whatever fleeting benefits may have appeared to have been achieved. And minority groups, I venture to suggest, are the ones who always have suffered and always will suffer most when street multitudes are allowed to substitute their pressures for the less glamorous but more dependable and temperate processes of the law. Experience demonstrates that it is not a far step from what to many seems the earnest, honest, patriotic, kind-spirited multitude of today, to the fanatical, threatening, lawless mob of tomorrow. And the crowds that press in the streets for noble goals today can be supplanted tomorrow by street mobs pressuring the courts for precisely opposite ends.

Minority groups in particular need always to bear in mind that the Constitution, while it requires States to treat all citizens equally and protect them in the exercise of rights granted by the Federal Constitution and laws, does not take away the State's power, indeed its duty, to keep order and to do justice according to law. Those who encourage minority groups to believe that the

United States Constitution and federal laws give them a right to patrol and picket in the streets whenever they choose, in order to advance what they think to be a just and noble end, do no service to those minority groups, their cause, or their country. I am confident from this record that this appellant violated the Louisiana statute because of a mistaken belief that he and his followers had a constitutional right to do so, because of what they believed were just grievances. But the history of the past 25 years if it shows nothing else shows that his group's constitutional and statutory rights have to be protected by the courts, which must be kept free from intimidation and coercive pressures of any kind. Government under law as ordained by our Constitution is too precious, too sacred, to be jeopardized by subjecting the courts to intimidatory practices that have been fatal to individual liberty and minority rights wherever and whenever such practices have been allowed to poison the streams of justice. I would be wholly unwilling to join in moving this country a single step in that direction.

[Justice Clark also dissented on the picketing statute, and Justices Harlan and White dissented on both statutes.]

Freedman v. Maryland
380 U.S. 51 (1965)

[The case involved the validity of Maryland's motion picture censorship statute.]

MR. JUSTICE BRENNAN delivered the opinion of the Court. . . .
In *Times Film Corp.* v. *City of Chicago,* 365 U.S. 43, we considered and upheld a requirement of submission of motion pictures in advance of exhibition. The [Maryland] Court of Appeals held, on the authority of that decision, that "the Maryland censorship law must be held to be not void on its face as violative of the freedoms protected against State action by the First and Fourteenth Amendments." 233 Md., at 505, 197 A. 2d, at 235. This reliance on *Times Film* was misplaced. The only question tendered for decision in that case was "whether a prior restraint was necessarily unconstitutional *under all circumstances.*" *Bantam Books, Inc.* v. *Sullivan,* 372 U.S. 58, 70, n. 10 (emphasis in original). The exhibitor's argument that the re-

quirement of submission without more amounted to a constitutionally prohibited prior restraint was interpreted by the Court in *Times Film* as a contention that the "constitutional protection includes complete and absolute freedom to exhibit, at least once, any and every kind of motion picture . . . even if this film contains the basest type of pornography, or incitement to riot, or forceful overthrow of orderly government. . . ." 365 U.S., at 46, 47. The Court held that on this "narrow" question, *id.,* at 46, the argument stated the principle against prior restraints too broadly; citing a number of our decisions, the Court quoted the statement from *Near* v. *Minnesota,* 283 U.S. 697, 716, that "the protection even as to previous restraint is not absolutely unlimited." In rejecting the proffered proposition in *Times Film* the Court emphasized, however, that "[i]t is that question alone which we decide," 365 U.S., at 46, and it would therefore be inaccurate to say that *Times Film* upheld the specific features of the Chicago censorship ordinance.

Unlike the petitioner in *Times Film,* appellant does not argue that § 2 is unconstitutional simply because it may prevent even the first showing of a film whose exhibition may legitimately be the subject of an obscenity prosecution. He presents a question quite distinct from that passed on in *Times Film;* accepting the rule in *Times Film,* he argues that § 2 constitutes an invalid prior restraint because, in the context of the remainder of the statute, it presents a danger of unduly suppressing protected expression. He focuses particularly on the procedure for an initial decision by the censorship board, which, without any judicial participation, effectively bars exhibition of any disapproved film, unless and until the exhibitor undertakes a time-consuming appeal to the Maryland courts and succeeds in having the Board's decision reversed.

Although the Court has said that motion pictures are not "necessarily subject to the precise rules governing any other particular method of expression," *Joseph Burstyn, Inc.* v. *Wilson,* 343 U.S. 495, 503, it is as true here as of other forms of expression that "[a]ny system of prior restraints of expression comes to this Court bearing a heavy presumption against its constitutional validity." *Bantam Books, Inc.* v. *Sullivan, supra,* at 70. ". . . [U]nder the Fourteenth Amendment, a State is not free to adopt whatever procedures it pleases for dealing with obscenity

. . . without regard to the possible consequences for constitutionally protected speech." *Marcus* v. *Search Warrant,* 367 U.S. 717, 731. The administration of a censorship system for motion pictures presents peculiar dangers to constitutionally protected speech. Unlike a prosecution for obscenity, a censorship proceeding puts the initial burden on the exhibitor or distributor. Because the censor's business is to censor, there inheres the danger that he may well be less responsive than a court—part of an independent branch of government—to the constitutionally protected interests in free expression. And if it is made unduly onerous, by reason of delay or otherwise, to seek judicial review, the censor's determination may in practice be final.

Applying the settled rule of our cases, we hold that a noncriminal process which requires the prior submission of a film to a censor avoids constitutional infirmity only if it takes place under procedural safeguards designed to obviate the dangers of a censorship system. First, the burden of proving that the film is unprotected expression must rest on the censor. As we said in *Speiser* v. *Randall,* 357 U.S. 513, 526, "Where the transcendent value of speech is involved, due process certainly requires . . . that the State bear the burden of persuasion to show that the appellants engaged in criminal speech." Second, while the State may require advance submission of all films, in order to proceed effectively to bar all showings of unprotected films, the requirement cannot be administered in a manner which would lend an effect of finality to the censor's determination whether a film constitutes protected expression. The teaching of our cases is that, because only a judicial determination in an adversary proceeding ensures the necessary sensitivity to freedom of expression, only a procedure requiring a judicial determination suffices to impose a valid final restraint. To this end, the exhibitor must be assured, by statute or authoritative judicial construction, that the censor will, within a specified brief period, either issue a license or go to court to restrain showing the film. Any restraint imposed in advance of a final judicial determination on the merits must similarly be limited to preservation of the status quo for the shortest fixed period compatible with sound judicial resolution. Moreover, we are well aware that, even after expiration of a temporary restraint, an administrative refusal to license, signifying the censor's view that the film is unprotected, may have a discouraging effect on the exhibitor. Therefore, the procedure must also assure a prompt final judicial decision, to minimize the deterrent effect of an interim and possibly erroneous denial of a license.

Without these safeguards, it may prove too burdensome to seek review of the censor's determination. Particularly in the case of motion pictures, it may take very little to deter exhibition in a given locality. The exhibitor's stake in any one picture may be insufficient to warrant a protracted and onerous course of litigation. The distributor, on the other hand, may be equally unwilling to accept the burdens and delays of litigation in a particular area when, without such difficulties, he can freely exhibit his film in most of the rest of the country; for we are told that only four States and a handful of municipalities have active censorship laws.

It is readily apparent that the Maryland procedural scheme does not satisfy these criteria. First, once the censor disapproves the film, the exhibitor must assume the burden of instituting judicial proceedings and of persuading the courts that the film is protected expression. Second, once the Board has acted against a film, exhibition is prohibited pending judicial review, however protracted. Under the statute, appellant could have been convicted if he had shown the film after unsuccessfully seeking a license, even though no court had ever ruled on the obscenity of the film. Third, it is abundantly clear that the Maryland statute provides no assurance of prompt judicial determination. We hold, therefore, that appellant's conviction must be reversed. The Maryland scheme fails to provide adequate safeguards against undue inhibition of protected expression, and this renders the § 2 requirement of prior submission of films to the Board an invalid previous restraint.

Mr. Justice Douglas, whom Mr. Justice Black joins, concurring.

On several occasions I have indicated my view that movies are entitled to the same degree and kind of protection under the First Amendment as other forms of expression. For the reasons there stated, I do not believe any form of censorship—no matter how speedy or prolonged it may be—is permissible. As I see it, a pictorial presentation occupies as preferred a position as any other form of expression. If censors are banned from the publishing business, from the pulpit, from the public platform—as they are—they should be banned from the theatre. . . . I would put an end to all forms and types of censorship and give full literal meaning to the command of the First Amendment.

A Book Named "John Cleland's Memoirs of a Woman of Pleasure" v. Attorney General of Massachusetts
Mishkin v. New York
Ginzburg v. United States
383 U.S. 413, 502, 463 (1966)

[In the first case the book, commonly known as *Fanny Hill,* had been adjudged obscene under Massachusetts law, in a proceeding directed against the book itself, not against any person. In the second case Mishkin had been sentenced to three years' imprisonment under the New York obscenity law for publishing fifty paperbacks found to be "sadistic" or "masochistic." In the third case Ginzburg had been sentenced to five years for violation of the federal law against sending obscene materials through the mails. The materials consisted of the magazine *Eros,* a biweekly newsletter entitled *Liaison,* and a short book, *The Housewife's Handbook on Selective Promiscuity.*]

MR. JUSTICE BRENNAN [speaking for himself, Chief Justice Warren and Justice Fortas in the *Fanny Hill* case, and for a majority of the Court in the *Mishkin* and *Ginzburg* cases]. . . .

We defined obscenity [in *Roth v. United States,* 354 U.S. 476] in the following terms: "Whether to the average persons, applying contemporary community standards, the dominant theme of the material taken as a whole appeals to prurient interest." 354 U.S., at 489. Under this definition, as elaborated in subsequent cases, three elements must coalesce: it must be established that (a) the dominant theme of the material taken as a whole appeals to a prurient interest in sex; (b) the material is patently offensive because it affronts contemporary community standards relating to the description or representation of sexual matters; and (c) the material is utterly without redeeming social value.

The Supreme Judicial Court [of Massachusetts] purported to apply the *Roth* definition of obscenity and held all three criteria satisfied. We need not consider the claim that the court erred in concluding that *Memoirs* satisfied the prurient appeal and patent offensiveness criteria; for reversal is required because the court misinterpreted the social value criterion. . . .

The Supreme Judicial Court erred in holding that a book need not be "unqualifiedly worthless before it can be deemed obscene." A book can not be proscribed unless it is found to be *utterly* without redeeming social value. This is so even though the book is found to possess the requisite prurient appeal and to be patently offensive. Each of the three federal constitutional criteria is to be applied independently; the social value of the book can neither be weighed against nor canceled by its prurient appeal or patent offensiveness. Hence, even on the view of the court below that *Memoirs* possessed only a modicum of social value, its judgment must be reversed as being founded on an erroneous interpretation of a federal constitutional standard.

It does not necessarily follow from this reversal that a determination that *Memoirs* is obscene in the constitutional sense would be improper under all circumstances. On the premise, which we have no occasion to assess, that *Memoirs* has the requisite prurient appeal and is patently offensive, but has only a minimum of social value, the circumstances of production, sale, and publicity are relevant in determining whether or not the publication and distribution of the book is constitutionally protected. Evidence that the book was commercially exploited for the sake of prurient appeal, to the exclusion of all other values, might justify the conclusion that the book was utterly without redeeming social importance. It is not that in such a setting the social value test is relaxed so as to dispense with the requirement that a book be *utterly* devoid of social value, but rather that, as we elaborate in *Ginzburg* v. *United States,* where the purveyor's sole emphasis is on the sexually provocative aspects of his publications, a court could accept his evaluation at its face value. In this proceeding, however, the courts were asked to judge the obscenity of *Memoirs* in the abstract, and the declaration of obscenity was neither aided nor limited by a specific set of circumstances of production, sale, and publicity. All possible uses of the book must therefore be considered, and the mere risk that the book might be exploited by panderers because it so pervasively treats sexual matters cannot alter the fact—given the view of the Massachusetts court attributing to *Memoirs* a modicum of literary and historical value—that the book will have redeeming social importance in the hands of those who publish or distribute it on the basis of that value.

[In the *Mishkin* case Justice Brennan said:]

The First Amendment prohibits criminal prosecution of the publication and dissemination of allegedly obscene books that do not satisfy the *Roth* definition of "obscenity." States are free to adopt other definitions of "obscenity" only to the extent that those adopted stay within the bounds set by the constitutional criteria of the *Roth* definition, which restrict the regulation of the publication and sale of books to that traditionally and universally tolerated in our society. . . .

[A]ppellant's sole contention regarding the nature of the material is that some of the books involved in this prosecution, those depicting various deviant sexual practices, such as flagellation, fetishism, and lesbianism, do not satisfy the prurient-appeal requirement because they do not appeal to a prurient interest of the "average person" in sex, that "instead of stimulating the erotic, they disgust and sicken." We reject this argument as being founded on an unrealistic interpretation of the prurient-appeal requirement.

Where the material is designed for and primarily disseminated to a clearly defined deviant sexual group, rather than the public at large, the prurient-appeal requirement of the *Roth* test is satisfied if the dominant theme of the material taken as a whole appeals to the prurient interest in sex of the members of that group. The reference to the "average" or "normal" person in *Roth,* 354 U.S., at 489-490, does not foreclose this holding. In regard to the prurient-appeal requirement, the concept of the "average" or "normal" person was employed in *Roth* to serve the essentially negative purpose of expressing our rejection of that aspect of the *Hicklin* test, *Regina* v. *Hicklin,* [1868] L. R. 3 Q. B. 360, that made the impact on the most susceptible person determinative. We adjust the prurient-appeal requirement to social realities by permitting the appeal of this type of material to be assessed in terms of the sexual interests of its intended and probable recipient group; and since our holding requires that the recipient group be defined with more specificity than in terms of sexually immature persons, it also avoids the inadequacy of the most-susceptible-person facet of the *Hicklin* test.

[In the *Ginzburg* case Justice Brennan said:]

In the cases in which this Court has decided obscenity questions since *Roth,* it has regarded the materials as sufficient in themselves for the determination of the question. In the present case, however, the prosecution charged the offense in the context of the circumstances of production, sale, and publicity and assumed that, standing alone, the publications themselves might not be obscene. We agree that the question of obscenity may include consideration of the setting in which the publications were presented as an aid to determining the question of obscenity, and assume without deciding that the prosecution could not have succeeded otherwise. As in *Mishkin* v. *New York,* and as did the courts below, 224 F. Supp., at 134, 338 F. 2d, at 14-15, we view the publications against a background of commercial exploitation of erotica solely for the sake of their prurient appeal. The record in that regard amply supports the decision of the trial judge that the mailing of all three publications offended the statute. . . .

This evidence, in our view, was relevant in determining the ultimate question of "obscenity" and, in the context of this record, serves to resolve all ambiguity and doubt. The deliberate representation of petitioners' publications as erotically arousing, for example, stimulated the reader to accept them as prurient; he looks for titillation, not for saving intellectual content. Similarly, such representation would tend to force public confrontation with the potentially offensive aspects of the work; the brazenness of such an appeal heightens the offensiveness of the publications to those who are offended by such material. And the circumstances of presentation and dissemination of material are equally relevant to determining whether social importance claimed for material in the courtroom was, in the circumstances, pretense or reality—whether it was the basis upon which it was traded in the marketplace or a spurious claim for litigation purposes. Where the purveyor's sole emphasis is on the sexually provocative aspects of his publications, that fact may be decisive in the determination of obscenity. Certainly in a prosecution which, as here, does not necessarily imply suppression of the materials involved, the fact that they originate or are used as a subject of pandering is relevant to the application of the *Roth* test. . . .

It is important to stress that this analysis simply elaborates the test by which the obscenity vel non of the material must be judged. Where an exploitation of interests in titillation by pornography is shown with respect to material lending itself to such exploitation through pervasive treatment or description of sexual matters, such evidence may support the determination that the material is obscene even though in other contexts the material would escape such condemnation.

MR. JUSTICE CLARK [dissenting in Fanny Hill; he concurred in *Mishkin* and *Ginzburg*]. . . .

It is with regret that I write this dissenting opinion. However, the public should know of the continuous flow of pornographic material reaching this Court and the increasing problem States have in controlling it. *Memoirs of a Woman of Pleasure,* the book involved here, is typical. I have "stomached" past cases for almost 10 years without much outcry. Though I am not known to be a purist—or a shrinking violet—this book is too much even for me. It is important that the Court has refused to declare it obscene and thus gives it further circulation. . . .

In my view evidence of social importance is relevant to the determination of the ultimate question of obscenity. But social importance does not constitute a separate and distinct constitutional test. Such evidence must be considered together with evidence that the material in question appeals to prurient interest and is patently offensive. . . .

The question of antisocial effect thus becomes relevent to the more limited question of social value. Brother BRENNAN indicates that the social importance criteria encompasses only such things as the artistic, literary, and historical qualities of the material. But the phrasing of the "utterly without redeeming social value" test suggests that other evidence must be considered. To say that social value may "redeem" implies that courts must balance alleged esthetic merit against the harmful consequences that may flow from pornography. Whatever the scope of the social value criterion—which need not be defined with precision here—it at least anticipates that the trier of fact weigh evidence of the material's influence in causing deviant or criminal conduct, particularly sex crimes, as well as its effect upon the mental, moral, and physical health of the average person.

MR. JUSTICE WHITE [dissenting in *Fanny Hill;* he concurred in *Mishkin* and *Ginzburg*]. . . .

In my view, "social importance" is not an independent test of obscenity but is relevant only to determining the predominant prurient interest of the material, a determination which the court or the jury will make based on the material itself and all the evidence in the case, expert or otherwise.

Application of the *Roth* test, as I understand it, necessarily involves the exercise of judgment by legislatures, courts and juries. But this does not mean that there are no limits to what may be done in the name of *Roth. Roth* does not mean that a legislature is free to ban books simply because they deal with sex or because they appeal to the prurient interest. Nor does it mean that if books like *Fanny Hill* are unprotected, their non-prurient appeal is necessarily lost to the world. Literary style, history, teachings about sex, character description (even of a prostitute) or moral lessons need not come wrapped in such packages. The fact that they do impeaches their claims to immunity from legislative censure.

MR. JUSTICE HARLAN [dissenting in *Fanny Hill;* he concurred in *Mishkin* but dissented in *Ginzburg,* a federal prosecution]. . . .

My premise is that in the area of obscenity the Constitution does not bind the States and the Federal Government in precisely the same fashion. This approach is plainly consistent with the language of the First and Fourteenth Amendments and, in my opinion, more responsive to the proper functioning of a federal system of government in this area. . . .

Federal suppression of allegedly obscene matter should, in my view, be constitutionally limited to that often described as "hard-core pornography." To be sure, that rubric is not a self-executing standard, but it does describe something that most judges and others will "know . . . when [they] see it" (STEWART, J., in *Jacobellis* v. *Ohio,* 378 U.S. 184, 197) and that leaves the smallest room for disagreement between those of varying tastes. To me it is plain, for instance, that "Fanny Hill" does not fall within this class and could not be barred from the federal mails. If further articulation is meaningful, I would characterize as "hard-core" that prurient material that is patently offensive or whose indecency is self-demonstrating and I would describe it substantially as does MR. JUSTICE STEWART'S opinion in *Ginzburg*. The Federal Government may be conceded a limited interest in excluding from the mails such gross pornography, almost universally condemned in this country. But I believe the dangers of national censorship and the existence of primary responsibility at the state level amply justify drawing the line at this point.

State obscenity laws present problems of quite a different order. The varying conditions across the country, the range of views on the need and reasons for curbing obscenity, and the traditions of local self-government in matters of public welfare all favor a far more flexible attitude in defining the bounds for the States. From my standpoint, the Fourteenth Amendment requires of a State only that it apply criteria rationally related to the accepted notion of obscenity and that it reach results not wholly out of step with current American standards. As to criteria, it should be adequate if the court or jury considers such elements as offensiveness, pruriency, social value, and the like. The latitude which I believe the States deserve cautions against any federally imposed formula listing the exclusive ingredients of obscenity and fixing their proportions. This approach concededly lacks precision, but imprecision is characteristic of mediating constitutional standards; voluntariness of a confession, clear and present danger, and probable cause are only the most ready illustrations. In time and with more litigated examples, predictability increases, but there is no shortcut to satisfactory solutions in this field, and there is no advantage in supposing otherwise.

MR. JUSTICE STEWART [dissenting in *Ginzburg;* he also dissented in *Mishkin* and concurred in *Fanny Hill*]. . . .

Censorship reflects a society's lack of confidence in itself. It is a hallmark of an authoritarian regime. Long ago those who wrote our First Amendment charted a different course. They believed a society can be truly strong only when it is truly free. In the realm of expression they put their faith, for better or for worse, in the enlightened choice of the people, free from the interference of a policeman's intrusive thumb or a judge's heavy hand. So it is that the Constitution protects coarse expression as well as refined, and vulgarity no less than elegance. A book worthless to me may convey something of value to my neighbor. In the free society to which our Constitution has committed us, it is for each to choose for himself.

Because such is the mandate of our Constitution, there is room for only the most restricted view of this Court's decision in *Roth* v. *United States,* 354 U.S. 476. In that case the Court held that "obscenity is not within the area of constitutionally protected speech or press." *Id.,* at 485. The Court there characterized obscenity as that which is "utterly without redeeming social importance," *id.,* at 484, "deals with sex in a manner appealing to prurient interest," *id.,* at 487, and "goes substantially beyond customary limits of candor in description or representation of such matters." *Id.,* at 487, n. 20. In *Manual Enterprises* v. *Day,* 370 U.S. 478, I joined MR. JUSTICE HARLAN's opinion adding "patent indecency" as a further essential element of that which is not constitutionally protected.

There does exist a distinct and easily identifiable class of material in which all of these elements coalesce. It is that, and that alone, which I think government may constitutionally suppress, whether by criminal or civil sanctions. I have referred to such material before as hard-core pornography, without trying further to define it. *Jacobellis* v. *Ohio,* 378 U.S. 184, at 197 (concurring opinion). In order to prevent any possible misunderstanding, I have set out in the margin a description, borrowed from the Solicitor General's brief, of the kind of thing to which I have reference.[1] See also Lockhart and McClure, Cen-

---

[1] "... Such materials include photographs, both still and motion picture, with no pretense of artistic value, graphically depicting acts of sexual intercourse, including various acts of sodomy and sadism, and sometimes involving several participants in scenes of orgy-like character. They also include strips of drawings in comic-book format grossly depicting similar activities in an exaggerated fashion. There are, in addition, pamphlets and booklets, sometimes with photographic illustrations, verbally describing such activities in a bizarre manner with no attempt whatsoever to afford portrayals of character or situation and with no pretense to literary value. All of this material . . . cannot conceivably be characterized as embodying communication of ideas or artistic values inviolate under the First Amendment. . . ."

sorship of Obscenity: The Developing Constitutional Standards, 45 Minn. L. Rev. 5, 63-64.

Although arguments can be made to the contrary, I accept the proposition that the general dissemination of matter of this description may be suppressed under valid laws. That has long been the almost universal judgment of our society. But material of this sort is wholly different from the publications mailed by the petitioner in the present case, and different not in degree but in kind.

The Court today appears to concede that the materials Ginzburg mailed were themselves protected by the First Amendment. But, the Court says, Ginzburg can still be sentenced to five years in prison for mailing them. Why? Because, says the Court, he was guilty of "commercial exploitation," of "pandering," and of "titillation." But Ginzburg was not charged with "commercial exploitation"; he was not charged with "pandering"; he was not charged with "titillation." Therefore, to affirm his conviction now on any of those grounds, even if otherwise valid, is to deny him due process of law. But those grounds are *not,* of course, otherwise valid. Neither the statute under which Ginzburg was convicted nor any other federal statute I know of makes "commercial exploitation" or "pandering" or "titillation" a criminal offense. And any criminal law that sought to do so in the terms so elusively defined by the Court would, of course, be unconstitutionally vague and therefore void.

Mr. Justice Douglas [dissenting in *Mishkin* and *Ginzburg;* he concurred in *Fanny Hill*]. . . .

The use of sex symbols to sell literature, today condemned by the Court, engulfs another exception on First Amendment rights that is as unwarranted as the judge-made exception concerning obscenity. This new exception condemns an advertising technique as old as history. The advertisements of our best magazines are chock-full of thighs, ankles, calves, bosoms, eyes, and hair, to draw the potential buyers' attention to lotions, tires, food, liquor, clothing, autos, and even insurance policies. The sexy advertisement neither adds to nor detracts from the quality of the merchandise being offered for sale. And I do not see how it adds to or detracts one whit from the legality of the book being distributed. A book should stand on its own, irrespective of the reasons why it was written or the wiles used in selling it. I cannot imagine any promotional effort that would make chapters 7 and 8 of the Song of Solomon any the less or any more worthy of First Amendment protection than does its unostentatious inclusion in the average edition of the Bible. . . .

Some of the tracts for which these publishers go to prison concern normal sex, some homosexuality, some the masochistic yearning that is probably present in everyone and dominant in some. Masochism is a desire to be punished or subdued. In the broad frame of reference the desire may be expressed in the longing to be whipped and lashed, bound and gagged, and cruelly treated. Why is it unlawful to cater to the needs of this group? They are, to be sure, somewhat offbeat, noncomformist, and odd. But we are not in the realm of criminal conduct, only ideas and tastes. Some like Chopin, others like "rock and roll." Some are "normal," some are masochistic, some deviant in other respects, such as the homosexual. Another group also represented here translates mundane articles into sexual symbols. This group, like those embracing masochism, are anathema to the so-called stable majority. But why is freedom of the press and expression denied them? Are they to be barred from communicating in symbolisms important to them? When the Court today speaks of "social value," does it mean a "value" to the majority? Why is not a minority "value" cognizable? The masochistic group is one; the deviant group is another. Is it not important that members of those groups communicate with each other? Why is communication by the "written word" forbidden? If we were wise enough, we might know that communication may have greater therapeutical value than any sermon that those of the "normal" community can ever offer. But if the communication is of value to the masochistic community or to others of the deviant community, how can it be said to be "utterly without any redeeming social importance"? "Redeeming" to whom? "Importance" to whom? . . .

Man was not made in a fixed mould. If a publication caters to the idiosyncrasies of a minority, why does it not have some "social importance?" Each of us is a very temporary transient with likes and dislikes that cover the spectrum. However plebian my tastes may be, who am I to say that others' tastes must be so limited and that other tastes have no "social importance"?

How can we know enough to probe the mysteries of the sub-conscious of our people and say that this is good for them and that is not? Catering to the most eccentric taste may have "social importance" in giving that minority an opportunity to express itself rather than to repress its inner desires. . . . How can we know that this expression may not *prevent* anti-social conduct?

I find it difficult to say that a publication has no "social importance" because it caters to the taste of the most unorthodox amongst us. We members of this Court should be among the last to say what should be orthodox in literature. An omniscience would be required which few in our whole society possess.

This leads me to the conclusion, previously noted, that the First Amendment allows all ideas to be expressed—whether orthodox, popular, off-beat, or repulsive. I do not think it permissible to draw lines between the "good" and the "bad" and be true to the constitutional mandate to let all ideas alone. If our Constitution permitted "reasonable" regulations of freedom of expression, as do the constitutions of some nations, we would be in a field where the legislative and the judiciary would have much leeway. But under our charter all regulation or control of expression is barred. Government does not sit to reveal where the "truth" is. People are left to pick and choose between competing offerings. There is no compulsion to take and read what is repulsive any more than there is to spend one's time poring over government bulletins, political tracts, or theological treatises. The theory is that people are mature enough to pick and choose, to recognize trash when they see it, to be attracted to the literature that satisfies their deepest need, and, hopefully, to move from plateau to plateau and finally reach the world of enduring ideas.

I think this is the ideal of the Free Society written into our Constitution. We have no business acting as censors or endowing any group with censorship powers. It is shocking to me for us to send to prison anyone for publishing anything, especially tracts so distant from any incitement to action as the ones before us.

MR. JUSTICE BLACK [dissenting in *Mishkin* and *Ginzburg;* he concurred in *Fanny Hill*]. . . .

My conclusion is that certainly after the fourteen separate

opinions handed down in these three cases today no person, not even the most learned judge much less a layman, is capable of knowing in advance of an ultimate decision in this particular case by this Court whether certain material comes within the area of "obscenity" as that term is confused by the Court today. For this reason even if, as appears from the result of the three cases today, this country is far along the way to a censorship of the subjects about which the people can talk or write, we need not commit further constitutional transgressions by leaving people in the dark as to what literature or what words or what symbols if distributed through the mails make a man a criminal. As bad and obnoxious as I believe governmental censorship is in a Nation that has accepted the First Amendment as its basic ideal for freedom, I am compelled to say that censorship that would stamp certain books and literature as illegal in advance of publication or conviction would in some ways be preferable to the unpredictable book-by-book censorship into which we have now drifted. . . .

Neither in this case nor in *Ginzburg* have I read the alleged obscene matter. This is because I believe for reasons stated in my dissent in *Ginzburg* and in many other prior cases that this Court is without constitutional power to censor speech or press regardless of the particular subject discussed. I think the federal judiciary because it is appointed for life is the most appropriate tribunal that could be selected to interpret the Constitution and thereby mark the boundaries of what government agencies can and cannot do. But because of life tenure, as well as other reasons, the federal judiciary is the least appropriate branch of government to take over censorship responsibilities by deciding what pictures and writings people throughout the land can be permitted to see and read. When this Court makes particularized rules on what people can see and read, it determines which policies are reasonable and right, thereby performing the classical function of legislative bodies directly responsible to the people. Accordingly, I wish once more to express my objections to saddling this Court with the irksome and inevitably unpopular and unwholesome task of finally deciding by a case-by-case, sight-by-sight personal judgment of the members of this Court what pornography (whatever that means) is too hard core for people to see or read. If censorship of views about sex or any other subject is constitutional then I am reluctantly compelled to say that I believe the tedious, time-consuming and unwelcome responsibility for finally deciding what particular discussions or opinions must be suppressed in this country, should, for the good of this Court and of the Nation, be vested in some governmental institution or institutions other than this Court. . . .

I would reverse this case and announce that the First and Fourteenth Amendments taken together command that neither Congress nor the States shall pass laws which in any manner abridge freedom of speech and press—whatever the subjects discussed. I think the Founders of our Nation in adopting the First Amendment meant precisely that the Federal Government should pass "no law" regulating speech and press but should confine its legislation to the regulation of conduct. So too, that policy of the First Amendment made applicable to the States by the Fourteenth, leaves the States vast power to regulate conduct but no power at all, in my judgment, to make the expression of views a crime.

Index

About The Author

THOMAS I. EMERSON is Lines Professor of Law at the Yale School of Law, where he has been a member of the faculty since 1946. Admitted to the New York bar in 1932, Professor Emerson has served as counsel for a number of government agencies, including the National Recovery Administration, the National Labor Relations Board, the Social Security Board and the Office of Price Administration. From 1937 to 1940 he served as associate general counsel to the NLRB. In 1940 he became special assistant to the Attorney General of the United States. During World War II he was deputy administrator for enforcement of the Office of Price Administration and general counsel to the Office of Economic Stabilization and the Office of War Mobilization and Reconversion. A Guggenheim fellow in 1953, Professor Emerson was also a visiting professor at the London School of Economics during that academic year and at the Brookings Institution in 1960 and 1961. A frequent contributor to legal periodicals on civil liberties and constitutional law, Professor Emerson is also co-author (with David Haber) of *Political and Civil Rights in the United States*. Professor Emerson makes his home in New Haven.